Shakespeare Stories

Shakespeare Stories

EDITED AND INTRODUCED BY
GILES GORDON

Illustrations by Robin Jacques

HAMISH HAMILTON
LONDON

First published in Great Britain 1982
by Hamish Hamilton Ltd
Garden House 57–59 Long Acre London WC2E 9JZ

Introduction and compilation copyright © Giles Gordon 1982

Individual stories copyright as follows: 'We that are Young' ©
Paul Ableman 1982; 'Affairs of Death' © Kingsley Amis 1982; *A
Mother's Lament* © Paul Bailey 1982; 'Extracts from the Journal
of Flying Officer J' © William Boyd 1982; 'De Bilbow' © Brigid
Brophy 1982; 'Justice Silence, now blind, wits wandering a little
. . .' © J. L. Carr 1982; 'Overture and Incidental Music for *A
Midsummer Night's Dream* © Angela Carter 1982; 'A Botanist's
Romance' © Elspeth Davie 1982; 'Rough Magic' © David
Hughes 1982; 'A Changeable Report' © Gabriel Josipovici 1982;
'His Everlasting Mansion' © Francis King 1982; 'Ossie: a Dumb
Black Ox' © Allan Massie 1982; 'The Second Best Bed' ©
Robert Nye 1982; 'Cross Over' © David Pownall 1982; 'Yorick'
© Salman Rushdie 1982; 'Letter from Leah' © Godfrey Smith
1982; 'What to Do about Ralph?' © Iain Crichton Smith 1982;
'Prize Daffs' © Emma Tennant 1982; 'The Queen of Infinite
Space' © Elizabeth Troop 1982; 'The Secretest Man of Blood' ©
Fred Urquhart 1982

British Library Cataloguing in Publication Data

Shakespeare stories.
   1. Short stories, English   2. Shakespeare,
   William, 1564–1616, in fiction, drama, poetry, etc.
   I. Gordon, Giles
   823'.01'08351[FS]   PR1309.S5
   ISBN 0-241-10879-9

Typeset by Rowland Phototypesetting Ltd,
Bury St Edmunds, Suffolk
Printed and bound in Great Britain by
Richard Clay (The Chaucer Press) Ltd,
Bungay, Suffolk

To the Royal Shakespeare Company,
and especially Peter Hall, John Barton and Trevor Nunn,
for having given so much pleasure

Contents

Introduction

Just as, nearly four hundred years ago, Shakespeare usually took his plots from earlier authors and historians, so does his unique power exercise its force and influence, direct or indirect, on today's writers. Tom Stoppard's play *Rosencrantz and Guildenstern Are Dead* (1966) brilliantly explored an alleyway and characters which Shakespeare hardly visited, and at the same time celebrated *Hamlet*. (And W. S. Gilbert wrote a little remembered play called *Rosencrantz and Guildenstern* in 1891.) Barbara Garson's *Macbird*, a reworking of *Macbeth* featuring Lyndon B. Johnson in the title role, John F. Kennedy as Duncan and Robert Kennedy as Malcolm, was staged by Joan Littlewood and Theatre Workshop in 1967. Robert Nye in his novel *Falstaff* (1976) hugely filled out the life of the fat knight. Literature feeds on literature as well as on life. Nothing, not even in Shakespeare, is original in the sense that it springs into being without an awareness and knowledge, whether calculated or instinctive, of what preceded it.

Writers in the centuries before and after Shakespeare relied to a considerable degree on a knowledge in their audiences of a wide range of folk tales and legends. It is something of a paradox that Shakespeare took it for granted that his audience would be cognisant with more than the bones of English and Roman history whereas, to today's readers and theatre-goers, Shakespeare's plots are one of the few areas of common ground in our culture: the history of Richard III's reign may not be known but Shakespeare's version is. *West Side Story* (1958) derives from *Romeo and Juliet*, and Kurosawa's film *Throne of Blood* (1957) from, again, the Scottish play. Musicals and films have both fed off Shakespeare, and are 'popular' forms today as was the theatre in Shakespeare's time. (With Derek Jarman's exotic film of *The Tempest* (1981) we are in an area somewhere between interpretation and adaptation.) Very occasionally, Shakespeare has inspired masterpieces: I would prefer, heresy though it will be to many, to listen to Verdi's opera *Otello* (1887) again than read or see Shakespeare's play once more.

If it be accepted that Mr W. S. is the greatest writer of them all, it seemed an intriguing prospect – or at least piece of programme planning – to suggest to twenty of our best writers that each should compose a story, inspired by or derived from Shakespeare. Whether they took a particular play or character, or mingled characters from more than one play (as Gabriel Josipovici has done); whether their stories were set at the time and place of the play's action or today or at any other time; whether the plays and characters were but metaphors or images or ideas for something quite removed (as in the cases of Brigid Brophy and William Boyd) was up to the individual writers. The results, I believed, would harbour a degree of criticism and comment on the plays in question, and – if any story turned out to be essential, even a masterpiece – quite possibly would affect our next reading or watching of that play, and in a more stimulating and lively form than much academic criticism.

I shall not be able to read or witness again what is to me the greatest of all tragedies in the language, *King Lear*, without recalling what Paul Ableman suggests was the relationship between Cordelia and Edgar before the action of the play begins – my understanding of Shakespeare's characters is, amazingly, enhanced. (I hoped, in vain, that someone might have provided a brief life of Lear's queen, the mother of Goneril, Regan and Cordelia. By way almost of compensation, Godfrey Smith essays Shylock's wife, Leah, mentioned once in *The Merchant of Venice*, as having given her husband the turquoise ring which his daughter, Jessica, purloins: 'I would not have given it for a wilderness of monkeys.')

Likewise, Fred Urquhart having revealed the full horror of the identity of the third murderer in *Macbeth*, I shall never again be fully convinced by a production of the play that fudges this time-honoured dilemma – and, for good measure, Kingsley Amis has discovered a hitherto unrecorded, or at least unacknowledged, secret visit by Macbeth to Rome to provide Pope Leo IX with an explanation of certain events in Scotland. Allan Massie's very *macho* Othello has his Desdemona meet her end in Brighton, and the part played in the proceedings by his Iago – a boxing manager – only clicks into place in the last few lines.

Three writers have tackled *Hamlet*, in as various ways as any three productions of a particularly intractable play are bound to differ. Perhaps Salman Rushdie has finally exorcised ('Rest, rest, perturbed spirit!') his Sternean preoccupations by delineating the phrenological affairs of Yorick, he of the skull. Iain Crichton Smith replays the domestic tragedy (the royal house of Denmark rather than the Poloniuses) within a Scottish school-master's family, and Elspeth Davie has her botanist protagonist (rosemary for him) funk a meeting with a twentieth-century Ophelia.

Three writers start from the English histories. J. L. Carr's terrible conclusion to the life of Francis Feeble, the woman's tailor – one of the Gloucestershire recruits of Sir John Falstaff in *Henry IV Part 2* – insists that, although Feeble by surname he may have been, by character and conviction he was steadfast to the end. Brigid Brophy depicts an almost Nabokovian obsession with a strawberry mark – de bilbow, indeed! – and presents *Henry V* as a sub-text for our times. David Pownall continues to explore the fascination he has shown as a playwright with excavating Richard III in purgatory.

Only one author has settled for a Roman or Greek play. (I had hoped for a latter-day Antony and Cleopatra – Brigid Brophy's couple are hardly that – not to say a Julius Caesar, and Brecht has presumably put anyone else off Coriolanus.) Francis King's misanthropic contemporary Timon inhabited, in more affluent days, a *dolce vita* jet set. This story (and Francis King reviews theatre for a Sunday newspaper), as is the case with more than a few others, could usefully serve as a director's introductory notes to his cast for a fresh interpretation of the play, background reading for a production.

As to the comedies, William Boyd sets his forest of Arden in an Audenesque, beleaguered England. Jaques, a sardonic, grounded airman, tells the tale. Angela Carter sheds anything but light on fairy goings-on in her glittering account of Puck's jealousy – a very midsummer nightmare. Gabriel Josipovici begins with Malvolio in prison (or is it Shakespeare? Which the creator, which the created?) and ends more darkly than *Twelfth Night* does.

Emma Tennant examines the father and daughter relationship – not neglecting the husband and wife, and mother and child ones – which so concerned Shakespeare in the magical, miraculous last romances as depicted in *The Winter's Tale*. David Hughes, exploring the island of *The Tempest*, has his actor playing Prospero exiled with his daughter's pornography on a Greek island (more than a touch of Lawrence Durrell's Corfu?) with the colonels' régime in evidence: 'And deeper than did ever plummet sound/I'll drown my book'. Paul Bailey's Sycorax presents a ghastly autobiography that leads, almost inevitably, to her son being born Caliban.

Which leaves the interpreters. To many of us, Shakespeare only comes fully alive when his lines are spoken 'trippingly on the tongue'. Elizabeth Troop provides an ironic memoir of Dame Laura Tate, 'the greatest Shakespearean actress of our time', whose roles began with Juliet – and ended with Juliet's nurse.

As to our author and on lie begetter, whoever he was, Edward Bond, in his play *Bingo* about Shakespeare's years of retirement at Stratford, asserted that the dramatist turned into an illiberal landlord. Robert Nye here presents hitherto unauthenticated facts (facts?) about the marital relationship of Mr and Mrs Shakespeare. Life begins in bed and tends to end there. Shakespeare, in his *Last Will* – now *there's* a potential pun – *& Testament* dated 25 March 1616, declared, 'Item, I give unto my wife my second best bed', hence Robert Nye's title.

PAUL ABLEMAN

We that are young

'What's the matter?' asked the girl.

The boy didn't answer. He lay still on his back in the barge and watched the afternoon sun twinkling through the branches of trees that overhung the sluggish stream.

'Eddy?' the girl tried again. 'Why have you gone so quiet?'

The boy didn't look at her but his shoulders moved slightly. She caught a faint sigh. She leaned down quickly and just brushed his lips with her own. He moved his head irritably as if to shake off the attention.

'What is it?' she cried.

At that he turned his head a little and contemplated her as she bent over him. He saw her lovely face with its bright, grey eyes and lustrous brown hair which had tumbled forwards to make a little cave. Inside this they gazed at each other, he from below and she from above. Then he reached up suddenly and pulled her down on top of him. But she was nimble and strong for a girl. She tore herself free and wriggled away. A moment later and they were kneeling, facing each other almost like combatants eager to begin the trial. But he shook his head with a wry smile and slumped back into a sitting position against the side of the barge. She remained kneeling, watching him uncertainly.

'I'm sorry, Delly,' he apologised sadly. 'I didn't mean to. It's just that – you looked so beautiful.'

She smiled and wondered. Was she beautiful? The servants said so and not just dutifully, as servants must, but often with what sounded like conviction. But she had been well trained. She had learned one of the first rules for girls in her position: never trust what servants say. Of course, men paid her compliments too but, again, she was not sure if they admired her person or her position. But Eddy –? He had never found her beautiful until today. They had been playmates since childhood, and no hint of romance had ever coloured their boisterous games. Until today –

'That's a compliment indeed,' she urged playfully. 'I mean, you have a true standard of comparison.'

He looked puzzled.

'What standard?'

'Why, your mirror, Eddy!'

She ducked quickly to one side. But she was not quick enough.

'Ah! Ooh!' she cried. 'Let go, you spiteful wretch.'

He had seized her by her hair and tugged it, hard enough to hurt but not hurt much. She knew how he hated being teased with his looks, which were indeed delicate as a girl's. He also loved reading and reciting poetry and it was said he could amuse little ones, and delight in them, almost as a mother could. But she knew he was not effeminate. He could outride some of the best horsemen in her father's entourage and often, at hunting, made the kill. He could swim like an otter. She felt herself blush as she considered this talent for, until that very day when the heat of the sun and the beckoning purity of the pool had lured them into the necessary impropriety of discarding their clothes, she had never seen him do it. Now an image of his white body, leaping and swirling in the crystal waters, entered her memory and reddened her cheeks. There had been no indelicacy. They had not touched each other in the pool. But when, fully clad once more, they had reclined against a grassy bank to warm up in the sun, he had taken her in his arms. And then they had lain in gentle, and prudent, dalliance for an hour or more until, looking up, they had found that their horses had disappeared. An hour later, they had reached the stream and, after following its course for a mile or so on foot, had overtaken the ox-drawn barge. Pretending to be the children of well-off farmers – for it would have been folly to have revealed their true stations – they had offered the bargemen money for a ride and the two peasants had readily agreed.

Eddy released her hair and said moodily:

'I shall go to Italy.'

'Why? To eat figs?' she asked with a laugh. She approached him again and, snuggling against his side, laid her head on his shoulder.

'Yes, if they're ripe,' he returned pertly. After a pause, he asked, 'Have you ever eaten figs, Delly?'

'Yes, often. There is a nobleman in France my father cut once and could have slain. He spared him and the grateful man sends every year some baskets of figs. Yes, and other Southern fruits too, fat melons and tough pomegranates. You must have tasted them when dining with us.'

'I have eaten quaint fruit at your father's table. But not figs, I think. Never figs.'

He looked down at her mournfully. Just then the ox drawing their rude craft bellowed twice. They laughed.

'He heard us and longs for daintier fare than oats,' suggested Delly.

'Perchance the brute can fathom our discourse. In London, so I've heard, they stall a mule called Westerley which understands and makes reply. Put it a question and it will nod for "yea" and shake its long snout for "nay". Well, so I've heard.'

'Is it craving for wonders that draws you South? They say Italy is strewn with marvels.'

She felt him go a little tense, and guessed why. He said brusquely:

'I care naught for such things. I just tell you what I heard.'

She must be tactful with him. He was her junior by two years. She must never seem to mock his boyishness. But that meant, alas, she could never admit how much his eagerness moved her. She said carefully:

'Italy is a long way to travel for blue fruit, Eddy.'

He laughed shortly.

'Aye, that would be a glutton's quest. I go for a different reason.'

'What reason?'

'To learn a craft.'

'What craft?'

He sat up abruptly, causing her to fall back and bump her head on the wooden hull of the boat. He failed to notice this result of his clumsiness, and she did not chide him. She sat up, rubbing her head, as he continued glumly.

'The craft of speaking words in character.'

'Acting?' she exclaimed in dismay. 'You seek to be an actor?'

He shook his head moodily.

'No, nor an ostler neither. But I saw them once, Delly. They came to my father's house – an Italian troupe but they spoke our English tongue quite well. They did some plays, in Latin first and then the same in English – comical English but you could take the sense. And – well –'

'Well?'

'It might be fun. I think it could be fun.'

She considered his words, trying to fathom the deeper reasons for them. She stood up and leaned on the side of the barge. At the water's edge the ox, regularly lashed by the yokel, plodded along the side of a tussocky meadow stretching to low hills some miles away. She glanced to the rear of the boat where the steersman plied his long oar. She was shocked to see how close the fellow rode to their snug hold. Could he have heard their discourse? Her mind darted swiftly back. Had they said anything to disclose their true identities? She thought not. She glanced again at the fellow. He sucked a straw and gazed stolidly ahead as if no more than rodents played in his cargo of hay and planks. Eddy stood up and joined her at the vessel's side. He said:

'It could be done, including the double voyage, in two years. Perhaps less.'

'Then we would not ride together again for two years – perhaps less,' she said evenly.

'Ah, but there's policy in it,' he urged craftily. 'I crave to be near you, Delly.'

'And so remove to Italy?'

'Just for two years. I'm eighteen now and would return at twenty with the means to remain in your company.'

'How?'

'Why, with a craft. When your father feasts in hall, I could caper and sing for his guests. He would be loathe to entertain without my spritely presence and so I would be near you every night.'

'As you may be without the detour. When was his table ever barred to you?'

'Aye, as my father's son. But he would set the dogs on me if I presented there as son-in-law.'

The girl drew from him in counterfeit shock and stared at him with round eyes.

'As son-in-law? I have but two sisters and they are both wed. This fellow's mad.'

The boy gazed at her in dismay. His lips moved falteringly.

'But – but I had thought –'

'As a fiend, I trow – all devious and dishonest. Which of my sisters would you defile, knave?'

'But – but, don't you – wouldn't you –'

'Connive in my family's disgrace? Nay, and you harbour such base schemes –'

'You, Delly! You,' he cried desperately. 'It's you I would wed.'

She clapped a hand to where her bosom glowed above her girdle's clasp and, as if in wonder, exclaimed:

'Me!'

He seized her free hand and, like a captured ape, chattered fiercely but made small sense:

'I thought – Delly – after today – after we lay – after we said – I thought –'

She could abide his grief no longer. Careless of the rude witness who kept his station at the tiller, she seized him by the hand and planted kisses on his lips.

'Dolt,' she chided, 'I mock your device, not your intent. If a greedy boy sees a ripe apple, does he journey first to Italy before he plucks it? I am yours. I have always been yours. Pluck me.'

'You mean –'

'I mean, I have waited through all the summers of our youth for your game-fellow to ripen into bride. I loved thee when we made little shelters of boughs and played they were our castles.'

He turned from her then, and his boyish face was hard.

'Does this not please you?' she cried.

'Aye, as the fellow, Moses, was pleased to see the goodly land he might not enter. Pleased and bitter too.'

'Enter, pluck, live,' she implored.

'Not without church!' he cried, seizing her by the shoulders.

'There are many hallowed precincts. Name but your favourite, and the day, and I'll be there awaiting you.'

He shook her then, quite hard:

'Your father would not have me!'

'Nay, cease!' she gasped, 'least you shake loose my love and squander it in the chaff. My father shall not have you. I want you all.'

He released her then and hung his head.

'Oh, Delly, don't mock me. Your father would not let us wed.'

'Why not?'

'Because you are great and I am low.'

'Not so low. Nor am I so lofty-perched but I can catch the serpent's wink. Eddy, my father dotes on me. He will grumble and accede.'

'You – marry a commoner.'

'If not, I'll marry a fish.'

'A fish?'

'As only fit companion for a cold bed. Which mine shall remain unless you warm it. Eddy, I love you and love before now has stitched high to low. Why, once in old Rome it bound with its strong thread an emperor to a slave. Our small discrepancy is naught to that. Your father is a loyal and honourable nobleman. My sisters have imported sufficient rank into our house and my father grows weary of dynastic toil. He'll welcome you.'

The boy shook his head sadly.

'I would rather cross the Alps than cross your father. For, if the former, I can return in good repute. But once his towering majesty is roused I'm barred from you forever.'

'I'll sound him on it –'

'Delly!'

'With great discretion. But I know he'll consent.'

'He's not the only range to cross. My father too will block our way.'

'How so?'

'Ah, a royal frown. The haughty princess yet inhabits the yielding maid. Be reassured, pinnacled lady, not out of disrespect but excess of it. He would not have me peep above my station.'

'Your father would consent to our union if the king commanded it.'

'Aye, then he might.'

'Well, so shall the king command.'

The boy shook his head with a rueful smile.

'It seems we must find staffs and stout boots for we have lofty peaks to scale. Delly, do you really love me?'

'No.'

'What?'

'Love is fits and figments, dreams and whispers and all things that are least real. If I really loved you then I would love you not. And yet I reel for love of you.'

Heedless of the peasants he drew her to him. But then, just as their lips met, they heard the drum of swift hooves and the shrill neigh of a spirited steed. Startled, they looked round and saw their mounts, still riderless, frisking in the meadow a little way from the barge.

'Our horses!' exclaimed Eddy and then, before Delly, swifter than he to sense the danger in this loyal reappearance, could caution him, he called out to the peasant with the ox, 'I say, draw us in there. Those are our steeds.'

He felt Delly tug at his sleeve and realised too late the message in her plucking. The fine harness and saddle-cloths on their horses could never have adorned farm-children's mounts. Something of their rank had been disclosed, enough perchance to bend the peasants' greedy minds to thoughts of ransom. The ox-man had halted his lurching tug and was gazing eagerly from the sleek horses, one brown and one dapple-grey, to his human freight. He called:

'Indeed, sir. Indeed, they are fine beasts. We'll have them for you, Sir. For you and the lady, sir. I only ever saw harness like that once before, sir. When I delivered corn to the great king's castle. But you are not from the castle, are you sir? Farming folk, I think you said, Sir?'

'Aye, in origins,' called back Eddy, his mind weaving swift figments. 'Now I am groom at the castle and this wench is the ostler's daughter. You will save us a whipping if you snatch the beasts. We had them out to exercise and lost them when we — you can guess —'

'True, good sir. I can guess.'

The barge was nearing the bank now, and Eddy saw the man's crafty eyes scouring their garments. He and Delly were dressed rough for riding but no groom or stable wench ever rode caparisoned as they were. Would he take the tale? Beneath his short tunic, Eddy wore a keen bodkin at his belt. Slowly, he clasped it now. Delly, sensing his intent, tightened her grip on his arm. The warning was apt. These were strong rogues. It would be a greater risk, which he would not have shirked for himself alone, to attack them than to cozen them. He released the steel.

When the barge touched the bank, the steersman leapt nimbly ashore. Then he turned to Eddy and Delly and bowed several times quickly from the waist, grinning and mouthing. It was over-obsequious salutation for a groom and ostler's whelp. But the man might be a half-wit. The ox-man hurried over and cuffed his subordinate.

'Get after the horses, Toby,' he urged brusquely, and then to Eddy and Delly: 'We'll have them for you presently, good sir. Stay aboard if you will or recline here in the shade of this cool elm. We'll take the beasts.'

And take them they did. The peasants knew the ways of horses and, with clucking and winning and stealing forwards, soon had the prancing steeds secured. Holding one each by the halter, the two rag-clad fellows pulled the snorting flesh back to its proper masters. Eddy once more grasped the hilt of his dagger, and whispered:

'If they but glance a menace, I'll gore the one that does so. Leap astride then, as I know you can, and prick hard away while I despatch the other. Then I'll follow.'

'No, I'll wait —'

'What, not obey? I'm glad to learn it this side the altar. She's no wife who won't heed her lord.'

'I'll gallop.'

'Good. Now smile. They're here.'

Eddy strode a pace forwards, and said heartily:

'Well done, my splendid fellows. You've spared us bloody backs. Here's gold. We have but little and yet prize our skin above our purses. Take it.'

The ox-man shook his head eagerly.

'Nay, sir. It is our pleasure to serve such a — good master as thee. But you know the castle?'

'Its walls and lesser huts I know well.'

'Aye, but, good sir, the steward — you must know the steward?'

'His boot's tip more than his voice. But he instructs me now and then.'

'The castle's just beyond yon wooded hill. Take your steed, sir, and the lady's too. Toby and I are right pleased to have served you, good sir. But if you see the steward —'

'Yes? What of the steward?'

'Tell him, Moss, the chandler, helped you. It fell out, sir, some corn we took him was a trifle mildewed and he's bought no more since then. Tell him, Moss, the chandler, and his man, Toby, have a barn of the finest grain to bestow. He can have this golden heap at chopped cost, sir. No better bargain will he find in England, sir. Will you tell him that?'

'Right willingly, good fellow. And though I am but lowly in his esteem, he trusts my scent for horse-food. Bring the grain soon and he'll inspect it.'

'It shall be done, sir. Oh, happy day. Mount, sir. And madam. Well met, good sir. Do tell the steward.'

'Your grain will soon be coin. Farewell!'

Eddy glanced swiftly aside to establish that Delly too was mounted. Then, with lusty slaps to the animals' flanks, the two young people arrowed away from the stream and the cringeing peasants.

Their buoyant hearts seemed to lift their mounts above the turf until they flew across the land. So swift their flight they could each scarce catch the gurgle in the other's throat, and only knew their common merriment when glances bridged the rushing air between them and disclosed laughing faces. When the first gust of their surge was spent they reined down their foaming mounts and, in a stately walk, exchanged stifled fragments of shared jest.

'Oh, happy day,' gasped Delly, 'Do tell the steward.'

'Indeed, good fellow,' moaned Eddy, 'Indeed, I shall. He'll devour your musty corn at chopped cost – that he will.'

Whereupon, releasing the reins so that the perplexed beasts ambled at will, they sat shaking with mirth until Eddy leaned aside and grasped Delly's bridle. Then he drew her mare and herself towards him.

'I now recall the rogue. Oft have I seen the grave steward frown at some wagon of mould he hath carted to the gates, and then push him forth unpaid. This same Moss is known throughout the weald as purveyor of rotten fodder.'

'Yet hath he served us. You must urge his case.'

'I will unstock him from my own pocket. His reeking produce can be strewn o'er the roses. He helps things grow, this Moss. Not only flowers.'

'What else?'

'Our love. My Delly – my Cordelia.'

With a brusque tug, Edgar stilled their platforms and leaned to drink her. When he unsealed he shivered and spake fearfully.

'Where was it, Delly? In what unsighted chest of air did it repose?'

'Did what repose, my heart?'

'Why, my cargo of love. I have shouldered it through the world until this day and never knew the burden. Who snapped the clasp? How did it break loose? What else is stored intangible that may, upon a word or glance, come tumbling out and bury us? If this time it be treasure, may not the next –'

She stilled his fearful musing with finger to lips.

'We only see the moment. The rest is mercifully eclipsed. But it is our moment, Edgar.'

'You must not tell.'

'Tell what? Tell whom?'

'Our love. Tell anyone. Keep it from the king. Let not Lear know.'

'We had agreed -'

'Not yet. I fear the moment may escape or be once more imprisoned in the casks of time. Not yet, Cordelia. Promise me as much.'

'If you like.'

'I do not like. I want you all and always. But I fear to lose what I have already won, more than I yearn to win all.'

'I think my father would condone –'

'Yet still I fear. Let us simulate indifference and meet next when we next meet. Then, one day, when the king's pleasure shines, I will demand you.'

'Be it so.'

'There. The castle gleams in the burnished glance of the departing sun. A final kiss and we are what we were when we rode out this morn.'

The kiss was long and the horses stamped faintly with impatience. Then, with a twitch of the reins, the handsome pair urged once more towards the castle. As they neared its gates, they were surprised to note uncommon stir in its precincts.

'Why,' exclaimed Cordelia, 'those men wear my sister Goneril's acquired livery. And those Regan's. I knew not the duchesses were summoned to the king. And what is that great cart, glittering with leaf?'

'I know that wagon. I saw it once in Calais. It is the transport of the King of France.'

'All converged here on Lear's castle? Some great business is afoot. Please heaven it be not war.'

No sooner were they passed under the portcullis than England's majesty was at their side. The frosty head crowned a sturdy frame, and tall, but one somewhat bowed with years. The commanding features were rich in strength and wisdom, and yet the kindly mouth moved sometimes independent of any thought. A royal hand was raised to greet a royal daughter.

'How now, Cordelia,' cried the king, 'where hast thou been? Thy sisters are arrived for council. Quick, girl, put off thy leathern weeds and deck thyself for the occasion.'

'What occasion, father?' asked Cordelia uneasily.

'Why, one that will not mar thy fortunes. I have a surprise for my daughters. Who rides with you?'

'Oh, father, it is Edgar, Gloucester's youngest son. You know him well.'

'My high intent obscures my memory. Forgive me, boy, and get thee gone. Commend me to thy father. But go, sprout. Only the loftiest rungs of state may attend me now. Jump, jump, jump, jump, jump.'

Hastily dismounting, Edgar bowed low in homage to his king and then hurried away with his courser towards the stables. Sorrowing, Cordelia watched him depart.

'Groom! You, boy,' called the king. 'Take the Princess Cordelia's mare. Come, girl, dismount. I am eager for the business.'

'What business, father?' probed Cordelia again, dutifully descending from her horse.

'Why, sport and profit. Sport for a loving father and profit for his loving issue. Dost love thy father, Cordelia?'

But the girl's thoughts were again with Edgar.

'Cordelia?' urged the eager monarch, 'Nay, thou'lt have time to testify presently. Get thee to thy chamber and wipe the road-dust from thy cheeks. We will not stay upon more intricate fashioning. When the sennet sounds, and that is but some minutes hence, attend us in my throne-room. Run, child, run!'

With demure haste, Cordelia paced to the castle and into the great entrance hall. There she spied, clustered in low controversy before the throne-room's portal, Edgar's father, the Earl of Gloucester, Edgar's brother, Edmund, and the good old Earl of Kent. As she skirted the little group, she heard Kent voice the opinion:

'I thought the King had more affected the Duke of Albany than Cornwall.'

She wondered if these words had any bearing on her father's mysterious project. Well, she would soon know.

Overture and Incidental Music for A Midsummer Night's Dream

Call me the Golden Herm.

My mother bore me in the Southern wild but, as you know, she died of me: 'she, being mortal, of that boy did die,' as my Aunt Titania says, though 'boy' in the circumstances is pushing it, a bit, she's censoring me, there. 'Boy' is correct, as far as it goes, but insufficient. Nor is the sweet South as wild as all that; child of the sun am I, and of the breezes, juicy as mangoes, that mythopeically caress the Coast of Coramandel far away on the porphyry and lapis lazuli Indian shore where everything is bright and precise as laquer. My Aunt Titania – not, I should tell you, my *natural* aunt, no blood bond but my mother's best friend to whom, before she departed, she entrusted me and therefore always called by me, 'auntie.'

Titania, she, the great, fat, showy, pink and blonde thing, the Memsahib, I call her, Auntie Tit-tit-tit-tania (for her tits are the things you notice first, size of barrage balloons), Tit-tit-tit-omania boxed me up in a trunk she bought from the Army and Navy Stores, labelled it 'Wanted on Voyage' (you bet!) and shipped me here.

Here! to – ATISHOO! – catch my death of cold in this dripping bastard wood. Rain, rain, rain, rain, rain!

'Flaming June,' the sarcastic fairies mutter, looking glum, as well they might, poor dears, their little wings all sodden and plastered to their backs, so water-logged they can hardly take off and, no sooner airborne than they founder in the pelting downpour, crash-land among the plashy bracken furls amid much piteous squeaking. 'Never such weather,' complain the fairies, grounded among the brakes of roses putting on – I must admit – a brave if pastel-coloured floral show in spite of the inclemency of the weather, and the flat dishes of the wild roses spill over with the raindrops that have collected upon them as the bushes shudder in the reverberations of dozens and dozens of teeny tiny sneezes, for no place on their weeny anatomies to store a handkerchief and all the fairies have got shocking colds as well as I.

Nothing in my princely, exquisite, peacock-jewelled heredity prepared me for the dank, grey, English midsummer. A midsummer nightmare, I call it. The whirling winds have wrenched the limbs off even the hugest oaks and brought down altogether the more tottery elms so that they sprawl like collapsed drunks athwart dishevelled fairy rings. Thunder, lightning, and, at night, the blazing stars whizz down and bomb the wood . . . nothing temperate about your temperate climate, dear, I snap at Aunt Titania, but she blames it all on Uncle Oberon, whose huff expresses itself in thunder and he makes it rain when he abuses himself, which it would seem he must do almost all the time, thinking of me, the while, no doubt. Of ME!

> For Oberon is passing fell and wrath
> Because that she, as her attendant hath
> A lovely boy, stolen from an Indian king;

> She never had so sweet a changeling;
> And jealous Oberon would have the child!

Misinformation. The patriarchal version. It was all between my mother and my auntie, wasn't it; all.

Besides, is a child to be given? Or taken? Or stolen? Or sold in bondage? Are these blonde English fairies the agents of protocolonialism, dammit?

To all this, in order to preserve my baroque integrity, I present a façade of passive opposition. I am here. I am.

I am Herm, short for *hermaphroditus verus*, one testis, one ovary, half of each but all complete and more, much more, than the sum of my parts. This elegantly retractible appendage, here . . . is *not* the tribade's well-developed clit, but the veritable reproductive article, while the velvet-lipped and deliciously closeable aperture below it is, I assure you, a viable avenue of the other gender. So there.

Take a look. I'm not shy. Impressive, huh?

And I am called, The Golden Herm, for I am gold all over; when I was born, tiny, playful cherubs filled their cheeks and lungs and blew, blew the papery sheets of beaten gold all over my infant limbs, to which they stuck and clung. See me shine!

Here I stand, under the dripping trees, in the long, rank, soaking grass among draggletail dog-daisies and the branched candelabras of the buttercups from whom the gusty rain has knocked off all the petals, leaving their warty green heads bald. And the bloody crane's bill. And the stinging nettles, those Portuguese men o' war of the woodland, who gave me so many nasty shocks when I first met them. And peaseblossom and mustard-seed and innumerable unknown-to-me weeds, the dreary, washed-out, pinks, yellows and Cambridge blues of them. Boring. In the underpinnings of the trees, all soggy and floral as William Morris wallpaper in an abandoned house, I, in order to retain my equilibrium and psychic balance, meditate in the yogic posture known as The Tree, that is, on one leg.

Bearer of both arrow and target, wound and bow, spoon and porringer, in my left hand I hold a lotus, looking a bit the worse for wear by now. My snake coils round my other arm.

I am golden, stark naked and bi-partite.

On my golden face, a fixed, archaic grin. Except when –
ATISHOO!
Damn occidental common cold virus.
ATISHOO.

*

The Golden Herm stood in the green wood.

This wood is, of course, nowhere near Athens; the script is a positive mass of misinformation. This wood is really located somewhere in the English midlands, possibly near Bletchley, where the great decoding machine was sited. Correction: this wood *was* located in the English midlands but the last of the oak, ash and thorn was chopped down to make a motorway just the other decade. However, since the wood existed only as a structure of the imagination, in the first place, it will remain, in the second place, as a green, decorative margin to the eternity promised by the poet. The English poet; his Englishness is his essence.

The English wood is nothing like the dark, necromantic forest in which the Northern European imagination begins and ends, where its dead and the witches live, and Baba-yaga stalks about in her house with chicken's feet looking for children in order to eat them. No. There is a qualitative, not a quantitative difference between this wood and that forest. It is not merely that a wood contains fewer trees than a forest, and covers less ground . . . those are just some of the causes of the difference and do not explain the effects of the difference.

For example, an English wood, however marvellous, however metamorphic, cannot, by definition, be trackless, although it might well be formidably labyrinthine – a maze. Yet there is always a way out of a maze, and, even if you cannot find it for a while, you know that it is there. A maze is a construct of the human mind, and not unlike it; lost in the wood, this analogy will always console. But to be lost in the forest is to be lost to *this* world, to be abandoned by the light, to lose yourself utterly with no guarantee you will either find yourself or else be found; to be committed against your will – or, worse, of your own desire – to a perpetual absence from humanity, an existential catastrophe, for the forest is as infinitely boundless as the human heart. But the wood is finite, a closure; you purposely mislay the way in the wood, for the sheer pleasure of roving. The temporary confusion of direction is in the nature of a holiday from which you will come home refreshed, with your pockets full of nuts and berries and wildflowers or the cast feather of a bird in your cap. That forest is haunted; this wood is enchanted.

The very perils of the wood, so many audio-visual aids to a pleasurable titillation of mild fear; the swift rattle of an ascending pheasant, soft drop of owl, red glide of the fox, may 'give you a fright' but, here, neither hobgoblin nor foul fiend can daunt your spirit, since the lobs and hobs reflect nothing more than a secular faith in the absence of harm in nature, and, since the last English wolf was killed, there is nothing savage among the trees to terrify you. All is mellow in the filtered light, where Robin Wood, the fertility spirit, lurks in the green shade; this wood is kind to lovers.

Indeed, you might call the wood the common garden of the village, a garden almost as intentionally wild as one of Bacon's 'natural wilder-nesses', where every toad carries a jewel in its head and all the flowers have names; nothing is unknown – this kind of wildness is not an otherness.

And always something to eat! Mother Nature's greengrocery store; sorrel for soup, mushrooms, dandelion and chickweed salads, mint and thyme for seasoning, wild strawberries and blackberries for dessert and, in the autumn, a plenitude of nuts. Nebuchadnezzar, in an English wood, need not have confined his appetite to grass.

The English wood, then, offers us a glimpse of a green, unfallen world a little closer to Paradise than we are.

*

Such is the English wood in which we see fairies, blundering humans, rude mechanicals; this is the Shakespearian wood of nineteenth-century nostalgia, in which the fairies look exactly like they do in those faked photographs of fairy folk that so enraptured Conan Doyle.

Enter these enchanted woods.

*

The Puck was obsessively fascinated by the exotic visitor. In some respects, it was the attraction of opposites, for, whereas the Golden Herm was sm-o-o-o-th, the Puck was hairy; on these chill nights of summer, Puck was the only one kept warm at all inside his hairy pelt. Hairy. Shaggy. Especially about the thighs.

Shaggy as a Shetland pony when naked and sometimes goes on all fours. When he goes on all fours, he whinnies; or else he barks.

He is the lob, the lubbar fiend, and sometimes he plays at being the nut-brown house-sprite for whom a bowl of milk is left outside the door, although, if you want to be rid of him, you must leave him a pair of trousers; he thinks the gift of trousers is an insult to his sex, of which he is most proud. Nesting in his luxuriant pubic curls, that gleam with the deep-fried gloss of the woodcarvings of Grinling Gibbons, see his testicles, wrinkled ripe as medlars.

Puck loves hokey-pokey and peek-a-boo; he has relations all over the place – in Iceland, the *puki*; the Devonshire *pixy*; the *spook* of the Low Countries are all his next of kin and not one of them up to any good. That Puck!

The tender little exiguities that cluster round the Queen of the Fairies do not like to play with the Puck because he is so rough and rips their painted wings in games of tag and pulls the phantasmal legs off the grey gnats that draw Titania's wee coach through the air, kisses the girls and makes them cry, creeps up and swings between the puce, ithyphallic foxglove spires above Titania's bed so the raindrops fall and scatter in a drenching shower and up she wakes. Spiteful!

Puck is no more polymorphously perverse than all the rest of these sub-microscopic particles, his peers, yet there is something peculiarly rancid and offensive about his buggery and his undinism and his frotteurism and his scopophilia and his – indeed, my very paper would *blush*, go pink as an invoice, should I write down upon it some of the things Puck gets up to down in the reeds by the river, since he is distantly related to the great bad god Pan and, when in the mood, behaves in a manner uncommon in an English wood.

By the Puck's phallic orientation, you know him for a creature of King Oberon's.

Hairy Puck fell in love with Golden Herm and often came to frolic round the lovely living statue in the moonlit glade, although he could not, happily for the Herm, get near enough to touch because Titania forethoughtfully had thrown a magical *cordon sanitaire* round her lovely adoptive, so that s/he was, as it were, in an invisible glass case, such as s/he might find herself, some centuries later, in the Victoria and Albert Museum. Against this transparent, intangible barrier, the Puck often flattened still further his already snub nose.

The Herm removed his/her left foot from its snug nest in her/his crotch and placed it on the ground. With one single, fluent, gracile movement of transition, s/he shifted on to the *other* leg. The lotus and the snake, on either arm, stayed where they were.

The Puck, pressed against Titania's magic, sighed heavily, stepped back a few paces and began energetically to play with himself.

Have *you* seen fairy sperm? We mortals call it, cuckoo spit.

*

And no passing, clayey mortal, trampling through the wood on great, heavy feet, scattering the fairies who twitter inaudibly as bats in their fright, just as he would not hear them, so he would never spot the unafraid Herm, sticking stock still as a trance.

And if you *did* chance to spy him/her, you would think the little yellow idol was a talisman dropped from a gypsy pocket, perhaps, or a charm fallen off a girl's bracelet, or else the gift from inside a very expensive pornographic cracker.

Yet, if you picked up the beautiful object and held it on the palm of your hand, you would feel how warm it was, as if somebody had been holding it tight before you came and only just put it down.

And, if you watched long enough, you would see the golden sequins of the eyelids move.

At which a wind of strangeness would rise and blow away the wood and all within it.

*

Just as your shadow can grow a bit and then shrink to almost nothing and then swell up, again, so can *these* shadows, these insubstantial bubbles of the earth, these 'beings' to whom the verb, 'to be', may not be properly applied, since, in our sense, they are not. They *cannot* be; cannot, themselves, cast shadows, for who has seen the shadow of a shadow? Their existences necessarily moot – do *you* believe in fairies? their lives lead always just teasingly almost out of the corners of the eyes of their observers, so it is possible they were only, all the time, a trick of the light . . . such half-being, with such a lack of public acknowledgement, is not conducive to any kind of visual consistency among them. So they may take what shape they please.

The Puck can turn himself into anything he likes: a three-legged stool, in order to perpetrate the celebrated trick ('Then slip I from her bum, down topples she') so beloved in the lower forms of grammar schools when the play is read aloud around the class because it is suitable for children since it is about fairies; a baby Fiat; a grand piano – anything!

Except the lover of the Golden Herm.

In his spare moments, when he was not off about his Master's various business, the Puck, wistfully lingering outside the Herm's magic circle like an urchin outside a candy shop, concluded that, in order to take full advantage of the sexual facilities offered him by the Herm, should the barrier between them ever be broken – and the Puck's motto was, 'Be Prepared' – if there were to be intercourse with the Herm, then the Herm's partner would require a similar set of equipment to the Herm in order to effect maximally satisfactory congress.

Then the Puck further concluded that the equipment of the Herm's hypothetical partner would need, however, to be attached in reversed order to that of the Herm, in order to produce a perfect fit and no fumbling; the Puck, a constant inquisitive spy on mortal couples come to the wood to make the beast with two backs in what they mistakenly considered privacy, had noticed there is a vexed question of handedness about caresses, that all right-handed lovers truly require left-handed lovers during the blissful preliminaries to the act, and Mother Nature, when she cast the human mould, took no account of foreplay, which alone distinguishes us from the beasts when we are being beastly.

Try, try as he might, try and try again, the Puck could not get it quite right, although, after strenuous effort, he at last succeeded in turning himself into a perfect simulacrum of the Herm and would, at odd moments, adopt the Herm's form and posture and stand facing him in the wood, a living mirror of the living statue, except for the fierce erection the satyromaniac Puck could not subdue when in the presence of his love.

The Herm continued to smile inscrutably, except when she sneezed.

*

But all of them can grow BIG! then shrink down to . . . the size of dots, of less than dots, again. Every last one of them is of such elastic since incorporeal substance. Consider the Queen of the Fairies.

Her very name, Titania, bears witness to her descent from the giant race of the Titans; and 'descend', might seem apt enough, at first, to describe the declension when she manifests herself under her alias, Mab, or, in Wales, Mabh, and rules over the other diminutives herself the size of the solitaire in an engagement ring, as infinitely little as her forebears were infinitely large.

*

'Now, I do call my horned master, the Horn of Plenty; but, as for my missus —' said the Puck, in his inimitable Worcestershire drawl.

*

Like a Japanese water-flower dropped in a glass of water, Titania grows . . . until you might imagine she herself was Mother Nature.

*

In the dewy wood tinselled with bewildering moonlight, the bumbling, tumbling babies of the fairy crèche trip over the hem of her dress, which is no more nor less than the margin of the wood itself; they stumble in the tangled grass as they play with the coneys, the quick fox-cubs, the russet field mice and the wee scrapes of grey voles, blind velvet moles and striped brock with his questing snout – all the denizens of the woodland are her embroiderings, and the birds that flutter round her head, settle on her shoulders and make their nests in her great abundance of disordered hair, in which are plaited poppies and the ears of wheat.

The arrival of the Queen is announced by no fanfare of trumpets but the ash-soft lullaby of wood doves and the liquid coloratura black-bird. Moonlight falls like milk upon her naked breasts.

She is like a double bed; or, a table laid for a wedding breakfast; or, a fertility clinic.

In her eyes are babies. When she looks at you, you helplessly reduplicate. Her eyes provoke engendering.

Correction: *used* to provoke.

But not *this* year. Frosts have blasted the fruit blossom, rain has rotted all the corn so her garland is not gold but greenish and phosphorescent with blight. The acres of the rye have been invaded with ergot and, this year, eating bread will make you mad. The floods broke down the Bridge of Ware. The beasts refuse to couple; the cows refuse the bull and the bull keeps himself to himself. Even the goats, hitherto synonymous with lechery, prefer to curl up with a good book. The very worms no longer make blind love in the turgid humus. In the wood, a chaste, conventual calm reigns over everything; as if the foul weather has put everybody off.

The wonderful giantess manifested herself with an owl on her shoulder and an apron-full of roses and of babies so rosy the children could scarcely be distinguished from the flowers. She picked up her defunct friend's child, the Herm. The Herm stood on one leg on the palm of Titania's hand and smiled the inscrutable, if rather manic, smile of the figures in Hindu erotic sculpture.

'My husband shall not have you!' cried Titania. 'He shan't! I shall keep you!'

At that, thunder crashed, the heavens, which, for a brief moment, had sealed themselves up, now reopened again with redoubled fury and all the drenched babies bundled in Titania's pinafore began to cough and sneeze; the worms in the rosebuds woke up at the clamour and commenced to gnaw.

But the Queen stowed the tiny Herm safe away between her breasts as if s/he were a locket, and commenced to diminish until she was a suitable size to enjoy her niece or nephew or nephew/niece *à choix* in the obscurity of an acorn-cup.

'But she cannot put horns on her husband, for he is antlered, already,' opined the Puck, changing back into himself and skipping across the glade to the heels of his master. For it is no roe-buck who now raises his head behind that gorse bush to watch these goings on; Oberon is antlered like a ten-point stag.

*

Among the props of the Globe Theatre, along with the thunder-making machine and the bearskins, is listed a 'robe for to go invisible.' By his coat, you understand that Oberon intends to remain unseen as he broods magisterial but impotent above the scarcely discernible quivering among last year's oak leaves that conceal his wife, and the golden bone of contention that has come between the elemental married pair.

High in the thick of a dripping hedge of honeysuckle, an attenuated creature was extracting a tritonic, numinous, luxuriantly perfumed melody from the pan-pipes of the wild woodbine. The tune broke off as the player convulsed with ugly coughing. He gobbed phlegm, that flew through the air until its trajectory was interrupted by a cowslip, on whose freckled ear the translucent pustule hung. The infinitesimal then took up his tootling again.

*

The Herm's golden skin is made of beaten gold but the flesh beneath it has been marinated in: black pepper, red chilli, yellow turmeric, cloves, coriander, cumin, fenugreek, ginger, mace, nutmeg, allspice, khus-khus, garlic, tamarind, coconut, candlenut, lemon grass, galangel and now and then you get – phew! – a whiff of asafoetida. Hot stuff! Were the Herm to be served piled up on a lordly platter and garnished with shreds of outer casing, s/he would then resemble that royal dish, *moglai biriani*, which is decorated with edible gold shavings in order, so they say, to aid digestion. Nothing so deliciously aromatic as the Herm has ever been scented before in England's green and pleasant land of boiled cabbage and bacon. S/he is hot; and sweet, as if drenched in honey, but Oberon is the colour of ashes.

The Puck, tormented for lack of the Herm, pulled up a mandrake and sunk his prodigious tool in the cleft of the reluctant root, which shrieked mournfully but to no avail as old shaggylugs had his way with it.

Distemperate weather! It's raining, it's pouring; the earth is in estrangement from itself, the withered buds tumble out of the Queen's apron and rot on the mulch, for Oberon has put a stop to reproduction. But still Titania hugs the Herm to her shrivelling bosoms and will not let her husband have the wee thing, not even for one minute; did she not give a sacred promise to a friend?

But what does the Herm want?

The Herm wants to know what 'want' means.

'I am unfamiliar with the concept of desire. I am the unique and perfect, paradigmatic Hermaphrodite, provoking on all sides desire yet myself transcendant, the unmoved mover, the still eye of the tempest, exemplary and self-sufficient, the beginning and the end.'

Titania, despairing of the Herm's male aspect, inserted a tentative forefinger in the female orifice. The Herm felt bored.

*

Oberon watched the oak leaves quiver and said nothing, choked as he was with balked longing for the golden, half and halfy thing with its salivatory perfume. He took off his invisible disguise and made himself gigantic and bulked up in the night sky over the wood, arms akimbo, blotting out the moon to menace his wife, naked but for his buskins and his great codpiece; the mossy antlers on his forehead aren't the half of it, he wears a crown made out of yellowish vertebrae of unmentionable mammals, down from beneath which his hair drops straight as black light. Since he is in his malign aspect, he has put on, furthermore, a necklace of suggestively little skulls, which might be those of the babies he has plucked from human cradles – do not forget, in German, they call him Erl-king.

His face, breast and thighs he has daubed with charcoal; Oberon, lord of night and silence, of the grave silence of endless night, Lord of Plutonic dark. His hair, long, it never saw scissors; but he has this peculiarity – no hair at all on either chop or chin, nor his shins, neither, but all his face bald as an egg, except for the eyebrows, that meet in the middle.

Indeed, who in their right minds would entrust a child to him?

When Oberon cheers up a bit, he lets the sun come out and then he'll **hang little silver bells along his codpiece and they go jingle jangle jingle** when he walks up and down and round about, the pretty chinking sounds hang in the air wriggling like homunculi.

And if these are not the creatures of the dream, then surely you have forgotten your own dreams.

*

The Puck, too, yearning and thwarted as he was, found himself helplessly turning himself into the thing he longed for, and, under the faintly twitching oak leaves, became yellow, metallic, double-sexed and extravagantly precious-looking. There the Puck posed on one leg, the living image of the Herm, and glittered.

Oberon saw him.

Oberon stooped down and picked up the Puck and stood him, a simulated yogic Tree, on his palm. A misty look came into Oberon's eyes. The Puck knew he had no option but to go through with it.

*

ATISHOO!

Titania wiped the Herm's nose with the edge of her petticoat, on which the flowers are all drooping, shedding embroidery stiches, the fruits are cankering and spotting for, if Oberon is the Horn of Plenty, then Titania is the Cauldron of Generation and, unless he gives her a stir, now and then, with his great pot stick, the cauldron will go off the boil.

Lie close and sleep, said Titania to the Herm. My fays shall lullaby you as we cuddle up on my mattress of dandelion down.

The draggled fairies obediently started in on a chorus of: 'Ye spotted snakes with double tongue,' but were all so afflicted by coughing and sneezing and rawness of the throat and rheumy eyes and gasping for breath and all the other symptoms of rampant influenza, that their hoarse voices petered out before they reached the bit about the newts, and after that the only sound in the entire wood was the pit-pattering of the rain on the leaves.

*

The orchestra has laid down its instruments. The curtain rises. The play begins.

FRED URQUHART

The Secretest Man of Blood

I am the most misrepresented man in the Shakespearean canon.
Besides being the most neglected and misunderstood man in history.
The English Bard gives me only six lines to speak, all short, a matter of
forty-two words in all. Forty-two words for one who helped to put a
king on a throne and swayed the destiny of a nation! Little wonder that
long ago this poor blood-spattered ghost put a curse on the work they
call in a whisper 'The Scottish Play'. It shall always be nameless like
me.

And yet, once, I had a name.

I never knew who my mother was. Sometimes, when I was a bairn, I thought she might be Macduff's lady from the way I caught her, on occasion, looking at me with a dark brooding glower. My sire himself would never tell me, even in our fondest and most secret moments. 'Ask no questions and you'll never be defiled,' he said once. 'Is it not enough for you that I acknowledge you as my bastard?'

Macbeth acknowledged me first before the whole world when I came as a stripling of ten years to King Duncan's court. I was brought there by the carline who'd looked after me since I was a babe, the carline I'd always called 'Granny'. Before she left, she warned me to look out for my father's wife. 'The Lady Gruoch is of royal blood,' she said. 'The grand-daughter of yon auld King Kenneth that ruled when I was a lass. She may greet you with sweet words and hail ye as stepson, but beware. She is never likely to forget that her man favoured another woman before he favoured her. 'Tis all very well for Gruoch herself to have been wed before and given birth, but what was right for a princess is not right for her man. So beware! Steer your barque clear of hers and never give her your confidence. Not that my warning will do ye any good, lad. Your dire destiny was writ large on your face when Macbeth took ye in his arms and kissed ye.'

And with a light slap on my cheek as her fond farewell, the carline gave an eldritch cackle and departed.

I took no heed of her last words. Though I did not forget her warning about the lady who had declared herself my fond stepmother.

Macbeth was proud of me. I was proof he had fire in his loins, something he could not prove openly now the Lady Gruoch had some female trouble that made her able to conceive no longer. Macbeth delighted in flaunting me before the world. I was his weapon against calumny. I was big for my age and comely, and all who saw us together paid a tribute to our likeness. He was a soldier, and I was a soldier's son. And because he was a soldier and fearless, I worshipped him for a hero.

Macbeth's arrogant pride in me may have aroused the Lady Gruoch's jealousy, but she cloaked it well. She was always careful to be kind to me, whether in company or not. The only times she railed were times when any reasonable mother, anxious for her offspring's good, would rail. Everything given to Lulach, the son of her first marriage, was given to me. No favours were shown between us; we were encouraged to be brothers and playfellows, though he was three or four years my senior; we shared the same chamber and, often, the same bed. And, indeed, for maybe a couple of years we were friends, and then I found that when he married Gruoch my father had, as a gift to the lady, adopted Lulach as his firstborn and decreed him heir to his own titles of Mormaer of Moray and Thane of Glamis. I can never say I hated Lulach, for, truth to tell, I always had a great fondness for him, a much greater fondness than I should have had for a stepbrother, a fondness that became irksome sometimes when Lulach showed he was aware and would have none of it; but once I learned he was to be Thane of Glamis when he came of age I grew wary of him, and swore to bide my time till I could make him regret he had ever claimed kinship with Macbeth.

In the same way, I have no doubt, Lady Macbeth's hatred grew of myself, though she could never have harboured the secret thoughts I had about Lulach. And the lady's hatred was not entirely because of my bastardy; I think she suspected I was her husband's lover.

Her suspicions were true. At periods when Lady Gruoch was parsimonious with her favours Macbeth would seek his way to my chamber. By then, having attained the age of fourteen, I no longer shared a chamber with Lulach.

I well remember the first time. We were at high table in the great hall of the old castle of Glamis. I was serving, as I often did, as my sire's cupbearer. After he had eaten and drunk to his fill – and I noticed he had drunk more than he should, and Lady Gruoch had also noticed – he pushed away his chair from the table and sat back in it, spreading his thighs apart and thrusting out his great legs. He was a fine big man with broad shoulders, and he filled his chair well.

'More wine, Callach,' he said to me, holding out his tankard.

I was obeying when Lady Gruoch cried: 'Enough, Macbeth! You have drunk more than the share of two men of your size.'

'Hear her, Callach!' he said, laughing, and he reached out and pulled me down between his speldered thighs. I struggled to get on my feet again, but he pushed me down firmly. I was now a big lusty lad, looking more than my years and almost as big as my father. Often, when at the ages of ten or eleven, I had sat thus between his thighs after **we had playfully wrestled. But for a long time now I had not come into** as close contact with him; I was over-aware of my own body and its strange longings. I was also aware of my father's body, and knew I should avoid touching him.

'Sit here a while, lad, and protect me from my lady's ever-thrusting tongue,' he said, and he held his tankard to my lips and whispered: 'Sup! Sup!'

He pulled my head against his fork. The nape of my neck could feel his secrecy swelling. I became overbrimful of cockiness. Looking to see my stepmother was not watching, I rubbed my cheek against my sire's thigh and put my hand on his ankle. My boldness rising, I stroked his calf. He bent over me and whispered laughingly: 'D'ye wish me to unbreech ye in front of the whole hall, ye lusty rogue?'

Lady Macbeth, who had been scowling down at the thin pale hands in her lap, the long fingers of which she kept smoothing disdainfully, said: 'Callach is behaving like a child. And you, husband, encourage him.'

Macbeth pulled me up, slapped my bottom and said: 'Get away, ye young rascal. 'Tis time you were abed.'

For a long time I lay in my chamber, rigid with lust. Towards midnight, after a quarrel with Lady Gruoch, he came to my bed. We wrestled for a while. Then I fell asleep in a state of happy worship in his drunken arms.

On many later nights when Lady Macbeth was seized by women's pains or unwilling, he would seek my chamber. And my boyish yearnings and fumblings progressed to wider and more splendid horizons. I was young and hot and eager for all manner of private capers that Macbeth, skilled in such matters and encouraged by my abandonment, got up to with me. Although he was a man of great courage, a martial man, a man brimming over with manliness and with no sign of the feminine in him, my sire had, like many soldiers, a softness, a gentleness that was best expressed in his liking for an emotional and physical involvement with a much younger man of his own sentiment. He had a soft eye for a pretty boy. Julius Caesar and Alexander were similarly disposed. And so, because of my overwhelming passion for him, and to prove that this passion was no mean thing, I killed King Duncan.

It is true that Lady Macbeth instigated Duncan's murder, but I was

the instrument that carried it out. And it was I who carried out the murders of Banquo and Lady Macduff and her bairns.

*

I am but a wisp of a ghost now, a flimsy creature spattered with gore, but those deeds and many others even more foul have crazed my mind for near ten centuries.

I am the most forgotten man in history. I am the most neglected man, the most eliminated man. Yet my life was filled with more horror than the lives of many others whose names bloom larger and more flamboyant in the garden of time's remembrance. Names like Macbeth's own.

My sire was a man of violent passions, a man brimful of ambition and not over-scrupulous as to how he attained his ends, but he never was the monster pictured by the legend-maker Holinshed or yon English bard, Master Shakespeare. When he penned his imaginary play about my father and my stepmother, Shakespeare was mistaken in giving me such a minor role. Indeed, it can hardly be called a role at all. He gives me no name, calling me only the Third Murderer. It is such a small part that many stage producers, short of cash or short of actors, sometimes short of both, cut it out of their productions. Master Shakespeare reckoned so little of me he gave me only stage atmospheric lines like 'Hark, I hear horses.'

He was in the gravest error. Lady Macbeth incited my sire to the killing of the king, but he was even more infirm of purpose than she said, so I took the dagger from him, entered Duncan's chamber and did the deed. Afterwards Macbeth regained his courage and killed the two drunken guards. Between us, suspicious and uneasy allies in the cause concerning both, the Lady Gruoch and I plotted the murder of Banquo and his son. Macbeth was against it; he would fain have warned Banquo and Fleance and let them escape into exile, even though the weird sisters had predicted that Banquo would be the ancestor of eight kings destined to follow Macbeth on the throne. Then, seeing his lady and I were adamant, he hired two murderers and hoped, secretly, they might prove inept. Full of foreboding, for I took great heed of the witches' warning, I joined the murderers in disguise, and when they asked who sent me I told them 'Macbeth'. This satisfied them well enough to let me carry out the stabbing of Banquo, but it must have added to their ineptitude, for Fleance had no difficulty in escaping. Had I not been concerned to see Banquo truly dead I would have been after the son quicker than the hired men.

In like manner I laid no trust in the assassins chosen to dispatch Lady Macduff and her brood. Again I disguised myself and went with them to the Thane of Fife's castle. When I stabbed Lady Macduff to the death I had in my mind the many times she had glowered at me so blackly when I was a bairn, and I wasted no pity on her and hers.

I was seventeen when I killed King Duncan. Six months after that, when I had likewise dispatched the Macduffs, my father, in gratitude – or maybe out of fear? – created me Thane of Glamis. This caused an almighty clash with the Lady Gruoch, for my father had sworn to her that Lulach would become Thane of Glamis when he attained his twenty-first year. But although she was queen, Lady Gruoch had little support at our court, and with Macbeth, the grateful father, and Macbeth's son against her she had to bide quiet and nurse her wrath. Lulach, who was then within a few months of twenty-one and not likely to relish being passed over for his younger bastard stepbrother, was not there to support his mother and his own claim; he was far away in the north dallying with the young woman who was soon to be his wife. And so no voice was raised when I became Glamis, for, next to Macbeth, I was the most feared and fawned-on man in Scotland.

*

By the time I was nineteen I had grown weary of my father's drunken embraces and the nightmares he often had in my bed after his visits to the three weird sisters. I was a big fellow and comely, a man bursting with lust. I had slept with my father often enough. I had killed a king. I had killed the man prophesied by the witches in their awesome cave to be the forerunner of kings. I was a Prince of Alba and Thane of Glamis. It was time I wed a lassie and had some weans. I wanted heirs to prove the witches in the wrong. I would be king and have kings to follow me.

The royal court was then at Inverness. I told my sire I fain would go to Glamis for a short visit to see my inheritance. 'Ay, go,' Macbeth said. 'But only for a whilie. Haste ye back. I need ye here ahint me to give me strength against my lady's constant cluckings like a sorely roused capercaillie, and her new habit of bleating as though she were a banshee when she sleepwalks.'

And so I came to Glamis for the first time on my own. Long, long over the slow-moving centuries have I regretted yon day. If I had not come then, alone and defenceless – though this description of my young self might strike some as woefully wrong, kenning what I'd already done – my shade might not be lingering here still but lying doucely in its tomb or consorting with other ghosts in a peaceable manner.

But I came to Glamis, and I met Maud and became accursed. On the third day of exhilaration at not being always watched by Macbeth and his lady and their courtiers I rode out alone. After I'd ridden ten miles or thereabouts I drew up my horse at a hovel beside a little wood and asked the beldame, who'd come peering out its door, for a drink from her well. The beldame, a well-built body still a few years below three score, watched as I drank from the not over clean tankard.

'I ken you,' she said. 'You are young Glamis. I've aye known ye would ride here one day to seek your destiny.'

'And what has my destiny to do with you, good wife?' I said.

She primmed her cracked lips as though she had a bite of sour apple in her mouth. 'Ye shall see in time,' she said.

She turned and skirled into the hovel: 'Maud! Haste ye here, Maud my hinny, and see what braw lad's landed on our doorstep.'

Maud did not seem to have been touched by water for aeons, but the dirt could not hide her wondrous beauty. Her long hair, matted by lack of brush and comb, was the colour of daffodils in the dew. Her eyes had yon greenish sheen you see in the sea and in some glass. She was tall and graceful: of such suppleness that her body arched this way and that, as if she were a bow ready to dispatch the arrows of desire.

'I am learning to be a witch like my granny,' Maud told me. 'But I fear I'll never be as skilled.'

'You are doing real fine, quean,' the beldame said. 'You will go on as you have begun and no man will ever be able to withstand your spell. The horned man himself should be jealous of the way this gowk is feasting upon you.'

It was true. Love for Maud flashed between us like a lightning bolt.

My lust rose as I drained the tankard and held it out to her. I loved her because she was like a jaunty pagan boy inviting rape. She reminded me of Lulach. Maud had the same boyish neck and shoulders I had always wanted to sink my teeth into when Lulach and I shared a bed-chamber. I had often lusted after him, and I still did, though by now he and I were enemies. He was bigger and broader and better-like than me, though I was a big and comely childe well over six feet by the time I was nineteen. I had often wished Lulach was a lowborn callant, a slave I could mount like a horse and whip yon big backside of his with loving strokes. The same overwhelming lust rose in me now with Maud.

Maud knew not who her mother and father were. She had been fostered since a babe by old Bertha. The beldame knew the secret, but she was not telling. I thought from the likeness to Lulach that maybe the Lady Gruoch had a finger in the mixing bowl, but Bertha said: 'You can rest easy on that score, Glamis. The quean has not a drop of yon lady's black blood.'

It was not until after I'd married Maud in the kirk at Glamis that I sent word of it to Macbeth. I knew the news would rile him, but I was scarce prepared for the violence of his reply: 'Never draw near me again, ungrateful mongrel. Bide at Glamis with your bride and consider yourself a prisoner there until I see fit to pardon you.'

It was more than a year and Maud was the mother of our first daughter when Macbeth and some attendants came unexpectedly to Glamis. I met him in the hall. He put his hands on my shoulders and kissed me. 'Marriage seems to agree with you,' he said. 'I swear you've grown, lad. You're taller now than me. A pity you should throw it all away on this lass of yours. Where is she?'

Macbeth paled when he saw Maud. I thought it was the sheen of lust, and I prided myself on being fleeter of foot than my father. I gave him a smirk of triumph, but before I could speak he said to Maud: 'Where did you come from, girl?'

Maud told him. Macbeth took a step towards her crying: 'Bertha! May she burn in hell for allowing you to do this sin!' And then he stepped back and said to me: 'Accursed boy, what ill fortune garred you ever clap eyes on her?'

And he left Glamis as though the foul fiend himself were pricking

him with a red-hot lance. I did not see him again for ten years.

In the next seven Maud gave birth to five daughters. Each time I prayed for a son, but it was never to be. Whenever she was heavy with child I knelt so often before the altar in Glamis Kirk that my kneecaps got as hard and cold as the stone flags. But it was of no avail. The seventh bairn, a girl again, was stillborn. And so were the eighth and ninth.

Maud was as avid for a son as I was, so to further this she slept with divers other men, hopeful that if she conceived a male child I would acknowledge it victoriously as mine. Our life together became a misery and a mockery. I bolted out of love with Maud as swiftly as I'd bolted in. We came to the time when we could not let our eyes rest on each other without blenching, and we got no joy out of our children. Besides everything else, Maud, not content with the power she wielded as lady of Glamis, took to practising witchcraft in a most abominable manner, filling the castle with stinking spells and companion witches and warlocks who reeked even more obscenely than the vermin they cast into their bubbling cauldrons.

I longed again for the excitement of Macbeth and his royal court, a venue where I might prance again, a proud stallion uncurbed by the leers and cold-eyed curses of Maud and her followers. The Lady Gruoch was long since dead, and Macbeth had taken no new wife. Thus I felt my sire might welcome me, even back into his bed. I had heard tell that Lulach was always at Macbeth's side and that Lulach's wife was forever eager to whisper her counsels into my father's ear. I felt I should be there to give greater and wiser words in the running of the kingdom.

I left the Lady Maud without a sign or a token and I rode through the moors and forests to Dunsinane, without attendants since I trusted none. As I approached my father's stronghold I was scarce overjoyed to see in my path the three witches who had given Macbeth warning on the blasted heath. They did not frighten me as once they had succeeded in frightening my sire with their dire forebodings. I saw them only as a harmless ill-favoured old man and two harmless ill-favoured old harridans, all huddled like hoodie-crows in shapeless bundles of filthy, evil-smelling rags. I would have ridden past without a greeting, but the old warlock hailed me:

'Hail to thee, Callach, motherless bastard, who shed blood to put thy father on the throne!'

The first witch cried: 'Hail to thee, viper and father of six vipers who sleeps with thine own sister!'

The second witch screamed: 'Hail to thee, monster of Glamis who shall lose thy manhood at the age of two score and three and be a monster for all eternity! Hail to thee, forever maimed and accursed!'

And before I could berate them for their insolence they vanished.

At Dunsinane I was stricken with guilt at the sight of Macbeth. Although he should have been still in his prime, he was an old man. He was like a child in need of love and protection. He greeted me with such affection, holding me to his chest and kissing me endlessly, that I forgot the chill and awesomeness of our last meeting and the ten barren years in between. My heart swam.

That night in bed I told him about the greetings of the witches. And so the truth about Maud came out. 'She is my own daughter,' Macbeth said, shuddering. 'Your half-sister. You have committed a grievous crime in marrying her and having issue. I will not tell you who her mother was, but she was not the lady who was yours. I dared not tell you before now. I was too late. You had already gone far along your doomed path to perdition.'

And yet, despite this blood-chilling pronouncement, this incestuous secret, my father and I became, if anything, closer than ever. And for the next seven years I remained by his side. I never went near Glamis, though on many occasions the Lady Maud sent urgent messages requiring my company, and several times she sent our daughters to court in the hope that they could woo me. But the hope was forlorn, for neither Macbeth nor I could bring ourself to look upon these girls without plunging into shuddering guilt.

Until, in the year 1057, Duncan's son Malcolm, him that was known as Canmore, or bighead, for he was a bragging callant, marched into Scotland at the head of an English army. Master Shakespeare has tellt the tale, and he has tellt it well. What else is there for me, this poor neglected ghost, to say?

While the battle at Dunsinane was raging, I saw all was lost, so I fled to Moray, where Macbeth had been Mormaer. The men of Moray looked after me well, and I lorded it as their new Mormaer until we

heard that Malcolm's soldiers were drawing nigh and there was high
value on my head. I raced northwards and shipped with a band of
Scandinavian pirates, donned a helmet with horns, and sailed for the
Mediterranean. The Scandinavians dreamed of reaping riches in the
southern seas, riches that would keep them in peace and prosperity for
the rest of their days on their farms above the Norwegian and Swedish
fjords. Whether they ever realised their desires I neither know nor care,
for after six months of their brutish company I left them in a port on
the Bosphorus.

It was there I met and became familiar with a young member of the
Varangian Guard. These guards are the personal property of the
Emperor of Rome, always in attendance in his palaces, ready to
protect him with their lives. Although mercenaries, they are not like
common soldiers. All the Varangians are of Nordic stock. All are tall
and virile, and all are of noble birth, not like some of the peasant scum
among the pirates. The randy young fellow I consorted with in yon
port in the Golden Horn, was a son of the King of Sweden's sister and
had fled from his uncle's court after a great blood-letting. He and I had
much in common. 'Is there any future in being a pirate?' he asked me.
'Why not throw in your lot with mine? We Varangians have an easy,
contented life, well paid and with plenty of time and opportunity for
loving. We have greater hopes of reaping fortunes than your pirate
friends. They can expect little more than death by axe or rope.' I
listened gravely, and let his cold blue eyes and warm blood lure me
away with him to Constantinople.

I took kindly to life among the Varangians; I liked the companionship of men like myself, big swaggering men with long pale golden
hair and brown faces. It was agreeable to live in a palace again, a
palace more comfortable and brightly appointed with fine pictures and
sculptures and sundry other decorations than any of the dreich castles
Macbeth had held court in. And I still had my good looks and the pick
of men, women and boys. For a while I was a favourite of the Emperor,
and I fell in easily with the eastern ways of making love. I began to have
dreams of being the greatest power in the empire, but, alas, the All
Highest's jealousy was aroused when he caught me wantonly handling
another guard. As a punishment we were sent with two hundred other
Varangians to Sicily to stop the ravages of Robert Guiscard.

In the days when I was a pirate I heard sometimes the name of Robert Guiscard, but little did I reckon that it would become such a dark, fearsome name in my destiny. It was when I came into the Varangian Guard that his name first started to mean something. His was a name that spread shivers through the Emperor's court. Robert Guiscard was a Norman knight who'd come to the lands south of Rome to carve himself a kingdom. He had not got that kingdom yet, but he was drawing close to it. He had made himself, or forced his fellow Normans to make him, Count of Apulia and Duke of Calabria. The Emperor feared him. He was a danger to the empire and the dynasty. And thus he had to be kept at bay in Italy lest his ambition caused him to take to sea and strike eastwards.

Our campaign was a disaster. I scarce saw Sicily. Our company landed at a coastal stronghold, and we had not time to settle before Guiscard's army besieged us. The stronghold was not as strong as the Emperor believed. It fell before the onslaught of Guiscard's troops, and there was fearful carnage. Of us two hundred Varangians only sixteen remained when we were hauled in front of the victorious Duke of Calabria.

Robert Guiscard was a huge man, taller than most of the Varangians, and none of them was below six feet. He too was of Scandinavian blood, a handsome flaxen-haired brute with the coldest of blue eyes. His heart was icy too, for there was not a scrap of pity in him for his vanquished countrymen. He scrutinised us like a butcher assessing the weight of the bullocks he will slaughter. Yet even with the brooding scowl that presaged disaster, he was a handsomer man than Macbeth was at the same age, and despite my sorry plight I lusted after him.

He shouted in one of the loudest voices I had ever heard:

'Castrate them and blind them.'

Although I knew this fate was only to be expected by prisoners like us, I could not let it happen without plea. I was forty-three years of age, strong and lusty and in my prime. I remembered the witch's warning. I thrust my guards aside and ran forward and flung myself at Guiscard's feet.

'My lord,' I cried. 'Spare me this shame. I am of the royal blood of Scotland. I am a Prince of Alba and Thane of Glamis. My wife, a king's daughter, will pay whatever ransom you demand for my miserable carcass.'

I pressed my slobbering lips against his spurred boots. He drew one back, and then he kicked so savagely he broke all my front teeth.

'Geld this horned northern boar,' he roared. 'Let him be the last to be gelded, so he can taste well what's in store for him. Let the piss and pride be taken out of him. This prince of Alba! But do not blind him. I wish him to see the look on his princess's face if he ever wends his way back to her.'

*

It was many years before I hirpled home to Glamis. The evil that was Maud, I felt, was maybe better than the evil that was in the world beyond Scotland. Perhaps she might have a peck of pity left for the once-loved couthy young childe? Fool that I was to think thus. Our daughters, all married to nobles unwitting of the ill-getted brood Maud and I had spawned, were set up in castles in every airt of the land, preparing to work out their own evil destinies. Maud herself, filthier and more fiendish than ever, laughed when she heard my tale, and straightaway she ordered her attendants to overpower me and bring me to this locked turret room, where I was chained to the wall and starved to death.

It was long, long after my last howls had died away and my body was mouldering that the door was unlocked. The chain was easy to pull away and the carrion was shovelled into a sack and cast upon a bonfire.

*

Macbeth said that blood will have blood. He knew this well, as he knew his own destiny. Yet he spoke no truth when he called himself the secretest man of blood. He was speaking instead of me, his wayward bastard son, more steeped in blood than my sire. Not all the perfumes of Arabia could sweeten Lady Macbeth's hands. Not all the perfumes of the whole eastern world could ever hope to sweeten those of poor dismembered Callach.

Once I was a free ghost and able to roam among my fellows through the ghostly spheres. But several decades ago the doom-laden shade of my wife Maud came back to Glamis from the nether regions, and she cursed me afresh. Since then I am a free ghost no longer. I can no more move from this chamber, where I am chained to the wall again, stark naked and stark mad, an apparition howling forever in pain and shame. Other ghosts cannot see me. Or if they can, they ignore. I am the most eliminated ghost in history. Even the English Bard allotted me less words than he gave to Duncan's horses that escape the chains in their stalls. Would that I could escape from mine with such ease and gallop away from all this blood. Who knows who the Monster of Glamis really was? None cares enough to listen to my tale. They laugh at my howls and turn away, leaving me in my misery and desolation. Yet I was once Callach, Prince of Alba. Must Macbeth's seed remain as nameless and accursed as the Bard's nameless play?

A Botanist's Romance

The botanist – a distinguished man on his own home ground – had only slowly discovered that he was also a welcome visitor to certain laboratories and botanical gardens on the Continent. At his age this was a bonus, for he had still a lot to say and more and more to discover about the rare plants of the world. He was not a particularly sociable man. In everyday life there was something dry about him as though the excitement he felt exploring the forms and origin of flowers had never been communicated in a large way to the amateur of these things. Although nowadays he could get as much teaching as he wanted, he **was at his best amongst small gatherings of experts. It was they who**

understood him and welcomed him. With enthusiastic persons who knew nothing of his subject except the colour and the smell of primroses, he was sometimes abrupt. His friends called him shy, his enemies – rude.

The botanist was unmarried and had lived with his mother – a practical and strong-minded Scotswoman – until she died at the age of eighty. Many people imagined there must be a magnificent flower-garden behind his house. This was not so. The old lady preferred vegetables to flowers, and had made it her duty to produce a plentiful supply of carrots, cauliflowers and turnips for the table. As for other growth, she liked it to be strictly contained – marrows and onions within chutney jars, exotic flowers and the like in pots and window-boxes. While she lived the botanist had not opposed her. Afer her death he planted a few bulbs here and there, quietly digging them in under the smooth front lawn. In the privacy of the back garden he flung up handfuls of seeds as though it were all one to him whether the birds got them or the earth. For the botanist it was an uncharacteristic gesture which he enjoyed but did not repeat. It was from this time that he started to move about more widely.

Although a life-long dedication had limited him to his own subject he had one other passion. He was a lover of the theatre. This too had a limit. He was devoted only to the Elizabethan theatre. So he said. Even that was taking it too far. What time had he ever given to the subject and what chance in his botanical wanderings to find it? No, if he was honest he had to narrow it still further, though narrow was the wrong word for this particular man. He was devoted to Shakespeare and to nothing else on the stage. When forced to it – and it was remarkable how persistent the pundits could be in digging out the reasons for people's choice – the botanist confessed that *Hamlet* was his favourite play. He went no further than that. Why should he? Many others had chosen it. Yet once in a while he could be heard proudly denying that his special interest in the play had anything whatever to do with the flower element. '*What* flowers?' he would ask irritably. 'Oh, I see. Yes, yes, I understand what you're getting at of course. But why should that be the memorable thing for me or the most important? Aren't there, in any case, scores of references to flowers in the other plays? Why would I pick on *Hamlet*?'

The experts didn't take up the question. Yet it seemed to the botanist, whose ear was tuned to plant-talk, that everyone else had something to say on flowers. He was constantly overhearing some casual reference to them – flowers and death, flowers and love, the place of flowers in city planning. People discussed the flower arrangements for wedding parties and civic banquets. Flowers were sent by way of apology or for thanks. They were sent by those too proud or shy to speak. The practical-minded came in with talk of wreaths and bouquets and the convenience for anniversaries of the city-to-city Interflora. Naturally, the botanist was involved with colleagues in professional discussion of his subject. But if certain flowers touched him too closely or were tossed about too carelessly in talk, he withdrew. He would return, his calm disturbed, to his own study.

The play the botanist had confessed to liking best could usually be found while he was on trips abroad. Indeed, in certain cities it was performed more often than at home. And when not in the main theatres as likely as not it was being done by some small group on the fringes or even in the depths of the country. He would discover it in schoolrooms, in church-halls and in ill-lit barns where you were lucky not to be smoked out by genuine taper lighting amongst geese and bats. As for costume, he had seen it in all guises and fashions. He rather enjoyed these changes, however bizarre they might be. This had something to do with the fact that his own clothes had always been of the most conventional kind – a tie which narrowed or grew wider by a millimetre, jackets whose subtle lapel-change was scarcely visible to the naked eye of woman. So it was almost with relief that he discovered the enviable vagaries of the Prince of Denmark who might appear on the city stage in pompommed cap, a knee-length knitted scarf and woolly gloves for the cold encounters with his father's spirit, and unexpectedly grace the barn in ruffles and black velvet, an ostentatious ring on his index finger.

All this hardly explained his feelings about Polonius's daughter. For this was how he often named her, as though 'Ophelia' was a familiarity he could scarcely bear to use himself, far less hear it from the lips of others. And no mere interest in her changing looks explained the half of what he felt as he waited for her to appear, though she too came on – like Hamlet – new from top to toe in every new production. She had appeared in Laura Ashley designs, in cotton meadow-dresses printed with purple daisies. She'd been a skeery schoolgirl in a tunic, a flower-collector, a débutante at court. He'd seen her once in a blue river-robe with darkened, flattened hair as though she had already risked the stream. The botanist, from dozens of dark seats, had seen it all. His own face could not be seen. But if the spotlight had been turned on him it would have shown a man lit up already. For though the town, the company, the actors had all changed, though the girl herself was always a different girl – her entrance never failed to be another shining encounter for this man. He had been waiting for Ophelia, and Ophelia was here again.

That was the one, fixed fact. And though love for an unknown and fragmented being was unaccountable, the botanist had found no reason to explain it. He would, in any case, have denied she was unknown – believing that her various shapes and voices gave all the more insight to her character. All the same he tended to avoid discussions of the play, having once or twice heard Laertes' sister described in negative terms, or sometimes put aside – dismissed almost as cursorily as the Prince had done it. An unstable girl from the start, some said, and unfortunately for herself unable to take a hint. A feminist view could also come up – of a girl totally unable to stand up for herself against any man: father, brother, lover – a pretty, passive girl with little in her head but love. There were those who'd questioned her innocence. What kind of thoughts had burst from these quiet, crazy songs? She was too forward. She was too backward. Some deplored her immaturity, others her knowingness. The botanist felt the injustice of these things. What time was there for growth in the short life? He'd seen the root pulled up, the buds stripped off.

Not that he was without some criticism himself. Her love of plants, real or imaginary, had been careless. Long before madness came on there was the rash, romantic streak. He agreed she had not too much to say for herself – believing no doubt that to offer some language of flowers could make up for it. This was not sensible. It was not safe. The botanist was sorry for these things in her, while knowing that they had one thing in common. Flowers in both their lives had been accidentally mixed up with an improbable love.

*

In many ways the botanist was a conventional traveller. Like other visitors he had his set routine on arriving in a strange place. He would take the usual before-dinner walk, looking a relaxed and self-sufficient figure as he strolled about. Yet this was something of a pose. Except in the vocabulary of his own subject his grasp of languages was not as good as it might be. He found his way around alone, often with guidebook in hand, drawing his finger down lists of churches and museums, checking on restaurants that were recommended and ones he had been warned against. In summer he would enter all public parks and sometimes, as his due, even the large private gardens that looked promising. If it happened that he missed the theatre in these ramblings there was always the chance that he'd come on bills and placards advertising what was on. He would scan these at a glance – his eye passing indifferently over the bright symbols of exhibitions, soloists' names, or the brash slogans of politicians up for election. Then after days and perhaps weeks he would suddenly come on a name on a poster. He would stand transfixed as though this paper nailed perhaps to a city tree had been a letter for him alone, left in a forest on the off-chance that he'd find it. Then, moving soberly on again, he'd ruminate on the double nature of his feeling – for a person always the same but always different, his contemporary from another age, a name behind a name. For in every search he made for her it was not her name that told him she was here. Always the name of the other man.

But sometimes months would go by before *Hamlet* appeared. Then the botanist might have to travel to the outskirts of some strange city – only to find he wasn't going to make it for the whole performance owing to difficulties of strikes or unfamiliar transport. Occasionally he'd arrive late and leave early – never leaving however until word came that Ophelia was drowned, as if between this performance and the last her fate might have changed. He would go back to town on top of a late bus looking down onto a network of strange streets, or staring from a suburban train which skirted the banks and bridges of black rivers. There was no knowing when he would see the girl again. The landscape of the return journey was always dark.

During the whole of one year following a particularly exacting tour on the Continent the botanist did not go abroad at all. When the time **for travelling came round he found he was tired and only too glad to** stay and feel the freshness of an English spring. This didn't prevent him from accepting the usual invitations. There were new centres of plant research to visit. He was pleased to attend the opening to the public of a Nature Reserve made from a large extent of parkland, noted for its trees. He gave a public lecture on conservation in general, and to various more specialised groups he talked of the history of plant discovery with reference to its bravest heroes. He spoke of the present-day problems of collecting and nursing rare seeds from around the world. To a select audience of librarians he gave a paper on the catalogues at Kew, including the computer storage of data on en-dangered species. To staff and students of an Art College he gave a talk on famous flower painters of the nineteenth century, bringing along his own copies of their books as illustration. More than one gathering of school-leavers heard him mourning the extinction of certain plants. He asked them not to tear branches from the trees, not to strip wild flowers from the hedges. Occasionally, there was something peculiarly old-fashioned about these exhortations as when he implored the older girls, who were trying out eye make-up in the back row, not to make wreaths or garlands for themselves from river-plants.

Towards the middle of April the botanist found himself in the west country being shown around a small estate, whose owner – a man he knew only slightly – was particularly proud of his rare cacti. He had built himself a desert in his garden – a long, narrow glass house, high enough to accommodate several thorny giants and under them a variety of the smaller kind, scattered in prickly bright green knots and bunches along the ground. The botanist found the atmosphere oppres-sive not for its dryness but because of the closeness of the tall cacti. For the first time he felt them not as plants but as tough, fierce presences reaching out aggressively from one corner. Together the two men walked the length of the house and back.

'My niece Ophelia will be here this evening for dinner,' the hot-house owner remarked as he bent to flick some sand from the heel of his shoe. The botanist lost his footing on a heap of pebbles, and sat down quickly on a large rock placed there for the benefit of a furry crowd of baby cacti clustering around it in the sand.

'*Is* there such a name?'

'**What do you mean, professor? That *is* her name.**'

'Outside the theatre, I mean. I have never met it.'

'It's rare enough I daresay. We are fond of our niece. I think you will like her.'

'She is interested in plants?'

'Plants of a different kind. She works with computers. As a matter of fact she is a very clever girl and holds down an excellent job. I can't say what other interests she has. I imagine she's got little extra time for anything at all these days. At any rate she'll be delighted to meet you.'

The botanist stared out from desert into spring. There was a flowering cherry on the grass slope beyond the house and a scattering of white narcissi. Through cages of cacti spikes he imagined he glimpsed a movement of poplar leaves.

'And she is not unhappy, is she?'

His host paused to stare at the botanist.

'Not that I know of. To tell you the truth, I don't see her all that often. And then young people don't exactly tell you every single thing they think and feel, do they? I would say she had her head well screwed on. I think she can look after herself. She's had to of course – seeing she has no mother now.'

'I hope she has a father to advise her.'

'My older brother – yes.' A shade of annoyance crossed his host's face. 'Though I think we can say, as her uncle and aunt, that we have not absolutely failed in our responsibilities.'

'And she has a brother?'

The owner of the garden moved rather firmly away from his guest and waited for him beside the door at the far end. He suggested, when the botanist joined him, that by this time he must be needing the fresh air. Perhaps he should take a walk by the river for an hour or so. As for himself, there were a few matters he would have to attend to before dinner – if the botanist didn't mind walking by himself.

The botanist was only too glad to be walking alone down the slope of the garden, breathing in the sweet and sour smells which for him were the very essence of spring growth. At the bottom a stream flowed between steep banks round the outer edges of the estate – sometimes visible in the clearings, sometimes hidden amongst oaks and willows. The path beside it, though it seemed part of the garden, was also a public way. The botanist walked slowly along this path, often stopping to look carefully into the growth on its bank. For whatever other thing might possess this man, the first and great enthrallment of his life continued undisturbed.

There were a few flowers near the water. He saw crowfoot and yellow woodstrife and the broad-leaved ragwort once named a wound-herb. Further up the bank he knelt to study the rarer purple orchis. The botanist, who was a bit of a prude, had never known or had forgotten what the liberal shepherds called it. He was absorbed for some time. When he looked up he saw a girl coming round the bend of the path. Still kneeling, he watched her gravely at first and rather absently like one who'd accidentally conjured up his own idea of spring. Her dress was dark blue with an ordered pattern of lighter leaves and neatly-outlined flowers. But as if rebelling against these tight designs she carried a scrappy armful of leaves and broken twigs with a few tough grasses thrown in, a stalk of wild garlic and a long white flower, still with its root attached. Ivy sprang from her sleeve like wilder leaves escaping the strict leaves of the dress. The botanist knew it was a huge mistake to notice her at all. Nothing but disillusion could come of this. Far better stay on his knees and pray he would neither speak nor be spoken to. As she came slowly on, the loose flower from her bunch got caught on a blackthorn bush and hung there, swinging behind her like a warning. He got to his feet and walked towards her.

'A fine afternoon,' said the botanist, his heart already sinking. On every side, from earth to sky, was the fierce, dark tangle of new life – so dense it was hard to see through to calmer fields. And the girl was close. No curtain or scene-shift now could separate him from pain.

'Yes, isn't it,' replied the girl, staring aside into a willow tree.

'I hope you weren't thinking of climbing up into that tree or anything like that,' said the botanist touching her arm with a despairing laugh. 'The branches are far too fragile to hold you, quite apart from the damage you might do to the tree.'

'I wouldn't think of anything so weird,' said the girl. 'And if I did I'd hardly make a start in shoes like these. Whatever made you suggest it?'

'Are you Ophelia?' said the botanist, with now no hope at all.

'No, I'm Agnes Donnelly,' she said. 'But I know who you mean of course – the Simpsons' niece. Ophelia's a friend of mine.'

The botanist was beyond caring about a proliferation of Ophelias –

how many or how few there might be around the place. For a long time he stood silently looking down the river, which a few yards on vanished under thick trees and reappeared far off as a dark pool between rocks.

'Well, people manage to survive somehow,' murmured the botanist, 'and you'd better tell your friend Ophelia that. The killings and sudden deaths! Dismissals are common. Dismissal by some unhappy and confused young man is not the end. Young men can be arrogant.'

'And old men very odd,' said Agnes. 'Odd and misguided. My friend seems perfectly happy at the moment and doing very well indeed. But I'll pass it on.'

'And people survive this so-called hopeless love quite well,' the botanist continued, ignoring her remarks and speaking encouragingly for himself, '. . . perfectly well, in fact, at the end of the day.'

But the girl wasn't listening. 'I'm looking at that cat up there,' said Agnes. 'It's here every day at about this time. I think it's got its eye on some bird or other. Either that or a fish. But it's too timid to make a move.'

The botanist's eye fell on the bunch of stuff she was holding. He looked beyond her to the trees on the other side of the water. These oaks had survived too. They had survived saws and blights and plans for hideous housing-schemes. He had even blocked such plans himself. For though the botanist had strange dreams he also sat on committees. Nor did he think the uprooting of rare plants was a small thing in comparison.

'You know about wild flowers, I believe,' he said to the girl. 'And surely you must have heard how rare they've become in some districts. Nowadays it's an offence to tear anything from a tree or a hedge for no reason at all.'

'Well, these are nothing,' said the girl, throwing some drooping leaves on to the bank. 'I hardly knew I was taking them. I was thinking of something else.'

'Exactly,' the botanist replied. 'And did you know, by the way, the connection between some birds and certain plants? Kill the bird and you kill the plant.'

'I've never killed a bird,' said Agnes. 'You must be thinking about the cat.'

'Of course some people might be forgiven a carelessness with flowers,' said the botanist. 'They don't know any better. But you – you know what you're doing. You've got all your wits about you.' The botanist knew it was so. This girl stood beside him as large as life. But long ago the witless one had floated off downstream.

Brightness had left the water. A chill gust swept the tops of the willows and – near the ground – faintly rattled last year's seedpods and twisted old leaves still hanging to the bushes. Only the botanist heard this melancholy undernote of spring. The girl was staring at the sky.

'Well, thanks a lot for the lecture,' she said. 'And I suppose you hadn't forgotten Ophelia and I are coming to dinner?'

'No, no, I hadn't forgotten. Certainly not.'

'Then I'll get along now if you don't mind. We'll see you later.'

The botanist watched her as she went off. She disappeared at once into the chequered dark along the path, and quickly the precise patterns of the dress were drawn further and further back into the web of the surrounding green.

In their bedroom at the top of the house, the Simpsons had been watching with interest from a window overlooking the whole of the garden and the steep slope which ran down to the water. The river was only visible where the vegetation was thin. But directly below them every inch of the path was plain.

'Really, he is a most unpredictable fellow!' exclaimed Simpson. 'Did you see how he approached young Agnes down there? – A girl he's never set eyes on in his life – grabbing hold of her arm!'

'I wouldn't call it grabbing,' said his wife. 'He put his hand on her for one second. He's very quiet, you know. If anything too reserved.'

'You'd be surprised what these reserved types can get up to at that age. The rest of us wouldn't get away with it for one moment. In full view of the house!'

'Exactly. He's got a certain peculiar unworldliness in some ways.'

'Oh, you think so, do you? Well I'm glad to say Ophelia isn't a girl to stand for any nonsense.' They left the window and started to get ready for dinner.

'Would you say I had a certain peculiar unworldliness?' said Simpson some time later as he drew on a mauve nylon sock.

'No,' said his wife.

'I mean, of course, in *some* ways.'

'In no way,' said his wife.

Simpson met the botanist as he came slowly up the steps leading from the lawn to the terrace of the house. A table and chairs had been set out for drinks.

'I'm sorry,' said the botanist, 'but I'm going to have to make the most profound apologies to you both, especially to your wife, and to your niece of course. But the fact is I've found I can't stay for a meal after all. Absolutely unforgiveable. I've made an extraordinary muddle about the time-lapse and I've got to get back to town at once. I have a man ringing me from Texas at midnight. About a plant.'

'A *threatened* plant,' said Simpson to his wife late that night. 'Very likely some girl or other. And "threatened" is probably the right word.'

'Don't be ridiculous,' she said. 'The poor man's simply running away. Couldn't bring himself to face two spirited young women over the dinner table.'

The botanist slowly recovered from his life-long attachment. Nowadays he might even listen to other people's problems, and had become easier to talk to himself – though it was difficult to make out from his detached and cautious murmurings whether his own experiences of this kind had been happy or not. For his references to persons were invariably mixed with something of the plant world. Occasionally he let himself go. He spoke of flamboyant characters he'd met, exotic blooms he'd discovered. Then he'd fall silent as if through the heavy scent of tropic plants he'd felt another breath, as cold as river cress. Once the sad girl had momentarily surfaced in his talk. He touched on her lightly – described her as some man's sister, another's daughter, the unfortunate girl-friend of a third. To some the touch was too light to be convincing. They felt the hint of breakdown, even suicide. But was it possible that this douce man himself had been the cause of the despair? This was unlikely. A wartime tragedy perhaps – brother and young man overseas or killed. And no doubt she herself by now long dead. But if it were the botanist's own love-affair? Well, everything disappears in time, they said. Even the memory of it gets blurred. And then he's getting on. Whoever she was, she could be totally forgotten when he dies himself.

But the botanist knew the drowned girl was safe. The stream was her place. And he was happy enough to let her go. She would float on through centuries with sticks and froth and waterweeds, drawing about her the endlessly-seeding drift of fantasies. Sometimes she would be waterlogged, with controversies dragging at her dress – but always moving on again past curious gardens, past new cities towards those future fields and forests which the botanist had imagined but would never see.

He grew old. He moved around less often. Even theatre-going had fallen to one or two performances a year. Though not out of the country himself, he received visitors from around the world – his interest in his subject and his eyesight being as keen as it had ever been. In his seventies he was awarded a substantial prize for a major contribution to Botany. He remained a staunch conservationist – still sitting on endless committees concerned with the saving of meadow and forestland. It was impossible to take on everything. Some people tried to interest him in the watering of deserts, or made it their business to remind him of the silting up of lakes. He had letters on the benefit of flowers as medicine, of flowers as friends, on the necessity of talking understandingly to roses. The botanist rather resented this last advice. He was a modest man and he loved his roses. He believed they would care no more for his ceaseless understanding chatter than would the neighbours on either side of him. He was still in demand, however, as a public speaker and continued to give his talks to schools, warning young people against the needless destruction of plants and trees. All the same he was not as exacting as he had once been, and as time went on he even broke some of his own rules. For sometimes on riverbanks the old man – never a one to throw bouquets around – would quietly pull up a few wild flowers from about his feet and, looking round to make sure he was undetected, would throw them out into midstream where a fast current might take them the more surely to their source.

GABRIEL JOSIPOVICI

A Changeable Report

Kent: 'Report is changeable'
King Lear, IV.vii.

I have been dead for five years. I say dead and I am trying to be as precise as possible. I do not know how else to put it. My hand trembles as I write but it is comforting to have pen and ink and paper on which to write things down. It is as if I had forgotten how to use a pen. I have to pause before each word. Sometimes I cannot remember how the letters are formed. But it is a comfort to bend over the white page and think about these things. If I could explain what happened I might find myself alive once more. That is the most terrible thing. The thing I really hate them for. They have taken away my life, though no court of law would convict them for it. When I think about that time, what they did to me, my insides get knotted up in anger and despair and I hate them not so much for what they did to me then as for what they are doing to me now, knotting me up with anguish and hatred at the memory.

I have tried to understand what happened. I thought that if I could put it all down on paper I would finally understand and I would be free of them for ever. But when I try I cannot continue. There is a darkness all round the edges. I think that by writing I will be able to shift that darkness a little, allow light to fall on the central events at least. But it does not work like that. It is as though the light follows each letter, each word perhaps, but no more, and in so doing moves away from the previous word, which is once again swallowed up in darkness. I pinch myself to make myself concentrate. I bite my lips and try to look as steadily as possible at what has occurred, at what is occurring. But the light moves along with the pen and I can never hold more than a small sequence in my mind at any one time. So I give up and wait for a better moment. But there is no better moment. There is just the urge to seize the pen again and write.

I did not think writing was so important. Till they shut me up. There was no cause. I had been gulled. But they bundled me in and locked the door. They told me I was mad. In the dark I felt about for windows, candles, but there were none. I was afraid of suffocating. I have always been afraid of that. I used to have nightmares about being shut into a basket and forgotten. I could hear them outside, chattering and laughing. I asked for pen and paper. I had to write and tell her what they had done to me. When they finally let me do so she had me released at once. I did not think I had changed then. I did not realise what it does to you to be shut up in the dark without hope or the ability to keep track of time. I vowed revenge on the whole lot of them. As I left I heard him start to sing. I went out into the night.

I had never had much time for his songs or his silly repartees. I do not know why she put up with him. Or with any of them. I need my sleep. I did my work well. I tried to keep them under control. I asked for nothing more. The noise they made. I could not stand that noise, that drunken bawling at all hours of the day and night. I cannot stand the sight of grown men who have deliberately befuddled themselves. It is degrading. Besides, she paid me to keep order in the house and I kept order as best I could. She should never have indulged him. Why put up even with a cousin if he consistently behaves like that? Why keep a Fool just because your father kept one? A hateful habit, demeaning to both parties. Let the Spaniards retain the custom, they are little better than beasts themselves. But that she should do so! And a foolish Fool at that. A knave. As bad as the rest of them, Maria and the cousin and his idiot friend. The noise they made. The songs they sang. Obscene. Meaningless. Vapid. Why did she let them? If it had been me I would soon have sent them packing. Restored some decency to the house. And her still in mourning for her brother.

I thought she had more sense. A page. A mere boy. Get him into bed at any cost. Forget her brother. Forget the injunctions of her father. What kind of life do humans want to lead, what kind of a . . .

My stomach has knotted up again. I hate them for making me hate in this way. I hate them for doing this to me. When I walked out into the night he was singing about the wind and the rain. I thought I would be revenged on them all. My stomach was knotted with anger. I wanted to scream, to kick and punch them, him especially, the fat cousin, the . . .

I have said to myself that I will keep calm. I have promised myself that I will control myself and write it all down so that I may understand and be free of the darkness. I am a survivor. I have not survived so long without learning a little about how it is done. I have the will. I have the patience. They think only of the moment. They drink and joke and sing. They did this to me. They tried to make me mad. They tried to persuade me that I was mad. They could not bear to have me there, watching them, I

At moments, as I write, I no longer know who I am. It feels as though all this had happened to someone else and it has simply been reported to me. I see things in my head. My stomach knots in pain and anger. But I am not sure if my head and stomach belong to the same person.

Never mind. I must use what skills I have and not be deflected. I must be patient. Men have burrowed out of dungeons with nothing but a nail-file. What are five years or ten years when life itself is at stake? I have always been patient. I have my pen and paper and I can always start again. And again and again until the darkness is dispersed and I can emerge into the light once more and live.

I remember the man I was. But he is like a puppet. I do not know what kept him going. Perhaps it was nothing except a sense of duty. I see him bustle. He was a great bustler. I sometimes think I am still there. That I still work there, do what I have to do about the house, take orders from him, from the boy now, while she stands simpering by. I hate her for that, for what she let them do to me and for standing by now and doting on that boy.

But I am not there. I know I am not there. I turned my back on them forever and walked out, vowing revenge. Yet I was not interested in revenge. I only wanted to forget them. To start again elsewhere. But I could not. The song would not let me go. It was like a leash he had attached to me when he saw that I was determined to go. I sleep and it comes to me in my dreams. I wake and it creeps up on me in the daytime. I plotted revenge. I thought I would find my way back there and take up my post with them again. I would steal her handkerchief and poison his mind. He would have killed her for that. Killed her first and then himself. He was capable of it, he went for Andrew the minute he saw him, broke his head and then lamed Toby. They would have taken me back. I know how she felt about me. I would have played on those feelings. I would have made him kill her and then, in despair, he would have done away with himself.

At other moments I thought of other, sillier kinds of revenge. I would have them all on an island. I would be able to control the winds and the waves. I would wreck them on my island. The two drunken idiots would be pinched and bruised and bitten by my spirits, and the others, the others would get their deserts – the whole lot of them. I would frighten them with ghosts made of old sheets, I would lead them into swamps and then reveal myself to them – It would be the silliness of the punishments that would be the most shaming.

Idle thoughts. I am surprised that I can remember them. At moments they were there, so strong, so clearly formulated. But I do not think I ever took them seriously. Because it was as if I had lost the ability to act. As if his song had drained me of my will. When it flooded through my head I cried. I cried a lot. There was another music too, unearthly, and fragments of speeches, but not speeches in the ordinary sense, not exchanges of information between two people, but somehow as if their souls had found words. I understood what they said, but not the meaning of individual words and phrases. In such a night was the refrain. The names of Cressida and of Dido, of Thisbe and of Medea came into it. The floor of heaven thick inlaid with patens of bright gold. I remember that. It was like a music I had never heard before and never imagined could exist. And then I was in the dark but it was peaceful, quite different from that other dark, and another song, fear no more the heat of the sun, and home art gone and ta'en thy wages. It merged with the other voices, telling of Dido and Medea and Thisbe and Cressida. But when I tried to hear them more clearly, to focus on them better, they faded away and finally vanished altogether. I went out through a door and instead of the garden I had expected there was desert, dirt, an old newspaper blowing across a dirty street, decaying tenements. I turned back and there was the music again, but now the door was locked and I could not get in. Why do I know nothing about music? Why have I always feared it? Not just the drunken catches but the pure sweet music of viols, the pure sweet melancholy songs. I fear them all.

I tried to walk then but my feet kept going through the rotten planks. I put my hand up to my head and the hair came away in clumps. I knew this was not so. I knew it was only my imagination. I fought against it. They are trying to do this to me, I said to myself. They want you to think that you are mad. You will not give them that satisfaction. But I woke up dreaming that my head was made of stone and I held it in my lap, sightless eyes gazing past me into the sky. My daughter had betrayed me. She had stolen all my jewellery and absconded with a negro. There was a storm and women spoke and tempted me. I looked at my hands and they were covered with blood. The storm grew worse and I was on a deserted heath and howling. An idiot and a blind old man held on to me, trying to pull me down, uttering gibberish, but I kicked them off, and then there was that song again, about the wind and the rain. In the rain my daughter came and talked. Something terrible had happened but all was forgiven. She talked to me. She answered when I spoke to her. But I knew it would not last and it didn't, she was dead in my arms, I held her and she weighed less than a cat. I pretended she was alive but I knew she was dead. I walked again and the rotten boards gave way, one leg stuck in the ground, it grew into the ground, and all the time I knew it was not so, that if I could turn, if I could return, and it required so small an effort, so very small an effort, then it would all change, she would be with me on the island and I would rule over the wind and the waves, she had only pretended to run away, only pretended to be dead. But I also knew that I could not make that effort, that I could not go back, that the door was shut for ever, hey ho the wind and the rain. I marked the days, the years. I sat at my desk and wrote as well as I could on the white paper. I was determined that they would not make me mad.

It has been like death. Time has not moved at all. Yet it cannot be long before the real thing. I try to put it down as clearly as I can but there is darkness behind and in front. Nothing stays still. I cannot illuminate any of it. I form the letters as well as I am able, but I cannot read what I have written. It does not seem to be written in any language that I know. The more I look at it the more incomprehensible it seems to be. As though a spider had walked through the ink and then crawled across the page. As though it had crawled out of my head and on to the paper and there could never ever be any sense in the marks it had left.

Perhaps there are no marks. Perhaps I am still in the dark and calling out for pen and paper. Perhaps no time at all has passed since they shut me up. I call for pen and ink and paper but they only laugh and cry out that I am mad. I do not know who I am. Except that I am a survivor. I will go on trying to write something down. This is a pen in my hand. I hold it and write with it. This is me, writing. I will not listen to their words. I will not listen to that music. I will try to be as precise as possible. I will write it all down. Then the darkness will clear. It must clear. The music will fade. It must fade. I will be able to live again. That will be my revenge on them. That I have endured. That I have not let them make me mad.

SALMAN RUSHDIE

Yorick

Thank the heavens! – or the diligence of ancient time papersmiths –
for the existence upon our earth of the material known as *strong
vellum*; which, like the earth upon which I have supposed it to exist
(although in point of fact its contacts with terra firma are most rare, its
natural habitations being shelves, wooden or not wooden, some dusty,
others maintained in excellent order; or letter-boxes, desk drawers,
old trunks, the most secret pockets of courting lovers, shops, files,
attics, cellars, museums, deed-boxes, safes, lawyers' offices, doctors'
walls, your favourite great-aunt's seaside home, theatrical property

departments, fairy tales, summit conferences, tourist traps) . . . like the earth, I repeat in case you have forgotten my purpose, this noble stuff endures – if not for ever, then at least till men consciously destroy it, whether by crumpling or shredding, through the use of kitchen scissors or strong teeth, by actions incendiary or lavatorial, – for it's a true fact that men take an equal pleasure in devising means of annihilating both the ground upon which they stand while they live and the substance (I mean paper) upon which they may remain, immortal, once this same ground is over their heads instead of under their feet; and that the complete inventory of such strategies of destruction would over-fill more pages than my ration, . . . so then to the devil with that list and on with my story, which, as I had begun to say, is the tale of a piece of vellum, – both the tale of the vellum itself and the tale inscribed thereupon.

Yorick's saga, of course; that same most ancient account which fell, near enough two hundred and twenty-five years ago, into the hands of a certain – no, a most uncertain – Tristram, who (although Yseultless) was neither triste nor ram, the frothiest, most heady Shandy of a fellow; and which has now come into my possession, by processes too arcane to be of any interest to the reader. Yes, a velluminous history! – which it is my present intent not merely to abbreviate, but in addition to explicate, annotate, – and also hyphenate, palatinate & permanganate, – for it's a narrative that richly rewards the scholar who is competent to apply such sensitive technologies. Here, dusty-faced and inky-fingered, lurk beautiful young wives, old fools, cuckoldry, jealousy, murder, juice of cursed hebona, executions, skulls; as well as a full exposition of the reasons why, in the *Hamlet* of William Shakespeare, the morbid prince seems unaware of his own father's real name.

Very well then: It appears that in the latter part of the reign of the illustrious king Horwendillus of Denmark, his chief jester, one Master Yorick, took to wife a toothsome goldhair waif, by name Ophelia; and there all the trouble began . . . what's this? Interruptions already? Did I not tell you, have I not just this moment set down, that the bardic Hamlet, that's to say Amlethus of the Danes, is quite mistaken in believing the Ghost's name to be Hamlet too – an error that's not only unusual but downright unsaxogrammatical? – But were you to be silent and hear me out you'd learn it was no mistake, but rather the secret key by which the tale's true meaning may quickly be unlocked.

I repeat: Horwendillus. Horwendillus Rex. – Still more questions? – Sir, of course the jester had a wife; she may not feature in the great man's play, but you'll concede that a woman's a necessary apparatus if a man would make a dynasty, and how else? – answer me that? – could the antique fool have produced that line, that positive monologue of Yoricks of whom the ill-named Tristram person's parson was but a single syllable? Well! You don't need ancient vellum to see the truth of that, I think. – Good lord: her *name*? Sir, you must take it upon my word. But where's the puzzle? Do you imagine, in a land where men were called such outlandish things as Amlethus, Horwend&c., yes, and Yorick too, that this 'Ophelia' was so blasted uncommon a name? So, so. Let's get on.

Yorick espoused Ophelia; there was a child; let's have no more disputes. In the matter of this Ophelia: she'd less than half his years and more than twice his looks, so it will instantly be seen that what follows may be ascribed to divisions and multiplications: an arithmetical tragedy, in sum. A grave tale, fit for gravesides . . . how did it come about that this old wintry fool got himself such a springtime of a bride? A noisome gale blows across the ancient vellum at this point; it is Ophelia's breath. The rottenest-smelling exhalation in the state of Denmark; a tepid stench of rats' livers, toads' piss, high game-birds, rotting teeth, gangrene, skewered corpses, burning witchflesh, sewers, politicians' consciences, skunkhomes, sepulchres, and all the beelzebubbling pickle-vats of hell . . . every time this youthful beauty, the frail perfection of whose features brought tears to the eyes, opened her mouth, there cleared all around her an open ground some fifty feet in radius at the least. So Yorick's path to wedlock was unobstructed, and a poor fool must get what wife he can. He courted her with a wooden peg on his nose; on their wedding day the King, who loved him, gave the jester a thoughtful gift, a pair of silver nose-plugs. That's how it happened; thus pegged and plugged, our fool in love assuredly looked his part.

So that's made clear. Enter Prince Amlethus, bearing a riding whip. The scene's a poor bedchamber at Elsinore; Yorick and his lady lie fast asleep in bed. In disarray upon a nearby chair: a cap, bells, motley, &c. Somewhere, a sleeping infant. Picture Hamlet now, tip-toeing to the bedside; then tensing; crouching; until at last he leaps . . . and now *Yor. (awakes)*: O, a! What whoreson Pelion's this, that, tumbling down from Ossa, so interrupts my spine? (There occurs to me a discordant Note: Would any man, awakened from deepest slumbers by the descent upon his back of a seven-year-old princeling, truly have such a command of metaphor and classical allusion as the text at this point indicates? It may be the vellum is not wholly to be relied upon in such matters; or perhaps that Denmark's fools were most uncommonly learned. Some things may never be known.) (Back now to our muttons:) *Ham.* Yorick, the day's awake; let's raise a chorus to the dawn. *Oph. (aside)* My husband never loved this prince; a spoiled short brat, and cursed with sleeplessness, which plague he passes on to us. Here's how we wake each morning, with royal fists a-tearing at our hair, or heir-apparent buttocks jig-jogging on our necks. Were he my child, I'd . . . good morning, sweet my prince! *Ham.* Ophelia, it is. A dawn chorus, Yorick, come! *Yor.* That's for the birds. I'm of too venerable feather, that's the truth; my years long since encrowed me, or made of me an owl. I sing no more, but only caw or hoot in most unseemly form. *Ham.* Now, none of this. Your prince would have a song. *Yor.* Still hear me out. Age, Hamlet, is a setting sun; and in my occidental years it is not right I hymn the orient day. *Ham.* No more. Up, sing. I'll ride upon your back and hear you croon. *Oph. (aside)* At seven he's the old man of the sea; who knows at twenty-seven what he'll be?

Yor. (sings) In youth, when I did love, did love, Methought it was very sweet, To contract, O! the time, for-a my behove, O! methought there was nothing meet. But age, with his stealing steps, Hath claw'd me in his clutch . . . *Ham.* Cease, Yorick, this foul caterwaul; instanter, hold your peace. *Yor.* Did I not tell you so? *Ham.* Enough; give me some jest. Yes, make it about a cat, just such a wauly mog as you just now surpassed. *Yor. (aside)* Now must I do this penance for doing what he willed. (*Aloud*) There's life yet in this old dog you ride; so tell me, Hamlet, why cats have nine lives? *Ham.* I know it not; but why they have nine tails, that I know well, and you shall find it out quick if the riddle be slow. *Oph. (aside)* This prince is sharp as his tongue; and

Yorick's blunter by the day . . . *Yor.* Then here's the answer. All cats will look at kings, but to gaze upon a monarch is to place one's life in their hands, and lives held in such hands do often slip through fingers and are spilt. Now, Hamlet, count the spaces on your hands, I mean twixt finger and finger, and finger and finger, and finger and finger, and finger and thumb; on two hands, count eight crevices through which a life may fall. Only nine lives will ensure that one at least survive; and so our cat, king-watching, must have nine. *Oph.* Husband, a fine conceit. *Ham.* So now a dance; discharge your jester's office and let's have a merry jig. *Yor.* You'll hang upon my back the while? *Ham.* I will; and ponder what I want. *Yor (aside, and dancing)* Hamlet, you want for nothing; yet Yorick finds you wanting.

*

. . . And all this spoken with filigree'd plugs up the nose, up princely nostrils as well as foolish ones! The child, crying in his cradle, cries as much for his bunged proboscis as for the noise of Hamlet's whip, whishing and whooshing through the air to encourage his dancing biped steed. Then what are we to think of this enraged prince? – It's sure he hated Ophelia; but for what? Her pestilential gusts? Her sovereignty over the fool, who doted on her very eyelashes? Or again: it could have been the swelling buds beneath her shift, that's to say her treasure of a chest; at seven, Prince Amlethus is disturbed by something in this girl, but cannot give it name. – So childish ardour turns to hate.

Perhaps all three: her stink; her theft of Yorick's heart, for as any fool knows the heart of a fool is his prince's possession, for who but a fool would surrender his heart to a prince?; her beauty, too. Why choose? Let's be gluttonous in our understanding and swallow the trinity whole . . . We shall spare him too harsh a judgment; he was a lonely child, who saw in Yorick a father as well as a servant, viz. the best, most perfect father, for every son would make his father a slave. In Yorick, singing, jesting, dancing, the pallid prince sees Horwendillus chained. He was a mother's boy.

The vellum hereabouts, – I should say the ink upon it – or more precisely the fist that held the pen – but the fist's long dead, and it won't do to speak ill of the dead – O!, let me say *the text* begins to ramble, to

list in grueful detail all the crimes committed by the prince upon the
jester's person: each imprint of heir-apparent boot upon his buttocks,
complete with itemizations of cause, effect, location, costume, contin-
gent circumstances (viz. the weather, or Hamlet's mother's absence
owing to the tyranny – yes, even over queens! – of the functions of
nature); descriptions of jesterly pratfalls, of the clump of turf with
which his nose collided, of subsequent searches for lost dislodged
nose-plugs . . . in brief, a most lamentable lack of brevity, which we
shall rectify here without delay. The point's well made, I think; to
labour it further would be to emulate that prince, who belaboured the
fool with sticks and whips and the Lord knows what . . . and would we
not be rash to treat our reader (being ourselves no prince) as if he were
a fool? (And being no prince, what business have I with this newly-
infiltrative 'we', this purple plural my sentences have – quite unbidden
– put on? Off with it; back to the common . . . if quite grotesque,
because cyclopean . . . I.)

Once – once will suffice – while riding Yorick, Hamlet with his whip
parted the fool's cheek's fleshy curtains, to reveal the bony stage
behind. It seems he was a feeling prince; enshouldered as he was, his
gorge rose at the bloody sight. – Reader, the Prince of Denmark (to
believe what's written here) puked generously on Yorick's dingling
cap.

*

Albeit, gentle reader, I have till now endeavoured to tell a delicate
tale of private character, with many fine touches of psychology and
material detail, still I can no longer keep the great World from my
pages . . . what ended in tragedy began in politics. (Which will be small
surprise.)

Picture a banquet at fabulous Elsinore – boar's heads, calves' livers,
parsons' noses, goose-breasts, venison haunches, sheep's eyes, pigs'
trotters, fish-roes (here's the anatomy of the table, which, were its
several dishes assembled into a single edible beast, would bear a
stranger monster than any hippogriff or ichthyocentaur!). – Tonight
Horwendillus and his Gertrude are feasting Fortinbras, hoping to stay
his territorial greed by satisfying his belly's equal liking for expansion,
the latter requiring only the murder of the above and mythical

monster, a happier and certainly a tastier strategy than war . . . and is it not conceivable that F., seeing upon the laden board the dismembered limbs of this fearsomely diverse and most occult of creatures, and constructing in his mind's eye a behemoth with antlers on his giant turkey's head and hooves set weirdly down beneath his scaly lower half, might lose all appetite for the fray (fearing to confront, on Danish battlefields, the mighty race of hunters who could slay so wild a beast), and so for Denmark? – It does not matter. I've lingered at the banquet only to explain why this Queen Gertrude, over-occupied by diplomacy and several types of meat, was unable to go upstairs and wish her son goodnight.

Now I must show you Hamlet sleepless in his bed, – but where's the fellow who can portray an absence? – that's to say, the absence of sleep, and of his mother's kiss upon his cheek, – for a cheek unkissed that should have been resembles in all respects a cheek for which no osculation had been hoped, and a boy shown horizontal in his cot (even were I to add the tergiversations and other frenzies characteristic of insomnia) may nevertheless be mistaken for a child plagued by a flea; or fevered; or surly, at being forbidden the grown-ups' table; or practising his swimming in this textile sea; or G— knows what, for I don't. But absence, as is well known, makes the heart grow fonder; so up Amlethus gets, and tiptoes down corridors thus (if each dot represent the conjunction of one toe-tip with the floor):

. . . ./. . . . ./. . . . ./. . . . ./, &c. &c.

– until (to be as quick as he) he reaches Gertrude's chamber, rushes in, and resolves to await her there so that what's absent from his cheek may be presented: a Lethe-kiss from mother, and then he'll sleep. As it turned out, this proved a lethal scheme.

– And now, in pantomime (for I'm afraid my pages' mean allotment may expire before my tale, and so in compensation for my own garrulity these characters may be obliged to rush through dumb-shows, tableaux, and other acceleratory devices quite unsuited to the tragic content of the story; – but still there's nothing for it – my present long-winded folly must make these ancients fools. Thus haste, enforced by our inevitable end, makes Yoricks of us all), let me recount what followed:

'*Hamlet Aghast*': There are voices at the door! – Not only his mother, but some fierce drunken sot! – Quick, hide! – But where? – The arras, not a moment to be lost! – He hides. (And so, in later life, he slays himself, his child-self's memory, grown hoary and Polonial in form . . .) – O, what he hears! The grunting, roaring man! His mother's squeals and shrieks; ah, frail maternal cries! – Who threatens the Queen? – Bravely, the prince peers round an arras-edge, and sees . . . *his father* falling wild upon the lady. A porky-snuffling Horwendillus, under whom Queen Gertrude sobs and flails, – and then falls quiet, while her breath sounds harsh in Hamlet's ears, as if her throat were stopped. – The prince hears death in her voice; and understands, with seven-year-old acuteness, that his father's bent on murder. – Now out he leaps! – 'Stop! Stop, I say!' – His father's springing back; his mother's hand flies to her throat, confirming Hamlet's fears of throttlement . . . the scene is clear enough. 'I saved her life,' Amlethus proudly thinks; but drunken Horwendillus takes his son and thrashes him and lashes and then thrashes once again. – A curious sort of thrashing, for it beats something in to the prince's hide, – whereas the nature of most punishment is to beat an evil out! – What's beaten in? – Why, hate, that's plain, and dark dreams of revenge.

'*Hamlet Alone*': (But I'll leave soliloquies to better pens; my vellum's silent on what Hamlet felt while locked and wealy in his room – you must infer his thoughts from what he did. – It's possible you may see him haunted: a Horwendillian phantom shimmers before his eyes, and seems to miss no chance of squeezing the life-breath from the Queen. – Amlethus' eyes, made visionary by fear, observe the frenzied spectre as it assassinates Queen Gertrude, oh, a hundred, no, more, a thousand times, now falling upon her to throttle her in the bath (soap bubbles burst upon her lips), now choking her at her mirror and forcing her to watch. You, reader, seeing Hamlet's dreams, look through his eyes at Horwendillus's chimæra as it strangles Hamlet's mother in gardens, kitchens, ballrooms, potting sheds; on chairs, beds, tables, floors; in public and private, by day and by night, before and after luncheon, while she sings and while she is silent, clothed and nude, in boats and on horseback, enthroned or on her pisspot . . . until, in short, he (Hamlet) sees his recent rescue's no end, but only a beginning, to his loving anguish; and appreciates the necessity of finding a permanent solution to this matter. – So a plot is born, conceived by nightmare urgency out of hate, its generative organ that royal whip that stung his royal buttocks, delivering upon those nether cheeks just such a yoricking as he'd often given the fool. And so the plot begins to converge on Yorick: bitter Hamlet will use the jester as revenge's tool. – And now you may see two hates coalesce; in Hamlet's angry brain his fury merges (that's to say marries) Ophelia and the King; the stone of his enragement will bring down both these birds, for this is a Medusan wrath, and will turn yoric flesh to fatal granite . . . at last, you hear the child pace round his room, a sullen riddle dripping from his lips:

> 'Nor liquid, nor solid, nor gassy air, –
> nor taste, nor smell, nor substance there.
> It may be turned to good or ill.
> Pour it in an ear and it may kill.'

– Now, reader, my congratulations; your fancy, from which all these dark suppositions have issued (for I began by swearing myself to silence), is proved by them more fertile and convincing than my own.)

*

. . . So well, so accurately have you supposed that my task's made very brief. It remains only to bring Hamlet and Yorick, the one upon the other's back as usual, to a Platform before the Castle at Elsinore. – Where the young prince pours such a magical poison into Yorick's ears that the fool starts seeing illusions. – Yes, you are right: the ghost of Hamlet's still-undead father appears to haunt poor Yorick; and another phantasm, too, is conjured by the venom: Ophelia, Yorick's wife . . . her clothes in disarray, her body twined in translucent, ectoplasmic splendour round the King's! – What was the princely poison? Solve your riddle, reader, and you'll know; – there, there, never mind, I'll solve it for you: reader, it was Speech. O deadliest venene! Being insubstantial, though very serpentine, it knows no antidote . . . to be plain, then, Hamlet persuades his father's fool that Horwendillus and Ophelia, that Dame Yorick and the King . . . and possibly (the vellum is unclear, smudged at this point by ancient tears or other salty fluid) the boy brought proofs – a pair of golden nose-plugs bearing the royal seal, wrapped in a billet-doux? – or was it a handkerchief? – no matter. The damage is done, and Yorick is multiply a fool: – for he was always a fool by trade, and is now a doubled dolt for being the prince's gull, and (in his own eyes) trebly and quadruply an ass (and a most foolish-looking ass, because of the horns that stand between the ears) for seeming, as he believes, a fool in the lovers' eyes . . . and here's the strangest thing, and the dark heart of the matter: by becoming a fool-actual, he sacrifices the privileges of the fool-professional. A jester was a curious sort of fool, permitted by his motley to speak wisdom and have men laugh at it; to tell the truth and keep his head, jingling as it was with silly bells. – Yes, fools were wise, as wise as clocks, for they knew their time for what it was. – But now this clock-wise Yorick changes round; fooled by the prince, he begins to play the fool – to play it truly, that's to say to rant, to roar, to act the jealous spouse in deadly seriousness. – Which was Hamlet's intention; to force the fool into a fatal folly. I've said he saw the jester as a second, clownish father; this surrogate parent is now unleashed by poisoned words against the royal sire.

You have understood the rest: Horwendillus sleeps alone in his gethsemane; enter Yorick, with juice of cursed hebona in a phial. – The poison Hamlet poured into his ears has precipitated, or so it seems, into this bottle – and from the bottle into the king it goes. – And that's Horwendillus dead; while Ophelia, accused by Yorick, loses her senses and wanders round the palace in a flowery madness till she dies of grief; – which madness gives the clue to Claudius, who then uncovers the crime, and it's to the block with Yorick, and that's that. – But here's a mystery, an unknown hand at work! For someone, whom I cannot name, retrieves the head; and with all necessary bribes and whispers secretly contrives to have it buried there, where after many years the prince will find it out, and be confronted by his grinning bony guilt. – So a faceless joker, some lover of the jester's heady wit, makes of his severed noodle a most *capital* (if unwitting) amusement.

*

Tumpty tum, tumpty tum, and a tumpty tumpty tum . . . reader, time's passing, and each of us passes the time in his own sweet way, whether by drumming of fingers, or in sleep, or courtship, or the

consumption of strings of sausages, or however we please; my own
habit is to hum, and so tum tum tumpty tum. (If the tune distresses
you, be off and pass the time in some other place; freedom's a spaniel
that grows weak and flabby if it is not exercised, so exercise your dog,
sir, that's the trick.) — But, returning after many years to our scene,
what do we see? Not Yorick; he's dead. Then Yorick's ghost? For he
seems to haunt the living, so that we may call him a will-o'-the-wits . . .
reader, how much has gone wrong at Elsinore! Gertrude, rescued by
her son from her first murderous spouse, remained in mourning many,
many years, while Claudius ruled. (In this it's true my history differs
from Master Shakespeare's, and ruins at least one great soliloquy. — I
offer no defence. — But this: that these are matters shrouded in
antiquity, and there's no certainty in them; so let the versions of the
story co-exist, for there's no need to choose. — Or this: that when
Queen Gertrude at last did marry Claudius, the intervening years (in
Hamlet's troubled mind) were by this action concertinaed, blurred
together, compressed; so that to him the passage of his childhood, his
adolescence and young manhood seemed to be no longer than two
months (nay, not so much, not two) . . . and this is wholly com-
prehensible, for have they not flown by in the brief space of time it
took to sing my tumpty tum? — Have they not passed in the few
moments it took to walk Freedom, your spaniel bitch? — Well, then,
you have two unanswerable cases instead of none; and that's enough,
I hope.

I was saying: Gertrude marries! And now dead Yorick's jealousy,
unhoused from the jester's corpse, and seeking a new home, finds one
in Hamlet. It's clear (so Hamlet plots) the King must be accused of his
brother's murder, and Yorick's execution must be shown to be the
camouflage, the arras behind which the truth was hid . . . so Murder's
spectre is invoked a second time, and Hamlet, in his mother-loving
passion, sees it walk the battlements of Elsinore. — But the ghost bears
his own name: by which the prince, the accuser, is accused. Haunted
by the phantom of his crimes, he starts to lose his reason. His own
Ophelia he treats badly, as you know; his cracking brain confuses her
with the unbearable memory of the fool's foul-smelling wife . . . and
(to cut this short) at last the prince, who once turned speech to poison,
drinks from a poisoned cup; — and then dead marches, and also

marches of the living: old Fortinbras, too long uninvited to a meal, eats Denmark up instead.

But Yorick's child survives; is brought to England; and generations follow; ending (I'll now reveal) in this present humble AUTHOR; whose ancestry may be proved by this, which he holds in common with the whole sorry line of the family, that his chief weakness is for the telling and re-telling of a particular species of tale: which learned men have termed *taurean*, and also *chanticleric*. – And just such a cock-and-bull story is by this last confession brought quite to its conclusion.

J. L. CARR

Justice Silence, now blind, wits wandering a little and very old, is visited by Sir John Falstaff's page, now a man, and asked for news of Francis Feeble, the woman's tailor, once unfairly conscripted for the army during rebellion.

'I care not, a man can die but once: we owe a death. I will never bear a base mind; if it be my destiny, so: if it be not, so: no man is too good to serve his Prince: and let it go which way it will, he that dies this year, is quit of the next.'

Henry IV, Part ii

Yes, I am Justice Silence. You say we've met before? Where did you say? Twenty years past, in Shallow's orchard? Speak more deliberately: I'm old. Robert Shallow . . . yes, yes, of course I knew him. Was he not godfather to my son, William, who was at Oxford (to my cost). And you seek news of Feeble? Frank Feeble, the women's tailor, once of this parish, at the town's end? Why do you come to me? Who sent you here? You served with him in France? And before, when Scrope and his rebels gathered at York?

You also were in France? Then saw you not my son, my William? Well, there were many there. He fell at Agincourt; I shall not see his grave. My daughter also, Ellen. Gone and within a twelvemonth of her wedding-day. Killed by a horse at Campden Fair, a Martinmass. Her child within her, too. They lie beneath the aisle close by our bench, Catherine my wife beside them. Come Sundays and a young child leads me there. William lies in France. I sit alone there now. And when I die, the name dies with me and Silence lost in silence. Well.

No, no don't hurry off. Sit down. Pour us some ale. Well, you can see I'm blind.

News of Frank Feeble? You are not the first. Another came asking for word of him. No, it was long ago – after the young King died. He came at shearingtime. Fluellen his name, a captain from the Wars. Or so he said. Well, I believed him. He said he saw my son, lantern in hand, heartening the outward watch, just before dawn that Crispin's Day. And next day saw him buried on the field at dusk. I told him all I knew of Feeble, gave him the writing Feeble gave to me before they trapped him here. I'd had it by me all those years, reading it nightly when I was alone. And, when I'd told him all, westwards he went to Wales.

He'd scarcely gone a day before men sent by our Bishop came, pursuing him. They swore he was a Lollard courier, reading the gospels in our English tongue wherever people met – on river-ferries, threshing-floors, at butts, in fields and inns. 'Eastwards!' I told him. 'Eastwards he went, coming from Wales.' They took the Oxford road.

You also were at Agincourt? And lived.

We met in Shallow's orchard, eh, when news of the old King's death came to these parts? And you were but a lad then, Falstaff's page? Well, neither you nor I will sit beneath those trees again. 'Bring out a dish of carroways, Davy,' he'd call. 'And, Cousin Silence, what will a yoke of bullocks fetch at Stamford Fair?' Davy! That was before servant was master, master, serving-man. Falstaff, your pigswill master, weighed things well. Did he not say, 'This Davy serves here for good uses, eh? He is this silly Shallow's husband; serves him well, I swear.'

And thus it was. When the Fleet Prison let them out and he came home, stripped of Authority under the Crown, the Lord Chief Justice's scorn stinging his ears, a thousand pounds the poorer, Shallow took to his bed. Then Davy served by night and ruled by day. So beds were changed and Shallow lay in a back garret. Others will tell you. He was my cousin, godfather to my son, William who lies in France. Captain Fluellen saw him there, out on the ramparts in the morning mist, answering the King. 'He was a worthy gentleman, your son, indeed he was. A stout heart he had and versed he was and observed well the disciplines of the wars he did,' the Welshman said. He said it sitting where you sit.

Ah, that was a black day for us when Falstaff's swaggering crew (you with them) came from the Cotsall Hills into these parts. But then it seemed heady breath of distant war. 'The Prince has northwards gone to York!' Ha! Had we but looked an inch before our silly noses! That leering braggart and his ragtag band! You knew him – name me that adjutant, that fire-faced man, that walking warming-pan! Bardolf! If you were Falstaff's page, then tell me how he died. Like an old rotten tub, riddled with pox? Come the Great Day, many will rise and damn his soul to hell. Shallow among them.

So Bardolf robbed a church and stole a pax? Wept as they dragged him to a tree? Well, I can picture it, his face all whelkes, bubukles and knobs, his blubber lips kissing a penny cord. That other one, that Pistol, unfrocked priest, sometime stage player? He had a cudgelling? From that same Welshman that I told you of, Captain Fluellen! A leek rammed down his throat! You heard them boast, 'To France, to France, to suck, to suck, to suck.' So one sucked hemp and one a stinking leek! Well, there is justice still.

Yes, you seek news of Feeble . . . I'll tell you in good time. You like our brewhouse ale? Then fill your can. Mine too. A song we sang that day in Shallow's orchard – do you remember it?

> 'Fill the cup and let it come.
> I'll pledge you a mile to the bottom.'

A silly song! You also were in France? My son lies there. I sold a river field to fit him out. That Lollard Welshman brought his broken sword. Look yonder on that wall. I had a fair voice for singing then. Or so folk said. I'm wandering.

Feeble was there, this Welshman said. You knew? Behind the lines guarding the baggage, when the fleeing French burned the King's tent and cut down the boys. And he fought well? You with him, back to back? No others lived? He never spoke of it. Ah, that's where he had that slash from ear to chin. Well. How did your swill-belly master, Falstaff, mock the man? 'Courageous Feeble! O most valiant mouse! Wilt thou (he said) prick holes in battles like a petticoat!' And Feeble answered, 'I'll do what's to be done and t'be my destiny. A man can do no more: we owe a death.' You were that boy attending us that day? Under the apple trees in Shallow's orchard? Well. 'Black as an ouzell-cock,' he called my girl, his god-daughter. Words, words . . . Words were the death of Shallow. Words took his wits away. Better he'd stuck to Silence.

So long ago! Under the trees! Yet you remembered me – old Justice Silence. For though I'm blind, I still hold office here under the King. Do you remember – *'Under which king, Bezonian, speak or die!'* Now here's a strange thing: Pistol lives in these parts. Yes, I am old but not so stupid yet. By Cock and Pye, I swear it. He had discharged his name and stuffed another into the breach. Well, I forget. When you are old, you too will grope for names. I swear I saw him in the street at Stratford Fair. Nick Cluff, a chandler there, told me he'd set up as a butcher in the town and laughed, saying that, when he slew a sheep he made a speech. They say he had a child out of Doll Tearsheet. Poor child – words will be all his inheritance. Well.

Frank Feeble . . . few here remember him. He might have never lived for all our youngsters care. A man of no account! Though a king's brother stood by him at the end. Yes, I was there and saw it. And I'll come to it presently. What took me the long road from here to Giles's Field that day? A gown! A grudge! My daughter Ellen, Shallow's godchild, plain as a pikestaff. (Is Pistol's name now Pikestaff?) But for her hair. Black like an ouzell's wing, my cousin said.

Ellen would have her gown made-up in Gloucester. 'Nay, that you shall not, chit,' I cried (her mother being dead). 'You shall have Feeble from our town's backend. Feeble shall cut both coat and cost.' Ah, what a bother for a wedding gown! She should have gone to Gloucester. And she wrapped in her shroud within the year! My grandchild too. Crushed where they stood at Campden Fair. That was a bad year for our Cotsall flocks. First, a long snow from Yuletide to Twelfth Night. Day after day of rain. Then footrot, then the scab. That's how it went. Else had she gone to Gloucester.

And all the fuss for nothing! She made me pay. By God, she made me pay. Feeble must buy blue Flemish silk from Stratford. Then she tormented out of him French lace he'd long put by. He dressed her like a golden toy, so when he brought his bill it was not Gloucester-sized. London would have come cheaper. And so I paid him twice. He scarcely had reached home to count the cash, when constables sent by me pressed him and, with Thomas Wart and Simon Shadow, (the parish idler and the parish fool), carried him off to Shallow.

I meant no more than frighten him – to pay him back. Shadow and Wart were charges on our parish; we were well rid of them. But Feeble! Feeble, a soldier! He was so slight, so miserably built, a scant cheese-paring of a man. How should I know that Falstaff could be bribed?

And, as they went, Frank Feeble turned. 'Ah, sir,' he said, 'Your daughter's gown – I shall not see her wear it on the Day. Tell her I wish her well.' Shadow was snuffling like a pup, Wart blubbering. He turned to them. 'Come, lads,' he said, 'No man's too good to serve his Prince. And let it go which way it will, who dies this year is quit the next. But never fear; this Bardolf's nose shall light us back to Badsey.'

Then they were gone.

Well, you were with them; you know as much as me. I heard the tale from Shadow. They came to Galtres Forest where the King's host camped near the Archbishop's. And when the rebels had gone home, the word went round, 'You summer soldiers sling your hooks and go. Follow your noses home.' And Shadow and Wart never afield further than Tewkesbury! But for Frank Feeble, only God knows what might have become of them. They were a month, more than a month on the roads. Money gone, shoes worn out, half-starved, beds on stacks, in barns! 'O, sir, methinks I dreamed it, sir. Sir, there were towns and rivers, sir. Sir, sometimes we slept; sir, sometimes we walked; sir, sometimes Frank Feeble talked.' So Shadow said.

'Talked, silly Shadow? Talked about what?'

'Sir, always the same, sir. Sir, always of Christ. Sir, he had some sheets of writing in his pack, had Feeble. Wart said nobody must be told: he kicked me, sir.'

That gave the game away. Did not John Wickliff, also Ball the hedge priest, come from those parts! York was a nest of Lollardy. Talked? Ha! Preached! That writing in his pack – scraps of the gospel copied down, the same I gave the Welshman. There's no doubting that. Wart, ragbag rogue tacked up with pins, came home another man. Feeble had dragged him through Jordan into godly cleanliness. And taught him how to sew. Why do you laugh?

You wish to hear the rest?

Well, Feeble came home. But not for long: a taste for wandering tickled his fancy now, to see new parts, talk with new folk of things he dared not here at home. So, when news came the King minded to go to France, Feeble was off. A woman, sleepless at night, heard him pass by, Wart grumbling at his heels. But Feeble turned him home. She heard him call, 'You have a wife; wars are for single men. Back to your bed. And pray.' And then was gone.

The rest you know. Captain Fluellen found no fault in him. 'He was no pigger than a poy,' he said, 'but had a great heart had Feeble. Indeed he did. And observant also in each eventuality in the true disciplines of the wars. Indeed he was. And read he could. And write a letter too. Your son, also, was a true soldier, sir. I saw him, sword in hand, with two or three (no more) stand about Erpingham, that ancient lord, when the French horsemen made a last attack. Here is his broken blade.'

Well, Feeble returned from France, helped Wart awhile; then, roundabout, I heard he preached in woods and heaths out Pebworth, Charlton, Cleeve and Cropthorn way. 'Our Lord said this. Not that. Look here – I'll read his very words as Wickliff wrote.'

The Bishop grabbed.

But Feeble had gone. Wart, knowing of the trap, sent word to Evesham. And so he wandered off, first to the Malvern Hills, then into Hereford, where that Lollard knight, Oldcastle, was Sheriff. There he was safe. Until the King, nagged on by churchmen, declared Oldcastle traitor-heretic, snared him in Powys, roasted him hanging on St Giles's Fields. There was a silly song,

> *Spit me right*
> *Yet dub me knight.*
> *Samingo!*

So, once again, Feeble came home. This time the Bishop snatched him. That wedding gown! She should have gone to Gloucester. I followed them. There, in the Chapter Court, he justified his heresy with Christ's own words. Three times the Bishop growls, 'The bread's Christ's flesh when the priest feeds your soul.'

'Nay,' Feeble answers. 'It's the same crust a ploughman munches out on the headlands by his blowing ox.'

I spoke to get Frank off.

'Wag not your beard at me,' he cries. 'This is *my* court. It may be you are one of the same persuasion as this rogue?'

He was a hard man, that bishop. There was no mercy in his heart.

And so I came to London, to St Paul's. There, the Archbishop got the same answer. NO.

It was so odd a sight. He was so small, a shrivelled pea-pod of a man. And they, his gilded judges, each in his chapter stall, like fat cats round a mouse.

At first, they purred. 'Come, little man, just say the word and off we'll pack you home. Candle in hand, you'll do a penance there in your own parish porch.'

'No.'

Then the fur flew. Out came the claws. 'We did not spare a knight. Your lord died screaming.'

'Aye,' Feeble answered them, 'aye, on the bitter cross, where priests like you lifted and nailed him. I have seen men die, serving their prince, at Harfleur and at Agincourt. We owe a death and if t'be my destiny, I must die too. For this I have been promised, like the thief: the day you burn my body, that same day my soul shall feast with Christ in Paradise. Wickliff has written it.'

And laughed.

And was condemned.

Words, words! Words ruined him.

You stand to stretch your legs? Tell me while you are on your feet . . . west where the Malverns rise, is it still light along the further ridge? That way the Welshman went.

Feeble? I followed him to Giles's Fields. 'Now, Frank,' I said, 'you have gone far enough. Think of the years ahead. Lie to them, lad: it's only claptrap. Let's turn our ways home west to the Severn.'

He could not speak for fright, yet shook his head.

Then, by the Rood, who should come there, remembering Agincourt and lads slain by the tents – Prince John of Lancaster, brother to the King. His folk forced back the throng, leaving the three of us by the heaped faggots.

'My Lord!' I said, 'William, my son, fought at your side that Crispin's Day.'

He did not hear. Brushed me aside.

'Now little tailor-man,' he laughed. 'Tell them bread becomes flesh, wine turns to blood. And say you'll learn some Latin. Then we can all go home.'

He did not answer. Oh, he was dumb with dread. No doubting that. He could not trust himself to speak. Then, forced between his teeth, another No.

You have seen Lancaster with his hackles up. 'On your head be it then,' he roared. 'The realm is one fool less.'

And, at a churchman's nod, Feeble was prodded up the heap and pinioned there. He stared at me as if he did not know what was afoot, why he was there. Then his lips moved. One of their butchers groaned.

'What did he say?' I cried.

' "It shall suffice. Jesu come quick." That's what I think he said. Yes, that's what he said.'

Must I go on? You will not stomach it.

A torch was flung. Fire flared from gorse heaped round his knees. God save us: I can see it still. And brighter now I'm blind.

'Let's have him down,' Lancaster yelled.

They leapt and dragged him off. Now he stood swaying. Smoke puffed from his rags.

'Come, man, say what they ask for. Great God in Heaven, man – yell anything and, by the Rood, I'll swear before ten thousand courts you uttered what the Church wants. Come man, I'll stick by thee. Speak, nitwit.'

Now, even now, all these years after, I still start up in bed and howl, remembering it. And Lancaster – God knows he had seen sights enough in France – yet now he shrank from that man's agony. Well, he is gone. God spare us every one.

The great scar he got at Agincourt shone on his filthy face. He did not speak. Then John of Lancaster grabbed at the wagging head. 'Your soul!' he cried. 'To let it go unshriven and unsummoned is a Great Sin. Your soul's in peril, man. One word!'

They stared one at the other like men mad. Think of it. Tailor and prince! Here's a strange thing: it seemed not strange. Now, yes; then, no.

And Lancaster stepped back. One long last look. Then he was in the saddle and away. Men scurried after him.

No, no, I could not look. Stopping my ears, I fled.

Who did you say you were? Well I am old. In Shallow's orchard all those years ago! Would that the times might turn and you a boy! He said my daughter Ellen sang like bird in bush. Shallow, her godfather, said it. You know I have no son? They flocked like wild geese, winging south to France; William among them. Well.

All of them gone now; some to the gallows, all to the grave. Frank Feeble? Brave words were his ruin. Where does the fault lie? So we are made, our ways are decided. Another hand dangles us, plays with us, tires of us. Down drops the curtain. Exeunt all.

You shuffle your feet: well, you've got what you came for. It's time you were off now? Give me your hand then. How lies the light now? What do you see? A child runs to supper . . . wains heaving homeward . . . rooks flying westward. Yes, you may leave me: I'm used to the darkness.

ALLAN MASSIE

Ossie: a Dumb Black Ox

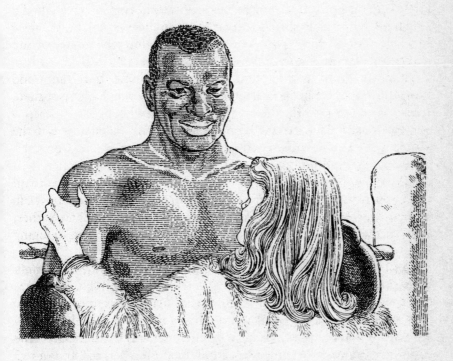

After the recording the talk relaxed. The television people were free to giggle among themselves; they had lost their brief authority. The four journalists who had made up the panel could now ignore them. By the time they were drinking their second gins, they might have been in the safe cocoon of a Fleet Street pub.

Their conversation turned anecdotal; inevitably; scurrilous, sometimes lewd, certainly slanderous. A young assistant producer, some sort of trainee, just down from university, hung round the fringe of the group, feeding off the crumbs they dropped.

Of course last month's scandal received an airing. Everyone

knew what had happened, or at least could chip in one piece of the mosaic, or had a version of the events. The *Guardian* woman spoke of CIA involvement; she had a colleague who had had it from a source in SHAPE. The trainee felt his skin glisten at the thought. The others seemed more sceptical; unlike the boy, they had long been accustomed to hearing the Company blamed for every sudden political death in the Free World or the Third World which might possibly seem to serve American interests.

'The strange thing is,' said the rather supercilious young-old man from one of the weeklies, 'that self-interest couldn't have had anything to do with it. Jeffers' self-interest ran all the other way. After all, nobody has been denying that Lionel was his patron, and Jeffers is pre-eminently the sort of little shit who needs to keep a good grip of all the patronage coming his way . . .'

'That's true,' *Guardian* woman admitted. 'but if the Company was blackmailing him . . . and all the evidence suggests Jeffers was very blackmailable . . .'

'I've heard tell,' said a serious young Scot, who might have been a bit out of his depth – did he, the trainee wondered, come from some provincial paper in Glasgow? – 'I've heard tell that Jeffers hadn't got the promotion he was counting on . . .'

'Oh promotion, who cares about fucking promotion?' *Guardian* woman asked.

'Och,' said the other Scot there, thickset Alec Macrae, veteran of a thousand and more crises, who had worked for the old Beaverbrook Press and been a protégé of the Lord himself, 'everybody's making too much of the strangeness, not that it's no' strange of course, but . . . well, there are precedents for this sort of thing. Does anyone call to mind the name of Ossie Bellow?'

Nobody did. The *Guardian* woman – she really was not what the trainee thought a woman should be, perhaps he was innocent – sniffed. As much as to say that anyone of whom she hadn't heard was better not raked up.

'Fill my glass, boy,' said Alec, 'and I'll tell you the tale. It's a rare one, and it takes me back to my youth . . .'

For a moment you could see the eager wee boy who had come out of Govan about the time of the General Strike.

'So you've maybe never heard of Ossie. Tempus fugit, no question. He was a big black bugger – sorry about the conjunction of noun and epithet, Hilda' – he ducked his head toward the woman from the *Guardian* – 'a real big black bugger,' he said, looking into his glass and disregarding his own apology. 'First time I saw him was in Ed Harkins' gym above the Black Dog pub in Islington. Pub's still there, but the gym's long gone. Gentrified. It was just after the war, we were all in our demob suits, Bruce Woodcock was the great heavyweight hope, the man who was going to end the tradition of the British horizontal heavyweight. And of course Ossie wasn't exactly British, not the way things were counted in those days. Jamaican in fact. As such then he wasn't eligible to fight for the British title. Which was as well for Bruce Woodcock, in my opinion. Ossie could punch like your proverbial mule. Mule was a fair way to describe him too.'

He took a sip of his gin.

'Can't remember who took me to the pub to see him spar. Somebody had said he was good. He was being rubbed down when I arrived, I remember that, a great shining ebony bugger. He looked at me over the ropes, lifting his head slowly and looking me straight in the eyes, and I turned to whoever brought me – Ed Spain of the *Sketch*, was it, yes, it was Ed – and said, "he's no champion. Not with that look." It was a victim's look, noble and self-regarding. You know that muckle great statue in Rome, the dying Goth or something. That sort of look. Admiring his own suffering. Not of course that Ossie was suffering. Not then. Maybe, I said to myself, he's just dumb. A dumb black ox.'

"To hell with that," Ed Spain says to me, "just you wait and watch his left hook. If you can see it travel, that is."

'So we settled down. They rubbed some oil on him and his body was sleek as a seal. And then I feel a hand plucking at my sleeve. Like a pimp's hand. There's too many people in the wee gym and a smell of sweat and oil and resin and you can hear the voices coming up from the bar below. I get a very curious feeling – why the hell do I remember it so clearly now, near forty years later? But I do, I get this feeling that none of it exists, none of the whole set-up is there, except for this pimp's hand plucking at my sleeve.

'Only of course it's not a pimp, or at least not the usual sort of pimp. I look round and I see this white-faced loon with big lemur's eyes and a widow's peak of black hair. He knows who I am and he calls me Alec.'

'For Christ's sake, Alec,' said the *Guardian* woman, 'what is all this nonsense?'

'Whisht, woman,' said Alec, 'it's a tale of passion and hatred. Self-love and self-hatred strangely mixed, and it explains to you why Jeffers acted as he did.' He raised a silencing hand. 'Furthermore,' he said, 'to resume my tale, the wee man knows who I am. "You're on the *Express*," he says, and I nod, looking for the offer of a dram. It doesn't come. "What do you think of him?" he says. "He's big," say I, not giving anything away. "Oh big," he says, "I'm his agent."

'Now that was a new one on me, I'd never heard tell then of a fighter wi' an agent. "You mean his manager," I say, but no, "that's his manager", he says and points to a grey man in a grey herringbone suit. And a yellow streak crosses his face as he says it.'

The other journalists started laughing, the *Guardian* woman with a shrill note of contempt that disturbed the young trainee – it was unkind and knowing – but did not appear to worry the old toping *Express* man.

'I'll tell you why you laugh,' he said, 'it's because you're uneasy. You're uneasy before the raw emotions of my tale.' His eyes twinkled. 'Anyway, before I can reply to him, Joe Hamlyn the guvnor of the pub steps forward and says that Ossie is now going to spar. He says a lot more besides but I'm more interested in seeing who they bring on for him to spar with. It's no one I know, a big Irish boy with red hair and a broken nose and a look in his eye like a poacher's dog. He comes out of his corner all bustle and action and lets fly a haymaker. Ossie just flicks his chin out of the way and smiles. Absolutely in charge, a man in his metier, as sure of what he's doing as a film cameraman. He snakes out his left, fast, three times, and the Irish boy blinks, and Ossie circles the ring on black panther's feet, and shoots out the left again and the Irish boy can't get out of the way. Okay, I say to myself, they're right, this boy'll make mincemeat of Woodcock . . .'

'Tell me, Alec,' said the young-old man from the weekly, 'do you suffer from total recall?'

But Alec, as the trainee who is a Romantic is pleased to observe, has now launched himself undeterrably, and he just waves the question aside . . .

'After a couple of minutes the Irishman's bemused and Ossie gives him a short right to the belly and snaps over a left hook and he goes down in a heap. And do you know, the white-faced loon that says he's his agent isn't watching. He's wetting his lower lip with the tip of his tongue and looking over the ring at the door to the back room. I'm no hand at describing girls, but the one who came through that door was like the Harry Lauder song, pure as the lily in the dell . . . "Who's the bint?" I say, "sure I've seen her before." But the white-faced loon doesn't answer. He takes his hand from my sleeve and moves round the ring and stands beside the girl. She takes one look at him with cornflower eyes under long lashes, and she's afraid and disgusted. You can see her mouth not quite able to shut. She's alarmed like a two-year-old filly in the parade ring. She's wearing one of those berets they wore in those days and you can see blonde hair bunching out at the side it's pulled down on, and she would look marvellous and secure in her black tailor-made if it wasn't that she can't shut her lips. And then she forgets the pimp or it looks as if she does, because she's now got her gaze fixed on Ossie. The big black bugger comes prancing up to her, and they sort of smoulder. It's as if they were the only two people in the room. You could imagine the pair of them getting straight on to the mat, and tupping there. That's what I'm trying to make you feel and see. Passion. Can you sense it? Can you sense it, boy?'

He turned to the trainee. The boy nodded. His throat felt dry and his skin hot.

The *Guardian* woman said, 'Really Alec, I had no idea you indulged yourself with these lurid Barbara Cartland fantasies.'

'Stop talking like a foolish virgin, Hilda, I know too much about you.'

The old man held out his glass for a refill.

'The girl was called Desi Lawrence,' he said.

'Desi Lawrence?' the man from the weekly caressed the name, reminiscently. 'Oh yes,' he said.

'Oh yes,' said Alec, 'the Honourable Desi Lawrence. You mind it now?'

'Don't want to spoil your story, Alec. Father was a judge, wasn't he?'

'That's right. Lord Chancellor briefly. And of course in a minute I had recognised her, and then the party broke up. The white-faced loon with his widow's peak was picking the Irish boy up – Cassidy his name was – and dunking his head in cold water, and Ed Spain was saying, "He's a prospect, isn't he, he's a real prospect. I reckon in two years he can take Joe Louis."

'"Joe's old," I say, "and that boy's not so young himself. Where's he been?"

'"Where have we all been? In the Army of course."

'"What's his record there?"

'"Exemplary," Ed says.

'Well, the boy goes on to win a couple of fights at Harringay, they wheeled on a couple of Yanks who may or may not have taken a powder, and then Joe Baksi half-murdered Bruce Wood-cock and broke his jaw, and that meant the fight for the Empire title wasn't on for a bit. There was talk of taking him to the States for a fight, but that never came off. They put him in against Cassidy who'd been his sparring partner and he won in two. But that proved nothing. Cassidy was often seen around with him and ignorant folks said it was a fix, but it didn't need any fix for Ossie Bellow to dispose of Mike Cassidy just when, where and how he chose.

'Somehow or other his romance with Desi was kept out of the papers. There was a sort of good-will towards the boy – it turned out he'd won a Military Medal with the Eighth Army in the de-sert, and in those days that sort of thing still commanded respect. And of course in those days . . .' His voice tailed off for a moment and the trainee saw it all in black-and-white; like a Carol Reed movie, he thought.

Hilda, the *Guardian* woman, was stuffing papers into the mock-Afghan shoulder bag she carried that was too young for her. 'This is fucking boring, Alec,' she said.

'I saw them a couple of times, Desi and Ossie, having lunch together at the Ivy. He wore a soft oatmeal-coloured tweed suit and a red tie, I remember, and his face glistening above it. He was out of place in a suit but not in the Ivy, it was a theatre restaurant. But, you know, I liked the way he looked at her. There was deference in his manner, but no inferiority. I watched them, covertly, all through their lunches and they never laughed, but when one of them put his or her hand on the white tablecloth the other would cover it and squeeze. And she kept looking at him as though she wanted . . . oh everything from him. And he knew he could give it and could hardly believe his luck at being allowed to supply it. It was a case of absorption. They really were besotted.

'Ed Spain told me how they were living. They'd moved into the Cavendish. Desi's grandfather had been killed at Second Ypres, and he'd been an old flame of Rosa's, so I suppose Desi could do no wrong. Not even if she was living with a nigger. Rosa's language, Hilda. But it wasn't at the Cavendish that it happened. That was down in Brighton.'

'What happened?' asked the younger Scot.

'Double tragedy in Brighton hotel. He killed her. Smothered her with a pillow and then cut his own throat ear to ear with a razor he'd bought from a barber's on the front not half an hour before.'

'On the banal side, surely,' said the young-old man from the weekly.

Alec shrugged his shoulders. 'If you like,' he said. 'Just as you please. Banal then. But it happened. And nobody knew why.'

'No suicide note?'

'No suicide note. Ossie couldn't write, it seemed. So no note. A chambermaid heard a great roar from the room, like a wild beast in the zoo she said, and ran for help. They'd to break the door open, and when they did there seemed to be blood everywhere and he was dead. They didn't see Desi at first. She was under the pillow and a muckle great quilt. Of course the obvious explanation was passed around. Jealous tempers these niggers, hotter blood than us white folks. But it didn't fit. They said Desi had been having it off with the sparring partner, Mike Cassidy, but apart from the fact that Cassidy was ruled with a rod of iron by one of these Irish bog-women of whom he went in mortal fear and was anyway under-sexed like most Irishmen, Desi wasn't that sort of girl. Of course there were plenty ready to call her a slut, nice, well brought-up, delicately nurtured Cheltenham Ladies girl shacks up with nigger prizefighter, what could she be but a slut? Only she wasn't. My first impression was right, she was as pure as the lily in the dell . . .'

The trainee picked up the old man's glass and took it to the side table on which the hospitality drinks were laid out. He filled it and pressed it into Alec's hand.

'Pure as the lily in the dell,' the old man said. 'I can still see her face looking at him. You know, it's a difficult thing to say, we're a' so cynical now, but they were indeed two noble natures . . .'

'Oh God,' said the *Guardian* woman, 'not again . . .'

The man from the weekly said, 'But look here, Alec, you started this rigmarolic anecdote, which is frankly of dubious interest – two noble natures indeed, what sort of cast is that for a story? – with the promise that it would shed some sort of light on Lionel and Jeffers. Not a glimmer, absolutely not a glimmer has been cast.'

'Patience,' said the old man, '*Pazienza*, my wee disciples. All will yet be revealed.'

He drank half his glass. The others sighed.

'So it was an unresolved mystery and, with no Old Bailey trial and Desi's folks' influence, got far less coverage than you might expect. It couldn't all be hushed up, it was far too sensational for that, but they found a sensible coroner and primed him well, and there was every evidence that right up to the moment of the catastrophe they'd been conducting themselves in perfectly seemly fashion, nothing scandalous. Not even the old *Sunday Pic* could construe orgies out of the evidence, they really had lived decently. Like man and wife or, as one hack preferred to put it, locked in a bower of love. So, apart from the résumés of their careers, and the poor bint had had no career at all, she wasn't even a bloody starlet, just a nice lovely girl who'd had the misfortune to fall for a nigger prizefighter with maybe a screw loose, and been murdered for it, straight from the schoolroom really, apart, as I say, from background stuff and the description of the murder venue and their last hours of love – breakfast had been sent up to the room but not eaten and there was sperm on the sheets, apart from that . . .'

The man from the weekly said, 'So what you're saying is that they'd made love just before he went out to buy the razor, do I understand you right?'

'Well,' Alec said, 'maybe and maybe not, but there was no harm in letting folks believe that was how it had happened. The reality may have been different . . .'

'You mean? . . .'

'That's right, the state he was in makes it more probable . . . you see the poor bugger really was obsessed by her, by her whiteness too. That was it for him. He wouldn't let her sunbathe even, I was told that later by a girl-friend of hers. It was the poor bint's only complaint against him, she said. So there we were, there was no story except background. Finis except for speculation, most of which – in those days – they couldn't print. It had just happened. You know I can still see her, she had these amazing eyes and soft curving lips. Like . . . oh I don't know what. I remember her as she came into the room of the gym over the pub and as I saw her at the ringside at Harringay watching Ossie put away that Yank. Then she got into the ring and hugged him. She was wearing a white fur coat. The fur on his black sweaty body . . .'

'Alec, this is obscene. You know it's obscene, *Playboy* sexist obscenity . . .'

'Ah well, but it happened. I'm telling you what happened and how I saw it. So . . . where was I? They were both dead, and time passed the way it does. Woodcock's jaw mended and folk soon forgot Ossie. He hadn't had enough fights to make him a popular hero, not really, and of course Desi was forgotten, except I suppose by her family, though maybe they preferred to forget her, for she had, after all, disgraced them by their way of thinking, and soon even I forgot her, though I'd sometimes in my mind's eye see the way she had come into that gymnasium, and go to sleep thinking of it. And the time passed, and my glass is empty again, boy . . . you're a good loon and thank you.'

The afternoon, the trainee realised, had stopped for all of them. With a sort of reluctant evaporation of their collective will they had been sucked into the old man's web of memory, his London of bomb sites and willow-herb, of old-fashioned pubs innocent of tourists, and of afternoon drinking-clubs, street-bookies and news cinemas.

'I was in the Highlander in Dean Street,' he said, 'with Ed Spain, as a pub where you could get Younger's Scotch Ale. I can even date it, the week Strathspey won the Cesarewitch, that would be about eighteen months after the tragedy in Brighton. Ed had come back from Newmarket where he'd had a winning double, and he was well on, lit up. Suddenly he stopped talking about the prospects for the Cambridgeshire – Sterope won it that year for the second time, carrying nine stone four – and pointed at a little man in a dirty mac and pork pie hat drinking beer at the far end of the bar.

'"Recognise him?" Ed says.

'"No," I say, "who is it? Should I?"

'"Take the hat off to him," Ed says.

'I do it mentally but it doesn't help. It's a white-faced wee bugger with great big innocent eyes and he's a thought drunk, the way he keeps building up piles of pennies and shuffling them around.

'"It's Charlie Jago," Ed says. "Used to call himself Ossie Bellow's agent. Remember? I wonder he dares show his face in Soho, I really do."

'Well, I remembered him then, though I'd never known his name, just christened him "the pimp".

'"What sort of agent was he?" I say, and why shouldn't he dare show his face here – I'd been abroad, you understand – the Lord had sent me to cover the emergent state of Israel and then take a look at how the Yanks were losing China . . .

'"Well, well, Charlie Jago," Ed says, "if you ask me, that's the rankest-smelling bugger unhung this side of the Rhine . . ."

'Mind you, at first I thought Ed's was only a figure of speech, the sort of hyperbole you might throw at anyone you didn't fancy, but then Jago looked up, and caught us gazing at him. For a minute he looked like a ferret that was ready to bolt, but then he picked up his piles of coppers, one by one, dropped them in his trench-coat pocket, and picked up his pint glass that was half-empty and sidled up the bar to us.

'"Ah, the gentlemen of the Press," he says.

'"You've a bloody nerve, Charlie," says Ed, "what makes you think I'll give you the time of day? Do you know what I've just told Alec here, that you're the ripest-smelling bugger unhung. And I meant it, no joke."

'Jago just looks at him with his great big eyes – and they really do look innocent eyes and awful big in that wee face. Of course they're not really innocent at all, they're spiv's eyes, wide boy's eyes, a pimp's, and he says, turning them on me,

'"You remember, Mr Macrae, we met at the gym above the Black Dog. I used to be Ossie Bellow's agent. Tragedy 'bout Ossie, wasn't it? You know I warned him that bint would drive him crazy. She wasn't his sort. I knew her whore's type and I knew Ossie. We'd been through the desert together."

'You know,' Alec said, 'it sounds corny but he enjoyed talking about them, he was gloating over it, and I couldn't forget how the girl had been frightened of him. She wasn't the sort of girl who should have been feared of a pimp.'

'"Course," he goes on to say to me, "Ossie never really knew himself. He was a child. It's no good being a child, is it, Mr Macrae . . ."

'Well, I didn't know him but it came to me that's what he was himself, a corrupt child, like a little monster from a novel by André Gide or a corrupted victim in a Henry James story – I've not lost you there, Hilda, have I? – the sort of wee horror that pulls wings off flies, to fall back on cliché. I don't know why I knew he was like that straightaway, but I did. There was a horrid irresponsibility in him, as though what he wanted was detached from consequence, and all he sought was the pleasure of hurting. And now he smirked, Charlie Jago smirked . . .

'"She wasn't really having it off," he says, "not with nobody, but Ossie was made to believe she was. It was his only way of escaping her . . ."

'"And what about you, Charlie Jago," says Ed, "it was you told him those lies about Mike Cassidy, wasn't it? What was your personal interest in that?"

'Charlie Jago took a wee pull at his beer. He had an Adam's apple that wobbled as he drank. I remember even in the bar he smelt of lavender water and old sweat . . .

'"It was me that made him," Charlie says, "me, not that cheesey bastard they called his manager. It was me found Ossie in the army, and me that got him through the war. Christ, he was so fucking innocent he couldn't draw rations without me, and then he fell in clover with that tart . . . shit-deep in clover . . . I told him it wasn't on, and, do you know, he smiled at me, Ossie smiling at me that made him . . ."

'Charlie Jago shuddered at memory of that smile.

'"Buy me a drink," he says.

'"I wouldn't buy you a drink, Charlie Jago," Ed says, "if Winston Churchill and Monty joined hands and told me to. I wouldn't buy you a drink if you were the last drinking companion left in Soho. I'd rather drink horse-piss alone than nectar in your company. That's how I feel about you, Charlie Jago."

'"Suit yourself," says Charlie, and gives me a little smile, a manufactured little smile, and puts down his glass, stretching between us to rest it in a pool of beer on the bar counter, and half-turns and sidles out of the pub. "There's others'd pay for my story," he says.'

Alec looked up.

'But the curious thing,' he said, 'is that nobody would, or did. Three weeks later Charlie Jago was found stabbed in the groin in an alleyway that runs off Greek Street. Nobody was ever brought to book for it. Nobody cared much. One rat the fewer. That was it.'

'Did he have a story?' asked the young Scot.

'Oh yes, he had a story.'

'Hadn't he tried to sell it sooner? Why not?'

'He was sent down soon after the affair in Brighton. Eighteen months for Black Market offences. He wasn't long out when we met him in the Highlander.'

'It's all fucking sordid,' said the *Guardian* woman, 'and boring, and I don't see the promised relevance.'

'But you do, don't you?' Alec turned to the man from the week-ly, 'you do, I'm sure.'

'Oh I can guess,' he said, 'it's pretty obvious. He worked on Ossie to murder the girl, just as Jeffers worked on Lionel, and in neither case can one identify any positive advantage. That's it, isn't it? What happened's not in doubt. It's the why. And we've got to fall back on some emotional or psychological explanation.'

'Was he gay?' asked the *Guardian* woman, almost (it seemed to the trainee) interested despite herself. 'After all, we all know Lionel and Jeffers were gay.'

'Gay?' said Alec. 'Dismal wee sod. I wouldn't think he had any sex-life.'

'Anyway,' the man from the weekly put in, 'it's far too simple to try to explain our more immediate case by saying Lionel and Jef-fers were gay. They certainly weren't lovers, and never had been.'

'But Jeffers would have liked it, wouldn't he?' said the younger Scot. 'Hell hath no fury like a poof that's spurned. Isn't there a case for saying he incited Lionel's treachery and then shopped him simply because they weren't lovers . . . ?'

'Anyway,' Alec said, 'Ossie was no queer.' He smiled at the trainee over the rim of his glass. 'What about you, boy? Can you account for it?'

The trainee was a Catholic and a bit naïve, shy, too, among these people he thought of as distinguished journalists (as they most of them were). He felt himself blushing.

'Well,' he said, 'it seems to me that if this Jago chap destroyed his friend on whose success any future of his own depended – it did, didn't it?'

'You could say that, boy, fire ahead . . .'

'And if jealousy didn't come into it, not sexual jealousy I sup-pose I mean, well then,' he blushed more hotly, 'we just have to fall back on wickedness, don't we, on original sin.'

The woman from the *Guardian* laughed, not from amuse-ment . . .

'Oh really,' she said, 'in this day and age . . .'

'In this day and age,' Alec said, 'we dress it up otherwise and blabber theories of social deprivation, but the boy's nearer right.

What's that line of Blake's – "some are born for endless night . . ." That was Charlie Jago, a creature of the night. He couldna stand the thought of Ossie and the girl being better folk than he was, of Ossie escaping to sunlight. Noble natures, I said, and they both had noble natures, and they made him feel the dark he was shut out in.'

'That's as maybe,' said the man from the weekly. 'Bit fanciful, though. You couldn't say Lionel had a noble nature, could you?'

'True, but what of Jeffers? He was a creature of the night too.'

'Fanciful is an understatement,' said the *Guardian* woman, 'you're romanticising the whole thing, like a Dickens novel or a Shakespeare play. Characters aren't black and white, explanations of human behaviour have to be more complicated than that . . .'

'Evil's too simple and ordinary enough for you, Hilda, is that it? It's no' for me. Some are born for endless night. Boy, you seem to have a good head on you and a grand understanding. Just fetch me another suppy gin, will you now.'

GODFREY SMITH

Letter from Leah

Venice
The first day of June 1593

Dearest Sara

Fond greetings to you from this most fair and cruel of cities! Bear with me while I unfold a story to you of such mixed fortune, such a confusion of comedy and tragedy, that you will hardly know whether to laugh or cry. But read me with attention, I pray you, for on your swift and ready accession to our aid lies all our hope for the healing of old wounds and the start of a new life.

Shylock sends you a devoted brother's love, but will not put his hand to this letter today. He lies resting after the most taxing day of his turbulent life and after his greatest triumph. You will know, dear Sara, none better, how I love this most gentle and unworldly of men; yet I never saw his greatness till now.

You will remember well from the days of our youth in Seville how much he loved learning, and how he esteemed your husband and his friend Roderigo above all men for his pre-eminence in scholarship. If it had not been for the black-hearted will of the Spanish king that drove us from their country, us to Venice, you to London, I believe he would have become a physician to rank with your Roderigo. As it is, in this most cold-eyed and venal of cities, he has been compelled to eke a living at a trade for which he is ill-fitted: putting such sums as he can spare at risk on the Rialto.

We must laugh, gentle Sara, at the hypocrisy of our Christian neighbours in this regard as in so many others; for we cannot cry. They call us usurers: who are expressly forbidden by our holy books from exacting excess in the settlement of a loan and were so bound for many centuries before they borrowed and bent our faith to their purposes. The difference is this: that the Jew must live within the strict tenets of his Law or he is doomed; the Christian feels no great need to practise what he preaches.

Let me tell you, dear Sara, what rates these merciful Christians exact in some of their great cities: in Madrid the legal rate is 25 per cent; in Paris it is 40 or 50 per cent; and I need not tell you that by an edict of King John of England it was fixed in London at 80 per cent. A German princeling could go to Holland, where he will pay 100 per cent; to Florence, where he will pay 200 per cent; or to one of his brother princelings who will charge him a charitable 300 or 400 per cent. 'O father Abraham!' Shylock has cried often, 'what these Christians are, whose own hard dealing teaches them to suspect the thoughts of others.'

This is why these magnificos come to the Jew for their money; whose rate is fixed by law and long use at between twenty and fifty per cent; whose word must be his bond; and whose network of family ties through Christendom has expedited the exchange of promissory paper. This must be honoured and so make all business flow and prosper.

Now you will know, Sara, for who does not, that this fair city of ours has made itself rich beyond all imagining. It has done so by the fine Christian act of exacting fat tribute from each and every holy crusade that has passed through on its way east. It has grown soft with luxury and is a stew of vice. In particular, our Moorish friends have instructed us in the sin which caused God to destroy the Cities of the Plain with fire and brimstone.

Three Venetians are at the centre of this web. Their names are Antonio, Bassanio, and Lorenzo. There is not much to choose between them; but I would say that Bassanio is the greatest hypocrite, Lorenzo the principal criminal, and Antonio the biggest villain of them all. So notorious has the evil triumvirate grown in Venice that not one of their Christian brothers is prepared to under-write their profligacy further. Antonio has therefore instructed his two young friends and catamites that they must forget their natural (or should I say unnatural – you will have my drift) inclinations and find rich wives to subsidise their future pleasures. Bassanio soon found his prey and boasted to all Venice that he would have her; nor did he dissemble about his motive: 'In Belmont is a lady richly left.' Lorenzo picked on our daughter Jessica.

Now it must seem to you a piece of outrageous *chutzpah* for Antonio to seek a loan from Shylock in such circumstances. He did it for two reasons: he believed that the liaison between Lorenzo and Jessica was a secret that would not be forfeited until it was too late for us to prevent it; and he was desperate.

He reckoned without me. No Jewish daughter conducts an affair of the heart under her own mother's nose and in her own house for long without her knowing. I did not need to be told: I had only to watch Jessica's face when we met Lorenzo by seeming chance at a play or in a masque; and I knew.

I could not decide whether to tell Shylock. I would watch him from our place in the synagogue, under the ever-burning lamp, and wondered what it would do to him to know that his only child loved a man she could never marry under the canopy; a stranger to us not only by want of faith but by dint of sex: an adventurer doubly damned who coveted his ducats and his daughter; but who would never remain faithful to the one when the other was gone.

In the end, I told him. I have never kept anything from him and I could not do so now. He grew old as I spoke, but I was glad it was done. I would rather he heard it from me than from a stranger, and he took it as well as he might. He was also ready when Antonio came to him on the Rialto with his impertinence and his importunity: Antonio, who spat upon his Jewish gaberdine like the fine Christian gentleman he was, and offered to do so again once he was accommodated with our cash.

A pound of flesh nearest his heart. How literal is our race of Christian brothers! For the pound of flesh nearest the black heart of Antonio lies not within his bosom but between his legs. What satanic deeds lie to the score of that dried neat's tongue, that vile standing tuck, that bull's pizzle! You will know, Sara, how one of the principal reasons for the hatred in which we are held by the Gentiles is our practice of circumcising our male children on the eighth day, though reasons of health and commonsense have recommended many other races and faiths to follow us, not least the Muslims. They see in our circumcision their primal fear of castration. They fear we will unman them.

Yet all mankind has benefitted from that most simple and most pioneer form of minor surgery. It gave our people the first knowledge of operative techniques, it taught them to use wine as antiseptic, led them to find drugs to silence pain, to prescribe diets and diagnose disease. It was thus the basis of those skills that have led your husband to be one of the first physicians in England and to the queen herself.

A man as devout as Shylock and raised in such a tradition would not have brought himself to unman Antonio, though he may well have been sorely tempted, nor even to have circumcised him. That would indeed have been poetic justice. What the trial did do was to bring us time.

For by now my Shylock had been doubly wronged: not only by the Christian contumely, by the rheum Antonio so graciously voided on his beard; but also by common and downright theft. For just as Antonio had not thought of keeping his desperate bond should he fail, so Lorenzo saw no harm, indeed good sport, in stealing from the Jew. Nor did anyone else in the majestic and law-loving city of Venice.

We are not rich. Shylock could not even find the three thousand ducats Antonio wished to borrow, but had to go to his friend Tubal, a wealthy Hebrew of our tribe. Indeed, the cause really lay between

Tubal and Bassanio, not Shylock and Antonio. Such wealth as we can find we keep in jewels, because they are small and can be easily moved as we travel the world. Beside, they have great beauty, and can be intricately worked, and given as acts of love. So it was that Shylock, who never speaks my name in the public places, cried out in pain when Tubal told him that in Genoa he was shown a ring that Jessica had sold for a monkey: 'it was my turquoise – I had it of Leah when I was a bachelor: I would not have given it for a wilderness of monkeys.'

Sara, I am no longer young. I do not profess to be learned in our laws. Yet I am glad to have lived to see us come through this sorry business, for it gave my husband the chance to find that eloquence he had always wanted to find from the holy books, that statement of common humanity which I wager will not be forgotten: 'Hath not a Jew eyes? hath not a Jew hands, organs, dimensions, senses, affections, passions?' Will men be able to read those words in ages still unborn and yet torment us? It beggars reason.

He lost the lawsuit, as he knew he would. They look after their own, here in Venice. They found a little doctor of law called Balthazar, a mincing fellow who is of their own persuasion I suspect, and threw out our case. The sentence of the court showed a large access of that Christian charity: half his goods forfeit to Antonio, half to the state, with Antonio renouncing his moiety in return for Shylock turning Christian. That, he must know, would be death to Shylock, but it will not touch him. For our berth is booked in a tall ship bound for England, and there, we know from your example, we shall find a new life. We may live for a while as crypto-Jews, covert faithful, as our fathers have done before in many lands, but in the end they will let us build our own synagogue and worship freely again. I am sure of that.

Venice will find scant comfort in the half of our goods they have so grandly confiscated. Our house is made over to Tubal's name, and they need Tubal for their further adventures far too much to take it from him by force or stealth. Jews always prove useful in the end, whether you need a book or a cure, a loan or a faith.

We have lost some few ducats to our wayward daughter and her fancy man. But what is one of our silver ducats? Three shillings and sixpence of your English money. We shall make it up again if our English neighbours allow us. As for those stolen diamonds, I think the young lovers may see the poetry in their life dissolve a fraction when they find they owe more to the paste-makers of Padua than the caves of Ethiope. That little service was the least a Jewish wife could perform.

We shall miss this beautiful, heartless city, with its palazzos and gondolas, its lanterns and its lutes, its rumours and its revels. But we look forward to sailing with these blue-eyed, long-headed men to our new life in London.

We look forward more than I can say to the markets and the theatres, the flowers and fields and rivers. We look forward to learning that strange, tongue-twisting language of yours. We look forward so much to seeing your house in Holborn and the hospital at St Bartholomew's where Roderigo practises and teaches, and need I say how much we long to see your girls and the boys at school in Winchester. All this in a few short weeks under sail; and meanwhile, have no fear for the turquoise. Tubal, a good Jew and a good friend, bought it back from the Genoan, and gave it again to Shylock as a farewell token of his love. It is on his finger now as he sleeps beside me.

Ever your devoted sister
Leah.

IAIN CRICHTON SMITH

What to do about Ralph?

'What on earth has happened to you?' said his mother. 'These marks are getting worse and worse. I thought with your father teaching you English you might have done better.'

'He is not my father,' Ralph shouted, 'he is not my father.'

'Of course, having you in class is rather awkward but you should be more helpful than you are. After all, you are seventeen. I shall have to speak to him about these marks.'

'It won't do any good.'

How sullen and stormy he always was these days, she thought, it's such a constant strain. Maybe if he went away to university there might be some peace.

'He has been good to you, you know; he has tried,' she continued. But Ralph wasn't giving an inch. 'He bought you all that football stuff and the hi-fi and the portable TV.'

'So I could keep out of his road, that's why.'

'You know perfectly well that's not true.'

'It is true. And anyway, I didn't want him here. We could have been all right on our own.'

How could she tell him that to be on your own nowadays was not easy? She had jumped at the chance of getting out of teaching and, in any case, they were cutting down on Latin teachers nowadays. Furthermore, the pupils, even the academic ones, were getting more difficult. She had been very lucky to have had the chance of marrying again, after the hard years with Tommy. But you couldn't tell Ralph the truth about Tommy, he wouldn't listen. Most people, including Ralph, had seen Tommy as cheerful, humorous, generous, only she knew what he had been really like. Only she knew, as well, the incredible jealousy that had existed between Jim and Tommy from their youth. Almost pathological, especially on Tommy's side. It was as if they had never had any love from their professor father who had been cold and remote, hating the noise of children in the house. They had competed for what few scraps of love he had been able to throw to them now and again.

She couldn't very well tell Ralph that the night his father had crashed he had been coming from another woman, on Christmas Eve also. She had been told that in the wrecked car the radio was playing 'Silent Night'.

Of course, in his own field Tommy had been quite good, at least at the beginning. He had been given a fair number of parts and later some minor ones on TV. But then he had started drinking as the depression gripped and the parts became smaller and less frequent. His downfall had been his golden days at school when he had been editor of the magazine, captain of the rugby team, actor. What a hero he had been in those days, how invisible Jim had been. And even now invisible in Ralph's eyes. And he had been invisible to her as well, though she often recalled the night when Tommy had gate crashed his birthday party and had got drunk and shouted that he would stab Jim. But he had been very drunk that night. 'I'll kill you,' he had shouted. Why had he hated Jim so much even though on the surface he himself had been the more successful of the two? At least at the beginning?

She should have married Jim in the first place; she could see that he was much kinder than Tommy, less glamorous, less loved by his father, insofar as there had been much of that. But she had been blinded by Tommy's apparent brilliance and humour, and, to tell the truth, by his more blatant sexiness.

Of course he had never had any deep talent, his handsomeness had been a sort of compensatory glow, but when that faded everything else had faded too. She herself had been too complaisant, declining to take the hard decision of leaving him, still teaching in those days, and tired always.

To Ralph, however, his father had appeared different. He had been the one who carried him about on his shoulders, taught him how to ride a motor bike, how to play snooker (had even bought a snooker table for him), taken him to the theatre to see him perform. Even now his photograph was prominent in his son's room. She had been foolish to hide from him the true facts about his father's death, his drunken crash when returning home from one of his one-night stands. She should have told him the truth, but she hadn't. She had always taken the easy way out, though in fact it wasn't in the end the easy way at all.

And then Jim had started to visit her, he now a promoted teacher, although in the days when Tommy had been alive not often seen except casually at teachers' conferences, but very correct, stiffly lonely, and certainly not trying to come between her and his brother, though she knew that he had always liked her. She had learned in the interval that kindness was more important than glamour, for glamour meant that others demanded some of your light, that you belonged as much to the public as to your wife. Or so Tommy had used to say.

She remembered with distaste the night of the school play when she had played the virginal Ophelia to his dominating Hamlet, off-hand, negligent, hurtful, almost as if he really believed what he was saying to her. But the dazzled audience had clapped and clapped, and even the professor father had turned up to see the theatrical life and death of his son.

But how to tell Ralph all this?

That night she said to Jim in bed,

'What are we going to do about Ralph?'

'What now?'

'You've seen his report card? He used to be a bright boy. I'm not just saying that. His marks are quite ridiculous. Can't you give him some help in the evenings? English used to be his best subject. In primary school he was always top.'

'I ran help him if he'll take it. But he won't take it. His English is ludicrous.'

'Ludicrous? What do you mean?'

'What I said. Ludicrous.' And then, of course, she had defended Ralph. No one was going to say to her that her son's intellect was ludicrous which she knew it wasn't. And so it all began again, the argument that never ended, that wasn't the fault of anyone in particular, but only of the situation that seemed to be insoluble, for Ralph was the thorn at their side, sullen, implacable, unreachable.

'I'm afraid he hates me and that's it,' said Jim. 'To tell you the truth, I think he has been very ungrateful.'

She could see that herself, but at the same time she could see Ralph's side of it too.

'Ungrateful?' she said.

'Yes. Ungrateful. You remember the time I got so angry that I told him I had after all bought him a television set and he shouted, "You're a bloody fool then."'

'You have to try and understand him,' she said.

'It's always the same. He won't make the effort to understand. His father's the demi-god, the hero. If he only knew what a bastard he really was.' Always making fun of him with his quick tonque, always taking his girls away from him, always lying to his distant father about him, always making him appear the slow resentful one.

That night she slept fitfully. She had the feeling that something terrible was happening, that something even more terrible was about to happen. And always Ralph sat in his room playing his barbarous music very loudly. His stepfather would mark his eternal essays in his meticulous red writing, she would sew, and together they sat in the living room hearing the music till eventually he would tell her to go and ask Ralph to turn it down. She it was who was always the messenger between them, the ambassador trying hopelessly to reconcile but never succeeding. For Ralph resented her now as much as he resented Jim.

She couldn't believe that this could go on.

Ralph sat at the back of his stepfather's class, contemptuous, remote, miserable. Quite apart from the fact that he thought him boring, he was always being teased by the other pupils about him. His nickname was Sniffy, for he had a curious habit of sniffing now and again as if there was a bad smell in the room. But, to be fair to him, he was a good, conscientious teacher: he set homework and marked it and it really seemed as if he wanted them all to pass. But there was a curious remoteness to him, as if he loved his subject more than he loved them. Nevertheless, he was diligent and he loved literature.

'This, of course, was the worst of crimes,' he was saying, sitting at his desk in his chalky gown. 'We have to remember that this was a brother who killed another one, like Cain killing Abel. Then again there is the murder in the Garden, as if it were the garden of Eden. There is so much religion in the play. Hamlet himself was religious; that, after all, was the reason he didn't commit suicide. Now, there is a very curious question posed by the play, and it is this.' He sniffed again.

'What was going on between Gertrude and Claudius even while the latter's brother Hamlet was alive? This king about whom we know so little. Here's the relevant speech:

'Aye that incestuous, that adulterate beast,
with witchcraft of his wit, with traitorous gifts,
 won to his shameful lust
 the will of a most seeming virtuous queen . . .'

The point was, had any of this happened in Hamlet's lifetime? He meant, of course, King Hamlet's. Had there been a liaison between Gertrude and Claudius even then? One got the impression of Claudius being a ladies' man, while Hamlet perhaps was the soldier who blossomed in action, and who was not much concerned with the boudoir. After all, he was a public figure, he perhaps took Gertrude for granted. On their answer to that question would depend their attitude to Gertrude.

The voice droned on, but it was as if a small red window had opened in Ralph's mind. He had never thought before that his mother had known his stepfather before the marriage which had taken place so suddenly. What if in fact there had been something going on between them while his father was still alive? He shivered as if he had been infected by a fever. He couldn't bring himself to think of his mother and stepfather in bed together, which was why he had asked for his own bedroom to be changed, so that he would be as far away from them as possible.

But suppose there had been a liaison between them. After all, they had both been teachers and they must have met. True, they had been at different schools but it was inconceivable that they hadn't met.

O God, how dull his stepfather was, in his cloud of chalk. How different from his father who inhabited the large air of the theatre. What a poor ghostly fellow he was in his white dust.

But the idea that his mother had known his stepfather would not leave his mind. How had he never thought of it before?

That night, his stepfather being at a meeting at the school, he said to his mother,

'Did you know . . . your husband . . . before you married him?'

'I wish you could call him your stepfather, or even refer to him by his first name. Of course I knew him. I knew the family.'

'But you married my father?'

'Yes. And listen, Ralph, I have never said this to you before. I made a great mistake in marrying your father.'

He was about to rise and leave the room when she said vehemently, 'No, it's time you listened. You sit down there and listen for a change. Did you know that your father was a drunk? Do you know that he twice gave me a black eye? The time I told everybody I had cut myself on the edge of the wardrobe during the power cut, and the time I said I had fallen on the ice? Did you know where he was coming from when his car crashed?'

'I don't want to hear any more,' Ralph shouted. 'If you say any more I'll kill you. It's not true. You're lying.'

For a moment there he might have attacked her, he looked so white and vicious. It was the first time he had thought of hitting her; he came very close.

Her face was as pale as his and she was almost swaying on her feet but she was shouting at him,

'He was coming from one of his innumerable lady friends. I didn't tell you that, did I? I got a message from the police and I went along there. He had told me he was going to be working late at the theatre but he was coming from the opposite direction. He was a stupid man. At least Jim is not stupid.'

He raised his fist as if to hit her, but she didn't shrink away.

'Go on, hit me,' she shouted. 'Hit me because you can't stand the truth any more than your father could. He was vulgar, not worth your stepfather's little finger.'

He turned and ran out of the house.

Of course it wasn't true. That story was not the one his mother had told him before. And for all he knew the two of them might have killed his father, they might have tampered with the brakes or the engine. After all, a car crash was always suspicious, and his father had been a good if fast driver. His stepfather couldn't even drive.

He went to the Nightspot where some boys from the school were playing snooker, and older ones drinking at the bar. He stood for a while watching Harry and Jimmy playing. Harry had been to college but had given it up and was now on the dole. Jimmy had never left town at all. He watched as Harry hit the assembled balls and sent them flying across the table. After a while he went and sat down by himself. He felt as if he had run away from home, as if he wanted to kill himself. He was tired of always being in the same room by himself playing records. And yet he couldn't bring himself to talk to his stepfather. The two of them were together, had shut him out, he was like a refugee in the house. He hated to watch his stepfather eating, and above all he hated to see him kissing his mother before he set off for school with his briefcase under his arm. But then if he left home where could he go? He had no money. He loathed being dependent on them for pocket money, which he used on buying records.

He hated his mother as much as he hated his stepfather. At other times he thought that they might have been able to live together, just the two of them, if his stepfather had not appeared. Why, he had loved her in the past and she had loved him, but now she had shut him out because she thought he was being unfair to her husband. He was such a drip: he couldn't play snooker, and all he did was mark essays every night. The house felt cold now, he was rejected, the other two were drawing closer and closer together.

'How's old Sniffy,' said Terry as he sat down at the same table, Frank beside him. They, of course, were unemployed and Terry had been inside for nicking stuff and also for nearly killing a fellow at a dance.

Then they began to talk about school and he had to sit and listen. Terry had once punched Caney and had been dragged away by the police. No one could control him at all. Frank was just as dangerous, but brighter, more cunning.

'Have a whisky,' said Terry. 'Go on. I bet you've never had a whisky before. I'll buy it for you.'

The snooker table with the green baize brought unbearable memories back to him, and he said,

'Right. Right then.'

'I'll tell you another thing,' said Terry. 'Old Sniffy's a poof. I always thought he was a poof. What age was the bugger when he got married? Where was he getting it before that?'

Frank didn't say anything at all, but watched Ralph. He had never liked him. He had belonged to the academic stream while he himself was always in one of the bottom classes, though he was much brighter.

'A poof,' Terry repeated. 'But he's having it off now, eh, Frank?' And he winked at Frank. Ralph drank the whisky in one gulp, and tears burned his eyes.

'Old bastard,' said Terry. 'He belted me a few times and I wasn't even in his class.'

*

The two of them took Ralph back to his house. Then they stood around it for a while shouting at the lighted window, 'Sniffy the Poof, Sniffy the Poof.' And then ran away into the darkness. Ralph staggered to his room.

'What was that? Who was shouting there?' said his mother. 'Some of your friends. You're drunk. You're disgustingly drunk.'

But he pushed her away and went to his bed while the walls and ceiling spun about him and the bed moved up and down like a boat beneath him.

He heard his mother shouting at his stepfather, 'What are you going to do about it then? You can't sit here and do nothing. He's drunk, I'm telling you. Will you give up those exercise books and do something?'

Later he heard his mother slamming the door and heard the car engine start, then he fell into a deep sleep.

At breakfast no one spoke. It was like a funeral. He himself had a terrible headache, like a drill behind his right eye, and he felt awful. His mother stared down at the table. His stepfather didn't kiss her when he left for school: he seemed preoccupied and pale. It was if the house had come to a complete stop, as if it had crashed.

'You have to remember,' said his stepfather when talking about *Hamlet* that morning, 'you have to remember that this was a drunken court. Hamlet comments on the general drunkenness. Even at the end it is drink that kills Hamlet and Claudius and Gertrude. Hamlet is at the centre of this corruption and is infected by it.'

His voice seemed quieter, more reflective, as if he was thinking of something else. Once he glanced across to Ralph but said nothing. 'I'm sorry,' he said at the end of the period, 'I meant to return your essays but I didn't finish correcting them.' A vein in his forehead throbbed. Ralph knew that he was remembering the voices that had shouted from the depths of the night, and he was wondering why they had been so unfair.

'Something's wrong with old Sniffy,' said Pongo at the interval. Ralph couldn't stand the amused contempt the pupils had for his stepfather and the way in which he had to suffer it. After all, he had not chosen him. His stepfather never organised games, there was nothing memorable about him.

When he went home after four, the door was unlocked but he couldn't find his mother. She was neither in the living room nor in the kitchen, which was odd since she usually had their meal ready for them when they returned from the school.

He shouted to her but there was no answer. After a while he knocked on her bedroom door and when there was no response he went in. She was lying flat out on the bed, face down, and was quite still. For a moment his heart leapt with the fear that she might be dead and he turned her over quickly. She was breathing but there was a smell of drink from her. She had never drunk much in her life as far as he knew. There was a bottle of sherry, with a little drink at the bottom of it, beside her on the floor. He slapped her face but she only grunted and didn't waken.

He didn't know what to do. He ran to the bathroom and filled a glass with water and threw it in her face. She shook and coughed while water streamed down her face, then opened her eyes. When she saw him she shut them again.

'Go way,' she said in a slurred voice, 'Go way.'

He stood for a while at the door looking at her. It seemed to him that this was the very end. It had happened because of the events of the previous night. Maybe he should kill himself. Maybe he should hang or drown himself. Or take pills. And then he thought that his mother might have done that. He ran to her bedroom and checked the bottles with the sleeping tablets, but it seemed quite full. He noticed for the first time his own picture on the sideboard opposite the bed where his mother was still sleeping. He picked it up and looked at it: there was no picture of his father there at all.

In the picture he was laughing and his mother was standing just behind him, her right hand resting on his right shoulder. He must have been five or six when the photograph was taken. It astonished him that the photograph should be there at all for he had thought she had forgotten all about him. There was not even a photograph of his stepfather in the room.

And then he heard again the voices coming out of the dark and it was as if he was his stepfather. 'Sniffy the Poof, Sniffy the Poof.' It was as if he was in that room listening to them. You couldn't be called anything worse than a poof. He heard again his mother telling him about his father. A recollection came back to him of a struggle one night between his mother and father. She had pulled herself away and shouted, 'I'm going to take the car and I'm going to kill myself. I know the place where I can do it.' And he himself had said to his father, 'Did you hear that?' But his father had simply smiled and said, 'Your mother's very theatrical.' For some reason this had amused him.

She was now sleeping fairly peacefully, now and again snorting, her hands spread out across the bed.

And his stepfather hadn't come home. Where was he? Had something happened to him? At that moment he felt terror greater than he had ever known, as if he was about to fall down, as if he was spinning in space. What if his mother died, if both of them died, and he was left alone?

He ran to the school as fast as he could. The janitor, who was standing outside his little office with a bunch of keys in his hand, watched him as he crossed the hall but said nothing.

His stepfather was sitting at his desk on his tall gaunt chair staring across towards the seats. He was still wearing his gown and looked like a ghost inside its holed chalky armour. Even though he must have heard Ralph coming in he didn't turn his head. Ralph had never seen him like this before, so stunned, so helpless. Always, before, his stepfather appeared to have been in control of things. Now he didn't seem to know anything or to be able to do anything. He had wound down.

Ralph stood and looked at him from the doorway. If it weren't for his mother he wouldn't be there.

'Should you not be coming home?' he asked. His stepfather didn't answer. It was as if he was asking a profound question of the desks, as if they had betrayed him. Ralph again felt the flow spinning beneath him. Perhaps it was all too late. Perhaps it was all over. It might be that his stepfather would never come home again, had given everything up. His gaze interrogated the room.

Ralph advanced a little more.

'Should you not be coming home?' he asked again. But still his stepfather retained his pose, a white chalky statue. It was his turn now to be in his own listening to his own questions. Ralph had never thought of him like that before. Always he had been with his mother, always it was he himself who had been the forsaken one. On the blackboard were written the words, 'A tragedy gives us a feeling of waste.' Ralph stayed where he was for a long time. He didn't know what to do, how to get through to this man whom he had never understood. The empty desks frightened him. The room was like an empty theatre. Once his father had taken him to one in the afternoon.

'You wait there,' he said, 'I have to see someone.' And then he had seen his father talking to a girl who was standing face to face with him, wearing a belted raincoat. They had talked earnestly to each other, his father laughing, the girl looking at him adoringly.

No, it could not be true. His father hadn't been at all like that, his father had been the one who adored him, his son. What was this ghost like when compared to his father?

He couldn't bring himself to move, it was as if he was fixed to the floor. There was no word he could think of that would break this silence, this deathly enchantment.

He felt curiously awkward as if his body was something he carried about with him but which was distinct from his mind. It was as if in its heaviness and oddness it belonged to someone else. He thought of his mother outstretched on the bed, her hair floating down her face, stirring in the weak movement of her breath. Something must be done, he couldn't leave this man here and his mother there.

Slowly his stepfather got down from his desk, then placed the jotters which were stacked beside him in a cupboard. Then he locked the cupboard. He had finished marking them after all and would be able to return them. Then he began to walk past Ralph as if he wasn't there, his gaze fixed straight ahead of him. He was walking almost like a mechanical toy, clumsily, his gown fixed about him but becalmed.

Now he was near the door and soon he would be out in the hall. In those seconds, which seemed eternal, Ralph knew that he was facing the disintegration of his whole life. He knew that it was right there in front of him, if he couldn't think of the magic word. He knew what tragedy was, knew it to its bitter bones, that it was the time that life continued, having gone beyond communication. He knew that tragedy was the thing you couldn't do anything about, that at that point all things are transformed, they enter another dimension, that it is not acting but the very centre of despair itself. He knew it was pitiful, yet the turning point of a life. And in its light, its languageless light, his father's negligent cheerful face burned, the moustache was like straw on fire. He was moving away from him, winking, perhaps deceitful. He saw the burden on this man's shoulders, he saw the desperate loneliness, so like his own. He felt akin to this being who was moving towards the door. And at that moment he found the word and it was as if it had been torn bleeding from his mouth.

'Come on home,' he said. 'Jim.'

Nothing seemed to be happening. Then suddenly the figure came to a halt and stood there at the door as if thinking. It thought like this for a long time. Then it turned to face him. And something in its face seemed to crack as if chalk were cracking and a human face were showing through. Without a word being said the ghost removed its gown and laid it on a desk, then the two of them were walking across the now empty hall towards the main door.

Such a frail beginning, and yet a beginning. Such a small hope, and yet a hope. Almost but not quite side by side, they crossed the playground together and it echoed with their footsteps, shining, too, with a blatant blankness after the rain.

His Everlasting Mansion

Come not to me again, but say to Athens,
Timon hath made his everlasting mansion
Upon the beachèd verge of the salt flood . . .
Timon of Athens, v.i.

Filth of the world, a world of filth. The detritus of cans, bottles, wrapping-paper, melon-rinds, orange-skins, lettuce-leaves, fishbones, rags and condoms lies, spread out and stinking, on the ash-grey sand under the huge evening sun and clogs the five rickety steps that lean away, no longer passable, at an angle to the jetty at which no boat ever moors. A valise – its last journey, like my own, long since done – nudges the lowest step of all, the labels of luxurious, far-off hotels (Ritz, Carlton, Ritz-Carlton, Waldorf, Astoria, Waldorf-Astoria) peeling away from it like shreds of scalded skin. A woman's satin shoe, heel-less but with the diamanté still aglitter within the rusty circle of its buckle, bobs just out of reach. A newspaper, streaked with grey-green lichen-like stains, shows the face of the famous and infamous General, shunted from siding to main-line and then back to siding like some locomotive of antique design but violent power. In the 'good' years, that were bad, I entertained him on my yacht, even larger than his, and in my house, far more resplendent than his palace; and in the 'bad' years, that were no less bad, I attempted to appease his fractious exile by ordering that money should be transferred from one numbered Swiss bank-account to another. Now I reach out for him, leaning out over the filth of the world, the world of filth, the fissured concrete of the jetty grating on my knees through my threadbare jeans and my scrawny arm extending splayed fingers on which the nails, uncut and dirt-seamed, curve like the talons of some bird of prey. The dog watches. I grasp. I gasp. I pull. But the section of newspaper held in my hand dissolves into a scum; and when I seize another section and another section, they too dissolve. The General's face splits precisely where the trim moustache divides, and then once more splits across those small, wary eyes, which are now gazing up at me as though yet again to beseech me *Save me, save me*. But I no longer have any wish to save him, even if I could do so.

I shall walk my little island, last and least of the many that once I owned, kicking out indiscriminately at the cans, bottles, wrapping-paper, melon-rinds, orange-skins, lettuce-leaves, fish-bones, rags and condoms. If there were human bodies, dead or alive, I should kick out at them too. But at the dog, the once magnificent boxer, his sides now fallen in, his tail broken and his eyes red-rimmed, I never kick out. He is my sole companion, if one excepts the silver-fish, the spiders, the flies, the mosquitoes, the fleas, the bugs, the cockroaches and the wasps that inhabit, along with the dog and me, the dry husk of my hut.

I shall slip off my shoes, trodden down at the heels and their ravelled laces long since abandoned, to paddle in that filth of the world, that world of filth, as once I would swim in it, swallowing, effortlessly and with no sense of nausea, all the nameless horrors that floated on its tide. Puffing, I shall mount the symmetrically rounded hill and, tiptoe, shall reach up, the dog patiently watching me out of his red-rimmed eyes, to pluck from one of the stunted trees a green apple that, as I bite into it, fizzes a corrosive vinegar, or from another an olive that, grating against my rotten teeth, seems to be all stone. I shall prostrate myself on the soil beyond the symmetrically rounded hill and, the dog beside me, shall join him in lapping at the brown, brackish water that has collected in the interstices of a gully. Then, perched on a rock, with that filth of the world, that world of filth outstretched before me and the dog outstretched behind me, I shall once again regurgitate and chew the bitter cud.

A shepherd-boy, I raced headlong down a mountainside with a crumble and crackle of stones, to the city fermenting as relentlessly with its filth as this sea all around me. I, too, was in a youthful ferment of ambitions, schemes and plots. I had only one thing, myself; and I must have everything. That one thing I sold: my youth to the ageing women, their steps dragging under the weight of their furs and satins and their arms limp under the weight of their encrusted, clanking bracelets; my strength to the ailing men, yawning and sighing away their lives behind nails buffed to a shiny pink; my enthusiasm to the effete women, men, half-women, half-men who had as little zest for the haggling of the market-place as for what it offered. Then I bought: ruined warehouses and ruined businesses, trinkets, pictures, carpets, flesh; and, finally, those scraps of paper, at first meaningless to me but later to be prized more highly than anything that I could touch or see or tread or fondle. I glittered, a column of pure gold smelted from an accumulation of numberless impurities.

Soon there were villas, chalets, apartments and mansions; Rolls Royces, Cadillacs and Lamborghinis; Titians and Poussins and Picassos. The dry husk of my life became loud with its human silver-fish, spiders, flies, mosquitoes, fleas, bugs, cockroaches and wasps. Film-stars, with opulent breasts and long, wet hair would clamber out of my swimming-pools, reaching up to clasp the hand that I chivalrously held out to them. On the deck of my yacht a long since senile statesman would suck, a swollen baby, at the teat of a Romeo and Giulietta that I had plugged into his mouth. A world-famous painter, inwardly fu-

rious but outwardly grateful, would listen, head bowed, to my ignorant criticism of the churning impasto with which he had depicted the
sea around one of my many islands. A Nobel prize-winning novelist
would drawl, eyes narrowed over the champagne goblet raised to an
ill-concealed grimace: *Ah, but you really are astute! How cleverly and
how cruelly you put your finger on precisely what is wrong with my
writing!*

Always there were the presents: the ties that I would toss contemp-
tuously to my valet to keep for himself; the watches (Omega, Piaget,
Longines) that I would drop negligently into the calloused palm of this
or that of my deck-hands; the cigarette-lighters and cigarette-cases and
cigar-cutters, all gold of course, that would clutter up my drawers until
someone had the initiative to steal them. Those who lavished these
gifts on me knew all about investment. With a wide gesture they flung
their bread on the waters of my generosity and with an even wider
gesture they scrabbled both it and its accumulations back. *Oh, but you
shouldn't . . . Oh, but I couldn't . . .* But I did; and they could. One of
my secretaries, a youth etiolated from the hours that he spent in a
shuttered room at a typewriter, fell in love with the daughter of one of
my associates. *I've nothing against the lad, oh nothing at all. But he
must see, you must see . . . One day my daughter is going to be an
extremely rich woman. . . . Well* – I laughed – *let me make him an
extremely rich man. How much should I settle on him?*

Your bounty is as boundless as the sea. That was the Nobel
prize-winner, smugly sure that I would not know the origin of the
quotation. He intoned the pentameter as he accepted the cheque that
would lubricate his passage out of one failed marriage and into
another. But my bounty, like this boundless sea about me, was one
soiled with the filth of the world, a world of filth. I had descended that
remote mountain-side with a crumble and crackle of stones, and it was
those same stones, obdurately unbreakable like myself, that I had
wielded with my scratched, bleeding, aching hands to gouge out the
channel through which this 'bounty' now flowed to irrigate their
parched and stunted lives. It was a bounty not of love but of hate.

I hated them for the nurseries in which they had been pampered; for
the schools in which they had been taught to quote from Shakespeare;
for the horses on which they had hunted and hacked; for the servants

whom they had always so effortlessly commanded; for their titles and commissions and degrees. I hated them for their delicate complexions, their soft hands and softer voices, their assumptions of command. I hated them, I despised them. *How far will you go? How far can I go? Will you allow me to give you this and this and this? Will you continue to entreat me for loans, advice, gifts, invitations? Will you beg me to take anything from you – your wives, your daughters, your sons, even yourselves – provided that I stretch out a hand to save you?* Oh, how I loved to witness the humiliation which you imposed on yourselves! It reminded me of the story, told to me by the Nobel prize-winner, of that vulgar nineteenth-century French *parvenu* whose mistress became more and more outrageous in the extravagance of her demands. At her insistence, he bought for her a Rajah's diamond and then invited her to dinner, in order to present it. Behind a screen in the lofty dining-room he concealed some of her most intimate 'friends'. The banquet *à deux* was resplendent and she was resplendent. A gold dish was brought in, covered, and taken to her. The waiter raised the lid. The plump cocotte gaped, wrinkling her little nose. There, embedded in excrement, glittered the Rajah's diamond. *If you remove it with your teeth, it is yours,* her lover told her. *But mind – no hands.* She half-rose from the table, tore at a handkerchief, shrilled at him, burst into hysterical weeping. Then, when he remained unmoved, she seated herself again, with the same resolution with which her chamber-maid mother would apply herself to some inevitable, if revolting, duty. She lowered her head. A lock of hair fell forward. Nose, lips and one cheek all became smeared. Then, as she triumphantly extracted the Rajah's diamond between those large white teeth, she heard a cachinnation from behind the screen . . . A *parvenu* myself, I know exactly how that French *parvenu* must have felt.

Soon, most of my wealth consisted of scraps of paper hoarded away in banks all round the world; and then, all of a sudden, an icy gust of wind swept through country after country and bank after bank, and those scraps of paper were scattered in all directions. It was not, I thought, impossible to retrieve them, indeed it should be easy – since my famous 'bounty' must have made me innumerable affluent and powerful friends. To some I sent emissaries; to some I went myself. *Ah, my dear fellow, if only you had asked at some other time. Nothing would give me greater pleasure but with this recession. You must know that I. You must realise that we. There's no one in the whole world that I'd more like to. If last month. If next month. Last year. Next year. The truth is. Skint. Cleaned out. Not a bean. But surely if you asked. But surely if you approached. But surely.* Like that newspaper by the jetty, disintegrating fragment by fragment as I tried to grasp at it, so my fortune and my friendships disintegrated at one and the same time.

If I now went into those clubs where once I had been welcomed with enthusiasm, eyes slid away and, in many instances, even the owners of the eyes slid away too. If I entered those hotels (Ritz, Carlton, Ritz–Carlton, Waldorf, Astoria, Waldorf–Astoria) where once an obsequious manager would himself conduct me to my suite, now a wary desk-clerk, riffling through his register, would tell me, *Sorry, sir, a muddle, there doesn't seem to be, there isn't.* The telephone in my mortgaged palace became preternaturally silent, having once rung continuously throughout the day. My former secretary cut me, as he strutted past me in the street with the wife whom I had bought for him. My mantelpiece was now bare both of ornaments and of the invitations that this man would once take so much pleasure in propping up along it. The Nobel prize-winner wrote a *nouvelle* about a vulgar upstart who cheated and lied himself to a fortune and then, one morning, woke up to find that it had gone. The painter gave an interview in which he expatiated on the lavish hideousness of the houses in which I had entertained him. The drooling baby-politician took his next cruise as guest of one my rivals. When I rang up the whore whom I had set up in a duplex across the road from me, I could see her sauntering through lighted rooms in her negligée even as her maid lisped that Madame had gone away on holiday and no, she had no idea when she would be back.

I sold my last picture and I planned my last party, taking into my confidence only my major domo – once a peasant like myself, from the village next to mine. He alone had remained faithful to me; and it was he who supervised the hanging of my garden with thousands of fairy-lights, the setting out of the tables and chairs under the resin-scented trees, with the sea glittering behind them, and the delivery of the heavily embossed invitations to all those people whose lives and mine had once been lapped together in those priceless sheets of paper now lost on the ravaging wind. There was general amazement, consternation, embarrassment and joy. *The old boy has somehow pulled through. One must hand it to him. Well, one always knew. Trust him to have a trick or two up his sleeve. One might have guessed.* The uninvited telephoned with invitations of their own, to remind me of their existences. My whore, following the custom of my affluent past with her, instructed her *couturier* to send me his bill. *(I'm sure you wouldn't want me to disgrace you.)* The Nobel prize-winner forwarded a copy of his latest book specially bound for me in the softest of calf. The painter had one of his churning pictures of the sea around one of my houses delivered to me. The baby-politician's wife telephoned to say that he would be staying with me on the night of the party – though he had not, in fact, even been sent an invitation.

Under the thousands of fairy-lights the hired waiters moved among these hired guests. A number of *paparazzi* had gate-crashed, as had a famous tennis-player and a couple of pop-singers. *(We knew that you had really meant to ask us.)* Flash-bulbs exploded as now this celebrity and now that linked an arm in mine or threw an arm around my neck. Chained in his kennel, my sleek boxer – the same dog that now lies outstretched beside me, his shrunken flank heaving like a dilapidated bellows and an opaque eye upturned to the sun – began to howl with an eerie persistence; but no one seemed to hear him.

Eventually the guests sought out their place-names at the tables set out, their napery glimmering and their cutlery glittering, under the thousands of little lights dangling from the resin-scented trees. *I'm sure I should. How strange that you and I. Oh, change the cards. Here, here, we're here! No, there!* The orchestra on the flower-wreathed platform on the brow of the hill swayed into a waltz. *Lehar! Strauss! But the Elder, not the Younger! But Richard, not Johann!* The hired waiters gravely made their way out of my palace, along the winding paths, towards the hired guests. They held aloft, on gloved palms, gold dishes like that gold dish that the *parvenu* Frenchman had had presented to his cocotte. Other hired waiters processed towards the hired guests with bottles wrapped in napkins. *I'm sure it must be Strauss. But the Elder, not the Younger. But Richard, not Johann!* The waiters ceremoniously removed the lids of the dishes, the waiters ceremoniously tilted their bottles. The guests stared, tittered, were aghast. Into each dish had been stuffed wads of Monopoly money of enormous denominations. Out of each bottle poured, not champagne, but nuggets of chocolate encased in golden foil. Unreal, totally unreal, the counters that I could never redeem. But it was a joke, of course it was a joke! Some of them began to laugh, others were smiling; but when – the once baying dog now on a leash at my side – they saw me, above them and above the abruptly silent orchestra, on the bare, brown hill, also laughing, laughing, laughing, their own laughter and smiles ceased. Singly or in groups, they began to rise. A woman with improbable orange hair scrabbled under her table for a high-heeled satin slipper with a diamanté buckle. Under one of the swaying bulbs the General's face seemed streaked with a green-grey lichen, like his face in that newspaper photograph. The Nobel prize-winner staggered against a spindly chair and sent it crashing to the ground, there to shatter, with the same unforeseen violence with which his literary reputation was soon to topple and shiver to fragments. The painter was short-sightedly examining one of the foil-wrapped nuggets, as though he still half-believed that they were made of solid gold. My whore had seized a handful of the Monopoly money (notes for £5,000, £10,000, £20,000) as though she still wholly believed that it was bankable. The dog gave a yank at his leash of plaited crocodile leather and reared up, fangs bared. Again and yet again he bayed, menacing and eerie. The General was one of the first to run. Then everyone was running. Still, still I laughed; and in wilder and wilder frenzy the dog still jerked at the leash now held in both my hands, repeatedly hurled himself forward and kept up that baying.

In a spluttering little caique, stinking of sheep, diesel-oil and vomit, the dog and I came to this island, clambered up the five rickety steps – they were then still passable – and made our way up to the husk-hut crepitant and murmurous with its insect life. The dog hunted through the sere bush, his coat growing mangy and his flanks lean, his eyes sinking within their red rims as a cobwebby penumbra settled on them. I bit on the vinegary apples, I tried to bite on the stone-like olives. I even grubbed for roots and rooted for grubs. The major domo had begged to stay with us but I had not let him. He had stood at the stern of the caique, his wide peasant hand shielding his narrow peasant face from the glare, as he gazed motionless at us, the hoarsely panting caique carrying him off through the filth of the world into a world of filth.

Months later, the major domo returned in a smartly gleaming motor-boat, with a panama-hat jauntily tilted above his narrow peasant face and an ivory-headed cane in his wide peasant hand. Some of the scraps of paper had been wafted back. They had settled, they had multiplied. An oil-prospecting company in which, as a kindness to the son of one of my hired friends, I had invested a few thousand pounds, had struck it rich. My whore had been decapitated in a motor-accident, hastening from one millionaire lover to another, and, her will unchanged since our separation, had left me the duplex that I had bought for her. A luxury hotel was being built on the stony ground of the small-holding that, for all my then wealth, my father had bequeathed to me, his eldest son, on his deathbed. But, perched on this rock, the dog panting on his side beside me, I was totally uninterested in the major domo's excited gabble. Later, other, bigger vessels came to the rickety jetty, with uniformed crews and gleaming brass-work and awnings under which their owners and their owners' guests could shield their delicate complexions from the sun. But the dog only bayed and I only laughed, as they interceded with me to give up all this nonsense and to return to 'civilisation', told me of some fool-proof investment (*Out of our long-standing friendship I want you in on the ground-floor*), or bleated about 'temporary' difficulties, a nasty little hitch or the sluggishness of cash-flow. Still perched on this rock, I watched them as, amazed, disconsolate, despairing or angry, they chugged, chugged back through the filth of the world into a world of filth.

My hatred and contempt for them had once been merely the obverse of my love and admiration for my own self. Oh, how I had loved and admired myself for my unbounded energy, my pristine youthfulness, my unwearying resourcefulness and my extravagant bounty; and how much easier it had been to love and admire myself for all these things if I could also hate and despise them for their effeteness and their senility and their ineffectuality and their avarice. Look here, upon this picture, and on this. (The Nobel prize-winner would be amazed to hear me quote those words.) But now my hatred and contempt for them have long since become an integral part of my hatred and contempt for myself. Call me not by my name but, if you must call me anything, in the language of my country call me 'Misanthropos'. The dog lies beside me and in his company I shall for a while live a dog's life – since that, despite what people say, is preferable to the life of a man. Together, he and I shall lap from the same stagnant puddle and together we shall scratch ourselves from the bites of the same fleas. We shall even defecate the same parasites. Perhaps we shall die together. Yes, I am sure that we shall.

Above the last of my mansions, on the last of my islands, there writhes a fig-tree long since dead and even longer barren. One day I shall have learned again to love myself enough to throw over the strongest of its branches the rope that the dog drags around with him, and to hang first him, so humane in his simple bestiality, and then myself, so beastly in my complex humanity. When that hour comes, these scraps of paper, as illusory as those other scraps piled high in innumerable banks in innumerable cities of the world, will have to stand as my gravestone.

But there is time enough for that. Of time, as of the filth of the world and of the world of filth, there is always enough.

KINGSLEY AMIS

Affairs of Death

My gaolers released me without notice on the morning of 26 October.
They acted without explanation also, merely indicating in their vile
French that I was free to go. Their continued and studied lack of
respect for my person, however, suggested that I owed my liberty to
some outside agency, which could have been nothing but the interven-
tion of my kinsman the Emperor. The prospect of this had been all that
had sustained me through the long months of my captivity. Henry, of
course, had held his hand on purpose, as much to underline his
disapproval of my recent actions as to weaken my prestige and power.

Autumn had come early and the weather had turned bleak and damp. My journey north from Benevento was wretched, its discomforts aggravated by irresistible contemplation of the contrast between it and my triumphant progress in the opposite direction that summer at the head of my troops. Who would have thought that a northern rabble like that could put those brave fellows to rout? More to the purpose was the question of my captains' bungling and treachery. It would receive my early consideration.

My delight at returning to Rome was tempered by apprehension about what might have been in store for me there. I need not have worried, however; Hildebrand the Benedictine had kept everything safe and I found the City perfectly quiet. I had sent ahead and he was waiting up for me in the yellow saloon, where a cold supper had been laid. He greeted me with a precise blend of reverence and warmth. He was a little thinner since June, I thought, perhaps a little harder too.

'You are not well, Lord,' he said with an intent look. 'Those Norman pigs have starved you. Was your highness at least dry?'

'Most of the time. I need rest and good food, fresh food.'

'Assuredly. Eat now, Lord. You enjoy these little birds.'

'No, I am too tired. Pour me wine.'

As he handed me the cup, he said quietly, 'I thought to have no ceremony. It seemed not to be called for.'

'Not after that, not after slinking back from prison, not after ignominious defeat on the field of battle. The papal forces in full retreat and the Supreme Pontiff a common prisoner. Hildebrand, arrest them all, all who are in Rome; hunt down the others and fetch them here. All – Gerard, Frederic, Valerian, Florentinus, Otho, the Spaniard and the one with the stutter. All my marshals, all those who robbed me of victory. Confine them here. All of them.'

'There, be calm, Lord. They shall be fetched, all of them.'

'See they are. Well, what awaits my attention tomorrow?'

'Many things, great and small. None pressing. Few pleasing. Some plaguing, as Peter Damian rebuking you for usurping the Emperor's function by your activities as a soldier.'

'Never mind him.'

'Perhaps we need not, but your highness will have to mind an accusation of heresy from the patriarch of the Eastern Church.'

'Michael Cerularius is an overweening fool. There must be something in the air of Constantinople that rots the brain. Does he know no better than to offer a direct challenge to my authority? I shall have to cut him off altogether, remove him from Christendom, him and his priests and all his Church. But I must first think long and seriously.'

'Let it be so, Lord. One pleasant matter. There is a king in Rome, most eager for an audience with your highness. I think I never saw one more truly eager.'

'What king?'

'Of Scots or Scotland, Macbeth by name. He has been here a week or more in hope and without the news of your release would very sorrowfully have given you up.'

'Or had something reached his ears?'

'In Scotland? All things are possible, Lord. It might be entertaining.'

'Entertaining or not, I will see him. Of course I will. I must make any friends I can. If he cares to call on me I will receive the king of Vinland. How is he attended, this Macbeth?'

'By nobody. By somebody I took for a kind of soldier. He was here, King Macbeth was in Rome, three years ago on purpose to see your highness, but you were abroad then, peregrinating beyond the Alps.'

'Yes, yes. Such persistence merits reward. Arrange it.'

'It is done, Lord. Provisionally. Noon, not tomorrow but the day following. Now your highness must retire,' said Hildebrand, summoning servants. 'And sleep late.'

When, somewhat refreshed after twelve hours in a good bed, I rose the next afternoon, Hildebrand was soon in attendance again with information about Scotland. The country, or the territory inhabited by Scots, was confined to that part of the mainland of Britain which lies north of the Firth of Forth. Here and over neighbouring regions from the furthest shores of the Irish Sea to those of the North Sea, there ranged at different times bands of Irish, Picts, Scots, Britons, Angles, Cumbrians, English, Danes, Norwegians contending in prolonged and obscure struggles. That end of northern Europe had been a violent place for centuries and seemingly still was.

At first sight Scotland was no concern of mine. The Church was well enough established there, and Macbeth had shown himself well disposed to her. I had no way of controlling events. There was only one bishop of the Scots, at St Andrews, and his influence was purely local. What monks there were had no power. Clearly, the key to control of the Scottish church lay in the sovereign. If I could win some personal regard from Macbeth, I might be laying the foundations of something that might, again, prove useful in any future trouble with England. And that there would be trouble with England, sooner or later, if not in my time then in that of one or other of my successors, I had not the slightest doubt. At any rate they, my successors, could not but regard with approval the notion I proposed, and the gaining of their approval was my second most urgent purpose in life.

I hardly know what I had expected to encounter the noon following, certainly not the tall, fair-haired, blue-eyed figure in his late forties who was presented; I thought he might well have had a Norse ancestor as well as Norse neighbours. His companion, introduced by my usher as Captain Seaton, short, broad, heavily bearded, with a look of stupid ferocity, was much more my idea of a Scotchman. As the two knelt before me I bestowed on each a salutation appropriate to his rank.

So as not to overawe my visitors excessively I had received them in a small throne-room built two centuries before by my predecessor Agapetus II and not two storeys high, none the less worthy of its function with sumptuous new frescoes, sculptures in the round and jewelled appointments. The soldier, if that was what he was, kept his eyes straight in front as though fearful of taking in what was about him; his master glanced here and there without disrespect, without astonishment either, his attention soon caught by the most unusual piece in sight, a grotesque carved-oak Calvary the bishop of Rennes took away from some church there and sent me for my forty-seventh birthday, my first after being consecrated. His dress gave further mild surprise; not deer-skins and foot-rags but a rich gold-edged surcoat that would not have disgraced the Emperor Henry himself, an inner garment of dark-red silk, high Spanish shoes, a short stout cross-hilted sword, plain but with some elegance in the workmanship, and below the throat a curiously shaped crucifix, evidently silver but of a pretty, bluish tinge, which I promised myself I would have off him before he took his leave. What manner of man was it who wore these things?

As was my custom when receiving royalty, I had had my seneschal position near the dais and at right angles to it a heavy chair with a high

and elaborately carved back representing scenes of martyrdom.
Mounted on a shallow platform, it was in no sense a throne but did
elevate the monarch in occupation a moderate distance above the
commonalty. Here King Macbeth sat, sat sufficiently at his ease with
his blue eyes reverentially lowered. Without much confidence in being
understood, I asked in simple Latin a question about his earlier visit to
the City.

Unexpectedly once more, he replied in fluent and correct French, my
own native tongue, 'I was desperately disappointed to be unable to pay
my respects to your highness. I had to be content with distributing
money to the poor of Rome.' His accent was no worse than those of my
late captors, indeed much resembled theirs.

'Do many of your countrymen share your majesty's remarkable
skill?' I asked in the same language, already in some degree impressed.

'Alas no, Holy Father. I have been fortunately placed. It so happens
that over the past two years I have sheltered at my court a number of
French-speaking fugitives from England, and I sent myself to school
with them. After all, this conversation, however memorable to me,
would have been much restricted otherwise. My Latin is rudimentary,
and I doubt if your highness's Gaelic is any better.'

I laughed, partly in unconcealed appreciation of this speech. Those
fugitives had of course come in the first place from Normandy, but
after my recent experiences it would have been less than tactful to
mention even the existence of that place. As for having learned French,
it seemed certain to me at this moment that Macbeth had done so in
order to be able to converse not with me, whom he had been prepared
to face three years before in ignorance of it, but with Duke William,
universally known to have been promised the English throne by King
Edward as soon as that throne fell vacant, and therefore a most
interesting personage to any king of Scotland. Whether William would
welcome such a conversation was another matter. 'Doubtless you
made other visits on your journey here, your majesty?' I asked,
deciding to probe a little.

He was on the defensive at once. 'Yes, Holy Father, one such, but it
was of no importance, not even comparatively so.'

'Nevertheless, I trust enjoyable?'

'I must ask your highness to pardon me,' he said, blinking fiercely.

This time I suppressed a smile. It was as clear to me as from a full description that what he had visited or attempted to visit was William's court, and no less so that he had been rebuffed – unseen, I judged, for it took no more than a glance to show that here was a man to be reckoned with, not the refined soul he took himself for, a barbarian still, but a remarkable barbarian. 'We hear pleasing reports of the state of Scotland under your majesty's stewardship.'

'Your highness is too kind. And you bring me to the object of this interview, or the secondary object, the first plainly being to be granted your blessing, Holy Father. I hope to be forgiven for making what must be an unusual request. It is that a clerk should be sent for to record the substance of what, if permitted, I shall say.'

I gave the necessary directions, and simply waited, mastering my curiosity as best I could.

'I suppose you know little of Scotland, Holy Father. It is a remote and obscure place, its people wild, ignorant, credulous, superstitious, not brutish but childish. They have no notions of probability, of consistency, of what is real and what is fancied. My reign has not been untroubled and some of the events in it, and even more those attending its inception, were violent, confused and ambiguous. Not long after I am dead the generally accepted account of it, of my reign, is likely to deviate absurdly and irrecoverably from historical fact. A like process has already distorted the years of my predecessor's rule. With your help, Holy Father, I intend to set on record the truth of these matters and to leave that record lodged in the bosom of the see of St Peter, where it will be safe for ever. What I have to say may also attract your highness's passing attention, for all Scotland's distance from the centre of the world.'

This last stroke, and the glance that went with it, caused me to reflect that such men as this were not very common anywhere, not even in Rome. Just then a clerk appeared, a Benedictine, and on my nod settled himself at Macbeth's left side. I spread the palm of one hand in invitation.

'Some things are seen, some things are put out of sight. It is seen that old Malcolm II, King of Scots, fortunate, victorious, praised of bards, had no son to follow him, but that he ruled so long that by the time he died his grandsons were grown up. For the succession, it is seen that he favoured the eldest, Duncan. This, when he might have chosen the third in age, myself, or even the fourth and youngest, Thorfinn Sigurdson, son of the Norwegian earl of Orkney. By the ancient custom of our royal house the eldest prince has no firm right to succeed, and I had a better claim, a double claim, a claim not only through my own lineage but also through that of my wife Gruoch, granddaughter of King Kenneth III, whom old Malcolm had deposed and killed. Such a claim as hers is also admitted by our custom.

'All this is seen. It is further seen though ill remembered, that old Malcolm made over to Thorfinn, with the title of earl, two fiefs on the mainland, this as a means of placating any ambition he might nourish, of restraining him. The old man had not reckoned that, once on the throne, the foolhardy Duncan would try to recover those places by force of arms. Scotland ran with blood, much of it that of my own people, some of it my own blood; I carried a sword for my king as a commander of his armies. One morning thirteen years ago, Thorfinn's Norwegians burst upon the Scots from the rising sun at Burghead in Moray and cut them to pieces on the beach in ten minutes. Duncan fled, and I and a party of my followers fled with him. Moray was my fief; by secret paths I led him to an abandoned fort at a place called Bothnagowan. There, one August night, we seized our chance, a dozen of us, and surprised him as he lay asleep out on the rampart, and stabbed him to death with our daggers. With no delay I had myself proclaimed king and was crowned at Scone, made peace with my cousin Thorfinn, made him my friend; indeed, he had been my friend before, he who always does what he has said he will do. And the Scots hung up their arms.

'This too is seen by some. What is not seen, what is already forgotten, what is put out of sight is Duncan as he was. Comely I grant him, with a bright eye and a curved lip, very like my father-in-law, as my wife often noted; both men were descended from Malcolm I, dead these hundred years. However, in all else Duncan was a wretch, mean of spirit, vengeful, I think a little mad; no one was safe from his sudden rages. Wasteful and indolent. Unclean in his person – he stank under our knives, not only from fear. Not kingly. It is put out of sight that his nickname of the Gracious was a jest, a taunt.

'Now Scotland is safe and at peace. This has not been customary; so fierce and prolonged have been her inner conflicts that, of her last nine kings, only old Malcolm died in his bed. The future holds some hope. Having no issue I have taken as my son the fruit of my wife's first marriage, young Lulach, a strong honest boy of twenty-one. I mean him to succeed me. Duncan's sons, Malcolm Broadhead and Donald Bane, whom I generously spared, shelter in the household of Siward, the English earl of Northumberland, a cousin of their mother's. They show no signs of moving to unseat me, nor can they ever contrive it while my friend and ally Thorfinn lives. Let them try and welcome. I will defend my country to my last breath.

'That all this is true I, Macbeth, King of Scots, swear on my honour.

'There remains the heavy matter of the killing of Duncan. It was done *more Scottico*, not in malice, it was done for Scotland, not for my advancement, it was done as an execution, not as a wanton slaying, but it was murder. If I am to bear the blame . . .'

As he paused I spoke. 'Of that you and I will speak in private, your majesty, at a later hour. I must consider your tale.'

'Thank you, Holy Father. Thank you, too, for giving me the opportunity of having it set down.'

'You justified your forecast that it would catch my attention.'

Macbeth nodded slowly, his thoughts on old wrongs and enduring hazards. It was more than half to himself that he said, 'Already they are telling one another that my gentle Gruoch had a hand in Duncan's death, when in truth she was in my castle at Dunkeld, over sixty miles away. If it were not for this record, who could guess what might be believed of me in centuries to come? That I took innocent lives, that I murdered my friend, murdered children, that I consorted with witches and saw visions, that I – how to put it? – supped full with horrors.'

Here he turned briefly to his man Seaton, and in a strange language spoke what I took to be some words of courteous apology for subjecting him to so much incomprehensible talk. The fellow gave a grunt of oafish surprise and faltered out a few harsh, graceless syllables, staring vacantly as he did so. Poor, poor King Macbeth; if that was his chosen associate, what must his daily company at home have been like? I would forgive him his murder; indeed, to have confined oneself to a single such crime in a country like Scotland, assuming the impression I had formed of it to be even moderately fair, indicated laudable restraint.

There were, of course, other considerations, other than the obvious diplomatic ones. A man likes to show mercy whenever possible. Then, at our private audience early that evening Macbeth relieved me of what might have been an awkwardness by tactfully producing un-asked a quantity of gold and suggesting that I should devote it to pious purposes of my own choosing. And, when all is said, one soldier is bound to feel a certain kinship with another. It was with a full heart that I pronounced him absolved and wished him a safe return, and I felt almost no reluctance in allowing him to keep the dainty crucifix I had noticed.

The next morning Hildebrand came to me with Macbeth's story written out fair. 'To my mind, Lord, a considerable person.'

'More so than his position calls for. I hope for his sake he sits as securely as he appears to believe.'

'Time will show.'

'Time will show many things of greater moment than the devices of a Scottish freebooter, however engaging.'

'Is your highness telling me that this is not to be put into the permanent archive?'

'We agreed to keep it as sparse as possible. Extract whatever is needed.'

'As your highness pleases. I hope you feel your time with Macbeth was not wasted.'

'It was most interesting, and we have his goodwill.'

'True, Lord. And now I have news of your marshals. Five are confined. Valerian died by his own hand before he could be secured. Frederic is believed to be at large in the Emperor's domain. I have a good man after him.'

'Let the matter be settled and over. It seems well it should be done quickly.'

Historical Note

Macbeth ('fair, yellow, tall') first visited Rome in the year 1050. This visit, unlike his second three years later, is vouched for by documents.

In 1054 his armies were defeated near Scone by those of Siward, Earl of Northumberland, but he continued on the Scottish throne another three years. Then his powerful ally Thorfinn died, and shortly afterwards Malcolm Broadhead murdered him. Macbeth's stepson Lulach became king, but after only a few months Malcolm murdered him too and took the crown, ruling as Malcolm III. Macbeth and Lulach were buried in the island of Iona, the ancient resting-place of the Scottish kings.

The health of Pope Leo IX had been shattered by his captivity in southern Italy and he died the following year, 1054, though not before he had excommunicated the Patriarch of Constantinople, thus making final and permanent the split between the Western and Eastern churches. He was canonised as St Leo in 1087.

Hildebrand became Pope Gregory VII in 1073 and also achieved sainthood.

De Bilbow

He lunged across the girl towards the Gauloises he had left on the bedside table.

'You are taking the book? You are helping now to make the preparation?'

'I just want a cigarette.' He lunged again, successfully. With some awkwardness, because he was lying on his back, he got a cigarette alight.

He blew Gauloise smoke and smell towards the curtains. They were closed but penetrated by the rich, soon-to-die sunlight of late afternoon.

The exotic smell and the intensity of the light, which came through the curtains like light glowing through one's own eyelids, seemed components of his sexual contentment.

'Barney?' the girl said.

'Mm?'

'I am having to go soon to the college. It is being tonight my class and I have not made the preparation. You are promising that you are helping.'

It was true he had promised. But then there had to be – they had both needed there to be – a pretext for getting her into his flat and his bed.

'Tell me the problem.'

'There is an English word I am not knowing. I am not finding it in the dictionary. And I am forgetting now.' He felt her stretch towards the bedside table. 'No.' Her hand was retracted. 'I am now remembering. "Bilbow."'

'Bilbow?'

'Yes.'

'There's no such word. It's a surname, not an ordinary word.'

'Please? You are not knowing this English word?'

'I *am* knowing,' Barney said. 'I'm knowing damn well the word doesn't exist.'

'I am shewing.' She felt for and found the book. It was a paperback inside a not very competently home-made brown paper cover.

She lay beside him and opened it. He saw it was a copy of *Henry V.* She turned the pages rapidly, seeking the right one.

'You have been reading this play?' she asked.

'Not since I was fourteen.' The image came into his memory of his school copy: a dark green cover, with enlarged canvas pores; a flyleaf bearing other people's names written in ink and then formally cancelled by an ink line drawn through them with a ruler.

He stretched his arm up at a right-angle to his supine shoulders and waved the Gauloise or perhaps, in his mind's eye, a school ruler.

'Follow your spirit,' he declaimed, making his voice ring in the small bedroom, 'and upon this charge, Cry "God for Harry, England and Saint George!"'

'I am not being able to find the page where this word is being.'

'Belligerent, patriotic, rhetorical rubbish,' Barney said without animus. *Henry V* struck him as an inept, indeed a positively insensitive choice of play to read with a class in English for foreigners. 'What sort of teachers are there at your college?'

'This class is being with Mr Reeson. Mr Reeson is being very nice.'

'But tactless,' Barney said. 'You should tell him it's a tactless choice. It'll give the students the impression the English are jingoists.' He reached across her again towards the table, this time in search of the ashtray.

She turned neatly turtle beneath his arm, taking the book with her. By the time he had finished stubbing out his cigarette, she was lying on her front, propped on her elbows, going through the pages of the book, which now rested on the pillow.

She had kicked free of the sheet and Barney looked at her naked back in the strong, filtered light.

All over the hollow of her back the skin was a deep crimson. For an instant he thought of a burn, as though he had stubbed out his cigarette there, but it was of course a birthmark, an exceptionally extensive one, and he wondered why such things were called strawberry marks when their colour was closer to mulberry.

As if to assure her he felt no repulsion, he put the palm of his hand on the mark. Simultaneously, she said:

'I am finding. Look, Barney.'

Without moving his hand, to which the girl seemed to pay no attention, he heaved and twisted in order to look at the open page.

His extended hand was not big enough to blot out the whole of the mark on her.

She pointed to a line of print.

'*Kath.*,' he read. 'Excusez-moi, Alice; écoutez: de hand, de fingers, de nails, de arma, de bilbow.'

'You are seeing, Barney. There is being this word.'

'But not in English there isn't. She's — what's her name? Katharine? — she's French.'

Something of the content of *Henry V* returned to his mind, where it looked strange because it had once been so familiar. Now it was easier to recall that he had once known the play well than to recall the play.

'Please? I am not knowing French,' the girl said. '"Bilbow" is being a French word?'

'No!' This time his voice rang involuntarily. Then he grinned at his own fury. 'She gets it wrong. She's learning English for foreigners. I suppose your Mr Thing – Reeson – finds that hilarious.'

'It is for making the examination.'

'It's a set book, do you mean?'

'Yes, a set book.'

Barney felt frustrated that he could not direct indignation at the unknown Reeson for the choice.

His hand rested on the girl's back like a saddle. He thought it curious that she could be so unconcerned about something she might easily, if mistakenly, consider a blemish.

Fragments of *Henry V* reassembled in his mind.

'After ten minutes I am making the bath. It is better I make the bath before I am going to my class.'

'Go ahead. Yes, of course. There's a towel in there.'

'You are being sad, Barney?'

'No.'

'You are being angered because I am not staying more time? Because I am making the preparation? If you are liking, I am coming tomorrow again.'

'Yes, do,' Barney said.

'I am finding very difficult the preparation.' She turned a page backwards. 'I try to make now the revision.'

He said, recovering the information as he spoke:

'Katharine asks Alice to teach her the English words for the hand, the arms and so forth. Then *she* tries to revise, and she gets it wrong.'

'We are having this lesson in my class also. "The parts of the body."'

'The parts of the body, yes.' Shifting his hand at last from her blemished back, he touched her hand, which was pinning the book to the pillow. 'De hand,' he said. With his finger he stroked each of her fingers, outlining each of the nails. 'De fingres, de nails.' His finger tumbled down her forearm. 'De arma.' He thought he was going to pull the girl towards him and make love to her again. Without taking a decision not to, he didn't. He wriggled his finger towards the folded elbow on which she was propped, but it was inaccessible in a depression of the bed and he said nothing.

'I am having to make now the bath or I am being late. When I am coming tomorrow, you are helping more the preparation?'

'Yes. All right.' He put his hand on the blemish again. 'You do know about this, don't you?'

'Yes, I am knowing.'

'Good. Not that it matters.'

'I am knowing. It is being called the back.'

*

How in the world could she not know?

How in a world of mirrors, vanity and self-examination could a girl grow to adulthood and not know that her back was stained the colour of mulberries? In a dozen places – in people's bathrooms, in the trying-on cubicles in clothes shops – the mirrors were poised in reciprocal pairings with the express purpose of introducing you to your back.

Waiting for the girl in the evenings, which were increasingly hot, which made his flat seem increasingly small, Barney composed and rehearsed informative speeches.

Some were tender, others flirtatious. They were usually allusive – usually to *Henry V*, the only subject-matter, apart from sex, he shared with the girl.

When the girl arrived, Barney would feel inhibited in the delivery of his speech by the very fact that it was rehearsed. He waded on through his inhibition – only to find his purpose splinter on the girl's sheer lack of comprehension of English.

'You are helping very much the preparation, Barney. Mr Reeson is saying I am being much better.'

Reeson must, Barney thought, be a lousy teacher.

'I am making now the revision.'

Bilbow: a hard little pilule, a carbuncle, a disfigurement of a word. Barney's allusiveness was forced back on him, crammed into the confinement of his own thoughts and obliged to do its reverberating there. 'De bilbow' became the way his thoughts alluded to the mark on the girl or perhaps to the duty with which it saddled him.

It seemed to him axiomatic that the girl had a right to know. To pursue the acquaintance, to go on making love to her, and not to tell her (or, alternatively, elicit unequivocally that she did after all, as sometimes he still reasoned she must, already know) was a form of taking unfair advantage of her, tantamount to laughing at her behind her blemished back.

Besides, to know something about her that she did not know was, somehow, a restriction on Barney's own freedom of action.

'When I will be making the examination, I am becoming perhaps an air hostess.'

'Surely Reeson doesn't think you're ready to take the exam yet?'

'Ah, Barney. You are not liking if I am going away?'

His prefabricated speeches became jocular to the verge of aggression. He fashioned fantasies of blurting the information, then of shouting it until he forced her to understand. He didn't try to make them come true, knowing her response would be 'Please?'

He wondered why the duty that was so impossible for him to discharge had not been performed years before by someone else: a previous lover, her mother, one of the other girls in the hostel where she lodged.

He took to questioning her, seeking to wring from her half-comprehension of the questions and half-expression of the answers (did 'since six years' mean 'during the past six years' or 'since I was six years old'?) an account of herself in which he might discern the people who ought to have informed her and could, moreover, have done so quite casually, without pain to either side. Perhaps he was looking for them in her history in order to blame them. He learned that she had come to London on an au pair arrangement but had quickly left the family she was placed with. She had taken a job in a café, which was indeed where Barney had, as a customer, met her. It was an amateurish job that didn't compromise her student status and didn't bring in much money either and was probably, Barney guessed, illegal in relation to her work permit. 'Ah, Barney, you are being so nice. You are wanting to know all the things that are being in my life.'

Sometimes he took her to bed and, instead of making love, gazed at de bilbow. Towards the edges there were patches of dark brown interpolated into the mulberry, like, indeed, fibrous bits in a soft fruit. Testing with his fingertips, he could detect no difference in texture between de bilbow and the golden flesh round its borders. He could not expect the girl to have discovered de bilbow by touch.

As he pored over her back, he longed for her to ask what he was dwelling on with such concentration. Yet if he were to find occasion to tell her now, it would already be impossible to explain to her why he had not told her before.

One weekend he held her prisoner in his wearisomely hot flat, forbidding her to get up and get dressed even for meals, and made love compulsively, without lyricism, in keeping with the feverish weather.

Yet when she next asked him 'You are helping now the preparation?', which had become her allusion to love-making, he pretended to take the question literally and opened *Henry V*.

'You are being so good, Barney. I am learning every day so much, Mr Reeson will be being very pleased.'

Nowhere in her confusing accounts could he locate her family. She had simply left them behind on some Baltic or yet more northern coast, effectively orphaning herself. Yet surely, he thought with brief hope, the communal, comradely life of the hostel must be capable of playing the part of siblings?

She brought the answer to his flat one Sunday morning in a carrier bag.

'It is being a dress which Gina is buying but she is not liking. I am trying and it is fitting with me and Gina is saying it goes well to me and so she is giving. And now I am trying and shewing for you, Barney.'

It was a sun-dress, with a wired top that made a brassière unnecessary. The upper part was without a back. Barney did up the hooks and eyes on the waistband for her. Half of de bilbow was exposed.

'You are liking?' She swished to left and right in front of the bedroom mirror, peering over her shoulder but stopping each swing just before de bilbow was bound to come in sight. 'Perhaps, when I will be making the examination, I will not be becoming an air hostess, I will be becoming a model.'

He saw her not only orphaned but castaway, marooned incommunicado among Ginas and Helgas whose latin or germanic languages she did not know and who themselves could understand neither her mother tongue nor her appalling English.

'And now we are going out, yes? It is being so hot, it is better that we are going into the park or the river, and for the change we are making the lunch in a café where I am not being a waitress, and you will be being pleased that you are being with a person who is having the nice dress and it is going well to her.'

'No,' Barney said.

'Ah, Barney, why?'

He saw that he had the opportunity to inform her. He had only to answer her question. And he could demonstrate his answer here and now, with the sun-dress, the mirror and de bilbow, appealing over the head of her linguistic incomprehension to her eyes.

He was, however, demoralised. He had watched for the opportunity too long and too intensely. And he was dispirited by perceiving that the Gina girl must have had the same opportunity this very morning, and must either have failed to take it or have taken it and failed to communicate de bilbow's existence.

'Just No,' he said. 'Just No, no, no, no, no.'

He found, to his astonishment, tears in his eyes and his voice: of fury? of disappointment? of failure?

'Ah, Barney, you are being so nice. I am understanding. You are not liking that other men are seeing so much of the parts of the body.'

*

He came to think of himself as ill.

Even to frame the thought seemed a surrender to his obsession. Yet to cede it might, he argued to himself, be necessary to beginning a cure, though he couldn't tell whether he needed curing of incipient insanity or merely of absurdity.

He nursed himself. He offered himself congratulations if he could get through a day's work without (so far as he knew) anyone's noticing at the office that his mind was absented from work, gripped, fixed and stained like a microscope slide; and he congratulated himself again if he could so much as get himself passively conveyed home from work and belched up, at the end of his journey, in one of the geysers of parched air liberated from the tube.

He never knew whether the girl, to whom he had given a key, would be in the flat when he reached it. The hours she worked at the café followed a complex, long-cycled roster, which was then thrown into unpredictability by last-minute exchanges of duties between the wait-resses which he thought resembled small, agitated transactions on the currency market. He lost track of the exchange rates and simply let the girl's presences and arrivals fall on him, like the heat.

He made no plans to use his holiday period. Because he would not commit himself, the girl did not even ask for leave from the café. At her college the regular courses were suspended but, when she sought Barney's advice ('You are thinking it is being necessary that I am learning more before I will be making the examination?'), he agreed she would do well to enroll for the summer school that took their place.

He could have afforded to take the girl away, at least briefly and without leaving England, and might have done so had the weather broken. But it went on burning and he knew that, wherever they went, the girl would want to swim or at any rate sunbathe.

When his holiday arrived, he simply stayed home from work.

Her hopscotch timetable surprised him at half past one on his first afternoon at home, when he heard her letting herself into the flat.

'My friend is asking me to be changing times with her. I am bringing you a present.'

She went into the bedroom, he supposed to change. He sat on in his armchair, looking at the punnet of raspberries she had given him.

He felt no desire to eat any, even though, through the same lack of desire, he had had no luncheon.

She came out of the bedroom wearing Gina's sun-dress.

'I am knowing you are not liking that other people are seeing, but I am liking that I am wearing it at home and you are seeing, Barney.'

She turned two rapid complete revolutions before him. Each time he glimpsed de bilbow. It rose out of the dress and tamed what was meant to be the fierce, jungle colouring of the material by being, in its fruity organicness, horribly much more vivid.

Barney perceived again that she was a very attractive girl; but he was no longer attracted by her.

He also perceived that, could he consider it soberly, de bilbow would seem a very minor matter for his thoughts to have made such a fuss about, since it couldn't seriously be held to take off from her attractiveness.

'I am being in this dress not so hot.'

Barney simply sat, while the afternoon steamed to a crescendo and the girl frittered it round them. She read half a page of *Henry V*; she ate several of the raspberries; she took an art book from the shelves and looked at three of the pictures; she boiled a kettle to make some lemonade but found Barney's kitchen devoid of lemons.

'I am making now the preparation, yes?'

Barney shook his head.

He had once felt dishonourable in making love to her without disclosing the existence of de bilbow. Now he felt still more dishonourable because he didn't – wouldn't and couldn't – make love to her.

'You are liking that we are going out? If you are liking, I am not wearing this dress. There is being much time before I am going to the café. It is being possible that we are going first to the cinema. It is being cool there.'

But Barney could raise no wish in himself to do anything. He sat on, while the day began to fade and shred.

He could no longer tell whether he liked the girl, any more than he could judge whether or not he thought her stupid.

He expected to be able to feel at least pity, for her unanchored state and her dependence on someone as feeble as himself. He could experience only a remote admiration, as he might for the exploits of an unknown athlete. Certainly she was brave to have cast herself on an alien world when she had so little gift for languages.

She took a bath, washed the sun-dress and hung it to dry outside Barney's bathroom window and, wearing jeans and a t-shirt, left early for the café.

Hoping to make her some amends, but in a public place where she could not expect making amends to consist of making love, Barney gave her half an hour's start and then walked round to the café himself.

He sat at one of her tables, which he had to share with unknowns because the place was crowded. He asked her for an iced coffee and a tomato sandwich. He didn't want but thought he ought to eat.

For the first time he noticed the unloveliness of the place. The tables jutted and butted between walls decorated by chipped whorls of aquamarine cement. The electric fan failed to reduce the temperature but at least its buzz and clicks interfered with the piped music.

Discommoded by the ungainliness of the furnishings and the meanness of the spaces between them, the waitresses seemed overworked. Barney suspected the café took advantage of the fact that the work permits of many of them could not abide scrutiny. Tonight it was easy to think of them as sweated labour.

At the far side, out of earshot of Barney, the girl bent over a customer to take his order, and Barney could see that he was flirting with her.

Barney bit indifferently into his sandwich and dipped his chin like a swimmer in an effort to keep the wafers of tomato either between the slices of bread or decently inside his mouth.

The girl moved away from the distant table, but the customer put out his hand to detain her a moment while he added something to the flirtatious exchange. His hand rested briefly on the back of her t-shirt at exactly the place where Barney knew de bilbow to be.

Barney suffered pure pain.

After a moment he identified it. It was not the stir of jealousy, which he would have welcomed. It was terror. His mind, which had earlier threshed about demanding why some previous lover had not informed the girl of de bilbow, had perceived the certainty that a future lover would. And then the girl, however stupid she might in fact be, would be bound to accuse Barney in retrospect of dishonourably keeping her ignorant.

Without finishing his sandwich, he signalled in panic to the girl for his bill and left hastily, obeying the obligation to tip which the girl had long before placed on him by explaining that tips were pooled but feeling that to pile coins on a table he knew to be tended by her was, now, insulting and a matter of shame.

He formed overnight the intention of warning the girl that the flirtatious customer had behaved too familiarly. But when she arrived at his flat the next day he found himself aware that he was himself a customer who had behaved too familiarly.

He muted warning into the question, to which he did not much want to know the answer, who the flirtatious customer had been.

'Please?'

'The thin one in brown denim.'

'I am not knowing what you are meaning, Barney.'

With pencil and paper he made a diagram of the disposition of the tables in the café and put an X at the place the flirtatious customer had occupied.

'Ah, Barney, I am now understanding. To begin, I am thinking it is being somebody I am not knowing. But you are meaning Mr Reeson.'

'Reeson? That was *Reeson*?'

There had never been any justification, Barney recognised, for his assumption that Reeson was safely fuddy-duddy.

'I am forgetting that you are not ever meeting him. He is being very nice yesterday in the café. He is saying there is being at another college a film club, and it is having tonight the film of *Henry V*, and Mr Reeson is knowing one of the teachers at that college, and he is getting two tickets, and he will be driving with me tonight with his car. This film is being very good for making the examination.'

*

At five-thirty, by which time he calculated that the girl must be in Reeson's passenger seat and out of the neighbourhood, he went to the do-it-yourself shop, which he caught just before closing, and sweated home carrying a tall, narrow strip of mirror glass.

He stood on the surround of the bath and hoisted the length of glass as though it were a rigid ballerina.

Teetering carefully round, he placed the glass flat against the wall next the bath, where it entered an oblique relationship to the smaller mirror that was already fixed across the opposite corner of the bathroom.

He held the long sheet of glass to the wall with the palm of his left hand, which deposited a sweaty palm print.

With his right hand, he poked a fragment of fuse-wire through the hole at the top left-hand corner of the glass and wriggled it to scratch the wall and thus mark where he must drill.

By stretching he managed similarly to mark the position of the hole at the top right-hand corner, and then, by bending, that of the one at the bottom left.

To mark the hole at the bottom right, he had both to bend and to stretch.

As he did so, the length of glass lurched. He realised he had made the scratch in the wrong place; and the uglily bevelled edge of the glass, which reminded him of the deckle on a wedding invitation, had drawn blood and shreds of skin from his knuckles.

He lowered the glass to the floor, leaned it against the bath, jumped down and ran his hand stingingly under the cold tap.

He forced himself to continue. It was impossible to align the holes in the glass with the three correctly placed scratches he had already made. He had to, he told himself without amusement, start from scratch again, and he made four new marks.

The flex on his electric drill was not quite long enough to reach the marks from the nearest plug, which was for safety's sake outside the bathroom. He thought of going out to buy an extra length, then remembered that the do-it-yourself shop was shut.

He shifted the sheet of mirror glass six inches along the wall and set about making new marks where the holes fell in the new position.

The muscles of his arms were tremulous after the weight of the glass. He worked fumblingly. He had no means of knowing how long Reeson would keep the girl out, but he had lost time and he forced himself to hurry.

He was distressed to notice furtiveness in his hurry. He was acting in rebellion against merely passively suffering. He had resolved by action to free himself. Yet he found himself nauseated by panic lest the girl should return before he had set up his fait accompli and ask why he was doing it.

As he drilled the four holes, he kept switching off the drill and listening, in case its din had masked the noise of her return.

He put the cone of old newspaper that he had been given in the do-it-yourself shop on the surround of the bath. As he unrolled it, his forearm convulsed into an involuntary jerk. The rawlplugs rolled on the bathroom floor, and he lost more time while he crawled after them.

Yet in the end the mirror was fixed, and the girl had not come back.

He stepped down from the surround. The muscles, the very bone, of the leg he put his weight on seemed to fold like paper, and he tumbled onto the bathroom floor, jarring his body and perhaps stunning himself for an instant.

He stood up. The back of his ribs felt bruised and grazed.

He pulled his sweat-sodden shirt over his head, which it hurt his ribs to do, and flung it on the floor.

Carefully, holding the edge as he went, he stepped into the bath. He stood there, seeking the image of his back reflected from one mirror into the other.

He ducked, painfully stretched and peered. The correct angle was difficult to hit on. His hope of obliging the girl to catch casual sight of de bilbow seemed falsified. He thought it perfectly possible that she could take a bath and even stand up to towel herself afterwards without ever glimpsing her back.

It would be ironic, he thought, if, when he located the image of his back, it were to disclose that he bore a birthmark which mother, lovers and friends had never informed him of.

At last he caught his reflexion. There was no mark on his back, permanent or temporary.

The bathroom door was pushed open. Perhaps it was because he had been stunned that he had not heard the girl enter the flat. She found him standing upright, wearing trousers and shoes but no shirt, in the dry bath.

'Ah, Barney, you are being here. I am being frightened when I am not seeing you.'

Feeling absurd, he stepped with care out of the bath and said:

'Did you have a nice time?'

'Yes, it is being nice. You have been being making the new mirror at the wall?'

'Yes.' To prevent questions, he asked:

'Did you enjoy the film?'

He had once seen the film but could remember nothing of it except the Nineteen-Thirties-lesbian hairstyle it attributed to the king.

'It is being very nice.'

'Reeson behave decently?'

'Mr Reeson is being very nice.'

'Good.'

'Barney, why you are being always so jealous?'

'I'm *not*,' he cried. He found himself bending down and hammering with his painful fist on the surround of the bath. 'I'm not, not, not, not, not.'

There was a sound from the wall above the bath. For a moment the
new mirror hung, lopsided, on one screw, like a person swinging by
one arm from a branch. Then it slithered down the wall into the bath
and burst into shards.

'You will be having to make carefully the tidying,' the girl said. 'It is
being very dangerous that there is being glass in the bath.'

He sub-noticed that she implied that she was not concerned in either
the tidying up or the danger.

'I am going now away, Barney. I am not coming more.'

'No,' he said, lunging for her wrist.

She shook him off. She opened her handbag, took out his door-key
and gave it him.

'I'm not trying to stop you,' Barney said. 'You're perfectly free. Of
course you're free. Only, there's something I've got to tell you first.'

'It is not being needed. I am knowing.'

'You *don't* know. I *know* you don't know.'

'I am knowing. I am knowing that you are not now loving, Barney.'

*

It was three weeks before he saw her again. The weather had
broken. Gusts of rain sent shudders down streets. Barney stood in the
second aisle of the supermarket, a wet umbrella hooked to his wrist,
his damp trouser legs furling about his legs, casting his thoughts over
the goods in the wire basket he held, about to approach the checkout.

He saw the girl, followed by Reeson, enter the shop. Each took a
wire basket from the stack.

In panic he strode back up the aisle: past breakfast cereals, past
pasta, past sauces, pickles, dried fruit and jams, past cakes. He halted
in front of the rear wall of the shop. There was nothing in view except
Tampax and sanitary towels.

He retreated the way he had come as far as pickles, wondered if he
could make a dash for the checkout, was alarmed by hearing the girl's
voice approaching up the other aisle and slipped into the little cul-
de-sac that abutted on pickles.

The cul-de-sac contained pottery mugs, clothes pegs and pet food.

Barney picked up a packet of dog biscuits but put it back. If the girl came upon him holding it, she would know he was hiding, because she well knew he had no dog.

He waited in his blind alley, listening. He heard no identifiable voices, no locatable footsteps.

He decided that if he was to be caught the cul-de-sac was the worst place for it. He put a mug he thought hideous into his basket, walked out of the cul-de-sac and turned down the aisle towards the checkout.

A spoke of his umbrella caught in the wire mesh of a basket that proved to be carried by the girl.

'Ah, Barney, it is being you.'

'How are you?' he asked. He saw that Reeson was delayed at cakes.

'I am being well.'

He longed to linger and spy on her reunion with Reeson beside cakes, so that he might gauge whether they were lovers. But he realised it was only in the sexology of the school playground that you could tell such things about two people from their public demeanour. And there was not even a folklore whereby you could tell if one lover had informed the other that she had a birthmark on her back.

'By the way,' he said. 'Your sun-dress is still at my flat.'

'It is not being important. I am not now needing.' She pushed past him, advancing her wire basket as a pregnant woman might her stomach, and made towards cakes.

He marched to the checkout, convinced that the girl had discovered de bilbow and thus the unsuitability to her of the sun-dress.

He stood at the checkout while his purchases were detailed out of his basket and their prices rung up.

An Arab woman came into the shop wearing a beaked face-mask and he felt pity as for caged birds.

His hideous mug was put into a paper bag which he hoped would do nothing to save it from being smashed. He heard the rain drip soggily from the awning outside the shop onto the strips of corrugated cardboard that had been placed on the pavement at the entrance, and realised that the girl's answer might have meant only that the weather was no longer suitable to a sun-dress.

Outside the shop he paused, struggling to put up his umbrella with a single hand. When he got it up, he tried to swivel it to the other side of his body, so that it would shield his shopping bag from the rain.

Wrenching his ribs, which were still sore from his tumble in the bathroom, he set off, halting, lopsided and oblique, his gait indicating, he thought, pretty much how he was emerging from the whole affair. As he moved away from the shop, a gust raised and let fall the awning with a strong crack, and he felt that he was being shaken out, like débris, from a huge bed.

PAUL BAILEY

A Mother's Lament

Done it up against an alley wall, me and his daddy did, didn't we. Silver his tongue was and his skin was olive. He wasn't quite white, but then again he wasn't black, he was – yes – olive, like an Eytie or a Greek, except that he come from Malta. Shows you what charm he had, coaxing me – not that I needed much – to do it in public, no thought of the consequences, up against Bright's candle factory. Anyhow, he was olive – you know, swarthy; looked as if he needed a shave just after he'd had one. It was the wartime, and though all of us girls down Deptford was flighty I never went with no Sanders of the River, I had too much respect for myself, it was only proper tarts done it with darkies. I mean to say, I could have gone with coons if I'd had a mind to, but as I say, I didn't, because I hadn't. I was a cut above that sort of thing, I can tell you.

Anyhow, where was I? In the alley, yes, alongside Bright's. As I say, he had a silver tongue, his daddy, it was his words more than anything else that got to me, and he certainly used them that night, he really did. I mean, he called my hair my raven tresses. I ask you, raven tresses! Oh, he buttered me up with his fancy talk in the saloon bar of the Kit Marlowe – you would have had to have been a fly on the wall to appreciate it. I got a bit tiddly, I have to confess. Nothing unpleasant: I was squiffy-eyed, yes, but I wasn't falling over my feet or bringing up my dinner. Nothing nasty like that. I wasn't far gone, I was happy, that's all. I was in the mood for a little romance.

So was he. I wasn't slow to catch his drift. Those words of his had to be leading somewhere, and you didn't have to be Einstein to guess where that somewhere was. Over my port-and-lemon, I pictured him taking me to some posh hotel up West – silk sheets and no po under the bed but a nice toilet in a pink bathroom. It was luxury I pictured. He was wearing two-toned shoes, and they're a sure sign of money. He had a smart suit on, too. I had high hopes of him; it wasn't every day you met his kind down Deptford. I couldn't believe my luck as I sat there, listening to him. And those eyes of his – dark pools. I swear I could see my face in them. 'I desire you dreadful, Susan,' he said. I couldn't remember nobody ever wanting me *that* bad. 'Honest?' I said, teasing him. 'No doubt about it, my love,' he whispered.

Anyhow, there I was, sipping my drink and taking in his sweet talk, feeling the silk sheets already, when I heard him ask in his next breath if I had a place we could go to cement our friendship. I thought that was funny, him mentioning cement after that desiring me dreadful stuff, but I reckoned it was because he was a foreigner. He made it sound ever so romantic, all the same. Well, I hadn't got a place, had I. I was living in a right poxy hole down Deptford – one room no bigger than a cupboard and an outdoors bog with bits of the *Daily Mirror* stuck on a nail for fifteen lodgers to wipe their arseholes on. Pardon my French. I couldn't take him there – not *him*. I'd have felt ashamed; I'd have died if he'd asked to be excused. 'No, Ambrose,' – that was his name; he shared it with the bandleader – 'No, Ambrose,' I said, 'I'm afraid I don't have nowhere.' Then, bold as brass, I let him know that I wouldn't be shy, not me, if he wanted me to stay with him in his posh hotel. That was how I found out, wasn't it, that he lived in Birmingham. He had a train to catch, he said, at eleven, if there was one running. It depended on Hitler.

I have to admit, I fancied him. What was I to do? His excitement was showing and I was in a pickle. 'There's always Bright's,' I said. I didn't let on that the alley was called Knee Tremblers' Paradise by everyone down Deptford. I didn't tell him neither that a couple had been slashed to pieces by God knows who the Friday before last. Anyhow, 'There's always Bright's,' I said. 'It's a sort of local Lovers' Lane.' A smile come over his face when I told him that. 'Let us have one for the road, my precious' – he had fog in his voice, he was that warmed up, and his eyes were misty. He had trouble walking across to the bar due to the state of his trousers. Anyhow, we clinked glasses when he got back and it was then that he promised that on his next business trip to London he would book a room – no, not just a room, a suite – at the Dorchester.

I believed him, didn't I. The two-toned shoes, the cigarette holder, the signet ring on his middle finger – it was hard for a girl not to. All the men who'd ever taken a shine to me had been the whip it in, whop it out and wipe it kind, and here was this gentleman, this toff, telling me the world was my oyster. I mean, I fell for it. I was putty in his hands after that. I was his plaything, wasn't I. He knew it, too. Every time he said 'Susan' I had the collywobbles – not 'Susie' or 'Sue', mark you, but 'Susan', he was that classy. Other blokes said 'Give us a quickie' or said they had something to slip you or told you to get your drawers off, but not him, not that Ambrose. He had a real command of words, he really did, didn't he. He said we would make music together, which I'd only heard in the pictures coming out of that Charles Boyer. I didn't have no idea that men spoke like that in real life until I met Ambrose.

Anyhow, we left the Kit Marlowe, the two of us, didn't we. Not staggering, like some I could name. He had his arm round me as we made our way along the High Street. 'Is it far to this Bright's?' he asked me. 'Down, Rover,' I said. 'You just be patient for a few more minutes; you just control yourself.' 'I am burning, Susan, burning,' he come out with then. He didn't laugh, did he, when I said that in that case we ought to go to the Thames and douse his flames.

Once we were down Bright's, I had second thoughts about what I was doing. I mean, there was no silk sheets, was there. I mean, with a smell of candle wax and cat's piss, pardon my French, getting up your conk it wasn't romantic by a long chalk. 'Let's wait till your next trip, Ambrose' – he didn't take kindly to the suggestion, I can tell you; he looked downright cruel when I said that. Anyhow, before I could shilly-shally any more, his hand was in, wasn't it. I won't go into details but I do remember we had a right old palaver undoing his buttons. While this was going on, I told myself that this wasn't just another knee tremble. This was the prelude (that was *his* word) to a life of bliss (that was how *he* put it) for all that it wasn't exactly pleasant being done standing up with only a greasy wall for support. I had to tell him to slow down, didn't I. I knew he had a train to catch, but the speed he was going was no fun for a girl, in fact it was bloody painful, if you'll pardon my French.

He come out with a sound like a war cry, you'd have thought he was Geronimo, when he shot his lot, didn't he. People must have heard it miles away, it was as loud as an air raid warning. Then he looked at his watch and then he unfixed himself even though he wasn't soft and I screamed, didn't I, with the pain of it. 'I must be off,' he said. That was all: 'I must be off.' At least he could give me a farewell kiss, I said. Anyhow, he managed a peck, didn't he, and then he vamoosed, didn't he, into thin air, as they say.

Well, I made my own way home, if you could call that dump a home. Six bob a week it cost me, out of the fifteen bob I was earning as a nippy. The landlord was a terrible Turk, always spying on you, a right tartar. I was still in a wine-and-roses mood when I got back and I lay on my bed picturing Ambrose beside me doing it slowly and properly, didn't I. He was in all my dreams from that night on.

Never saw him again, my Ambrose. No billy-dos, even though he took my address off me over the third drink in the Kit Marlowe. I haunted that pub, spent what was left out of my wages there, week in, week out, waiting for my toff from Malta to turn up. No sign of him, though, with his two-toned shoes. Not a peep; not a whiff. No one down Deptford knew him from Adam. 'He was just a ship what passed in the night, Susie,' said a bloke I give it to for ten bob on a Wednesday, seeing as how I had Thursday to get through until pay day, which was on a Friday. We was alongside Bright's as well, in Paradise I don't think, but not on the same spot I done it with Ambrose, that would have brought back too many painful memories.

I was sick in the mornings, wasn't I. Didn't take me long, did it, to put two and two together. I had Ambrose's bun in my oven. Couldn't have been no one else's: they was just flotsam and jetsam to me, and anyhow they all wore French letters. I fancied Ambrose so much I threw precautions to the wind. Tell the truth, I didn't give no thought to precautions at the time, did I, you don't when you're in that state, do you. Anyhow, what was I to do? I didn't have no family to lean on, I'd been an orphan ever since my Mum was knifed in a caff down Wapping, and people were in the habit of looking at me sideways because of my gypsy blood. I had no friends to speak of and the only decent blokes down Deptford was away, wasn't they, fighting for King and country. Anyhow, as I say, I was being sick mornings. The times I cried, sitting there, the strips of *Daily Mirror* stuck on a nail.

Tried to get rid of it, didn't I. Went with a spiv for three bottles of black market gin. Knocked it back neat, I did, and jumped down a flight of stairs when the Turk was out. Didn't do much good. Ended up with a bad back, made my life as a nippy hell on earth, I can tell you. Used a button hook, too, but I got scared and stopped. Took a day return to Birmingham, didn't I, horrible place, walked the streets looking for Ambrose, not hide nor hair did I see, no lights on the train coming home, hands all over the shop, two young privates give me some Woodbines and had their fun, I was worn to a frazzle by the time I was down Deptford again.

Kept my job, I did, till I was eight and a half months gone. The Turk called me a slut – 'common doxy' was the expression he used – and shoved up my rent by four bob to ten. Anyhow, I felt the birth starting and got myself into the Anti-Vivi hospital, didn't I, the maternity was full, so I had to go to the Anti-Vivi, which everyone called the Butcher's. Thought I would die having him.

When they showed me what I'd been carrying I screamed my bloody head off, didn't I, pardon my French. He didn't look human. I could see he was a boy because of the willy on him, but the face, the face – I know new-born babies aren't always pictures, but his moosh was all twisted; I mean, even the nurses, who are used to horrible sights, found it hard to coo over him. And he wasn't olive, like his father – he was *black*. My son was black as, well, pitch.

People down Deptford thought I'd given Sanders of the River a paddle on my canoe, didn't they. That Susie, they said, would throw it anyone's way, including darkies. I got a reputation all of a sudden. 'Syphy Susie' I was known as, and they sang a filthy song about 'Syphy Susie' doing things with soldiers, I couldn't repeat it even if I wanted to, you'd have to pardon my French for a fortnight if I did. The Turk, he sent me packing. 'You nigger's fancy woman,' he shouted so the whole of Deptford could hear. 'You black-haired gypsy sow,' he said.

I worked up Soho for a bit, keeping body and soul together, and earning enough to put food into him. I had to get him off tit as soon as I could, because he was sucking me dry, my Colin. That was the name I give him: Colin. It sounded nice and normal, even if he wasn't. I was determined to bring him up decent, ugly as he was.

Never stayed anywhere for long, the two of us, did we. We was – what's the word? – ostralised. You know, not wanted. Cast to one side, so to speak. He was a burden on me, I can tell you. I still had my gypsy good looks, I was quite the Esmeralda, but he put people off. It was that mouth of his being halfway up to his ear, that was the cause. And when he was at an age when other kiddies would be saying their first words – well, he was grunting. I mean what I say – he grunted like a pig. And in public. I blushed, didn't I, from the shame of him.

If that old merchant seaman, Harry, hadn't crossed my path, I'd have done for myself and him as well, I tell you no lie. I was all for doing the pair of us in. I met Harry up Hammersmith, coming out of the Palais, which was daft when you think of it, seeing as how his left leg was wooden. Anyhow, that's where it was. He come over to where I was waiting for a bus and asked me for a light. We got talking, didn't we, and he invited me to his place for a tinned salmon tea the following Sunday, didn't he. He didn't seem to have malarkey in mind, he certainly didn't mention it, so I said yes, where did he live, and I had a son, Colin, who was a bit on the deformed side. 'Poor little mite,' Harry said. Well, it turned out that he had a house all his own on the Isle of Dogs.

Harry made me a respectable woman, even though there's people still alive down Deptford who think different. I became his housekeeper, I did, didn't I. Due to his leg, he couldn't make love all comfortable like, so I helped him as I've never helped no other man before nor since. I might have done what I did for him for Ambrose if he hadn't taken a two-toned flit, but then again I might not have. After all, Ambrose did have both legs working. Harry was an invalid.

Like a father to Colin he was, Harry was, wasn't he. Treated the boy like a son. It was difficult for him at times, what with those grunts, but Harry had the patience of a saint. If he'd known the trouble Colin was going to bring me, he wouldn't have been so patient, I can tell you.

Sent him off to a special school, Harry did, in 1949, when the lad was five. Still he wasn't speaking, Colin wasn't – it was as if his mind had no room for words. Not like his olive-skinned Daddy, who barely drew breath. Grunt, grunt, grunt. No sense at all. Eyes that never looked at you, although I did catch him smiling at me once in a while.

Heard from the school, didn't we, that Colin would never be intelligent. That was no news to me. Retarded, they said he was. Thank God I had Harry beside me, to help me with him in the holidays. I'd have gone spare otherwise. Colin could speak a bit now, you see. Gibberish, like. Oh, it did upset me.

Harry died, didn't he, unexpected, soon after I'd given him his special help. Colin wept, he really did. So did I – buckets. We was his only mourners at the funeral.

Harry going made a hole in my life. My dear old sailor boy left me his house and his money, a tidy pile, but I missed him tap-tapping from room to room, watching him eat the food I'd cooked for him. I missed those things. I missed him most when Colin started on his funny behaviour.

I can't trace when it began, can I. He was finished with school when he was fifteen, which was when he took up with this posh crowd from up West who bought a big place down here and done it up like they was living in Chelsea. Took him on as servant, didn't they, this man and his daughter did. Fancy handles they had: she was called Miranda, just like that mermaid that Glynis Johns played in that daft picture Harry and me went to see at the local flea pit. *His* name escapes me, though I do believe he was a professor, his head never out of dusty old books. Must have been murder, cleaning that place! Anyhow, my Colin with his twisted little moosh and his black skin that I can't reckon on, he was butler and houseboy and all sorts and sods, pardon my French, to them, wasn't he.

I had my suspicions he was veering towards the barmy when he come home (and it *was* a home, no Turk on the stair, no cut-up bits of the *Daily Mirror* – *his* arse never went short of proper paper to get wiped on, pardon my French) – as I say, he come home one night and called me 'Man'. Well, it stands to reason, you don't call a woman 'Man', least of all your mother. 'Listen to me, man,' he said, 'I'm the King of the Isle of Dogs, man. I'm King Cal, man.'

I give him a mouthful, I did, didn't I, I can tell you. I told him to cut out that 'man' stuff straight away, and I reminded him he'd been christened Colin, a good clean English name. 'I've changed it, man,' he said. 'I'm Cal now. Colin's cissy and I'm a m-a-n, man, that's me!' That's when he sat down and spread his legs and said, 'You an old witch, man. That guy with one leg, there's no way he was my Daddy. You got a secret from me, man. I'm a child of l-o-v-e, I am, ain't that the story, Witch?' Well, what with 'witch' and what with 'man' I didn't know what I was about, did I. 'I don't understand nothing you're saying, Colin,' I said.

That professor, I told him, had been filling his head with daftness. 'Your real father was killed defending his country,' I said. 'Like shit, man,' he said. You must pardon his and my French. 'Like s-h-i-t. You old Sycorax.' 'Who's she when she's alive?' I asked him. 'You too damn thick and ignorant, white woman, to ever know, man,' he said. At least he was calling me a woman again, even if he was taking it back in the next breath. 'My lord and Master,' he said, and he was laughing like some crazy animal, wasn't he, 'he says you're Sycorax. That's his little joke, man.'

Left the professor, didn't he. 'Was you sacked, Colin?' 'King Cal, he abdicated, man,' was the bloody stupid, pardon my French, answer I got for my civil question. Sat around the house all day with these two other darkies (except I still don't see my Colin, black as his skin is, as a coon like them) smoking and drinking, didn't he. Stevie and Trick. No one civilised goes through the world as Trick. They called me 'man', too. 'Man', 'man', 'man', in their hateful voices. Yes, hateful. That's what they were.

He was their king, they said. 'You just curtsey to King Cal, man,' I heard that streak say over that noise – boom, boom, boom – they call music. It must have blasted every single ear on the Isle of Dogs, the volume they was playing it. 'We got plans, man,' that Stevie said.

Well, anyhow, we all know what those plans were, don't we. My own flesh and blood, my Colin for who I done my best despite his Daddy leaving me and him being born in the Anti-Vivi and all the ups and downs I lived through before dear Harry took us in and shared his every loaf of bread with us, my Colin, who I tried to love despite his colour and the twist on his face, he and that Stevie and, worse, that Trick went and cut up the professor and his daughter and three of their friends, what's more, and they made a record of the screams, didn't they, and it was played in the court, wasn't it: the professor moaning, the daughter moaning, the three who'd come for a quiet dinner moaning and moaning and moaning.

People stand outside sometimes and shout filthy things at me. They blame me for Colin. I try and take no notice. If I hear what they say, I pardon their French. People shouldn't jump to conclusions, should they, and condemn out of hand, when they don't know the half. A little consideration and a little respect – they're not much to ask for, are they? Without them, I can't see a future worth living in. I can't see myself making old bones without them, can I, long as I've lived already without them. I've never asked for much from life. I've certainly never asked for more.

EMMA TENNANT

Prize Daffs

'There's scarce a maid westward but she sings it . . .' *The Winter's Tale, IV.iv. The New Penguin Shakespeare commentary: 'westward, in the West Country. In Shakespeare's mind England, not Bohemia.'*

You could see him best in early spring, before the hedges at the back of the garden filled out and the catkin fell, you could see his head, high and narrow and set in a frizz of white hair, as he walked up the garden with his wheelbarrow. You couldn't see much else: Mr Leontes cared for privacy. But the leaves did go, and winter exposed him much as it did the trees: frail in the cold, a little older each time the cold puff came down from the north, bent and skeletal and silly.

There had been a scandal. The village slept on it, under grey stone steps to houses strung in a rope over the Dorset hills. In eaves of snow and tombstones where the writing was nearly gone, wind and rain taking the old news back to nothingness, the scandal had filtered and lain down. One day it will be gone. But it is an old tale that comes up again and again, and finds a new owner. Mr Leontes, who was said to have murdered his wife, could have been two thousand years old or seventy. Watch him as he walks in the long garden at the back of his house, stooping over his wheelbarrow – the Winter King. Under the ragged coat, long fingers are poking out, grimy as twigs. Could this man have murdered his wife? And does it matter when? His own sap is gone, his youth impossible to imagine as the beginning of time.

The thing that overlies the scandal, that people think of when they see Mr Leontes, is daffodils. He is highly thought of in the village, for the sheets of yellow and white, the rare breeds, the nodding pheasant's eye and high-stinking narcissus. He doesn't sell . . . he's a recluse . . . this makes him all the more respected in the village. Sometimes an expert will come, a visitor from the Botanic Society, and stay an hour or two. The village is impressed. Somehow, the red stain of the scandal has faded – into the brittle white petals of the flowers, in a white line of ghosts and yellow trumpeting faces under the trees on the hill.

As you peer through the hedges and pull your scarf closer in the terrible March wind, it becomes clear that for all the dancing and swaying and paleness of the daffodils, they only (in Mr Leontes' garden at least) serve to accentuate the winter. Never has Mr Leontes, as he pushes the weeds in a trug to the site of the bonfire, looked nearer to extinction. He could be blown away, lifted like an early frail blossom and puffed back up to the north. The trees are black as crows.

So, in this scene of desolation, where the daffodils lie in a winding-sheet on the hard ground and the wind tortures the trees, we step back with a certain surprise when a voice calls from the house and Mr Leontes turns uncertainly to listen to it. A young voice, at that, strong enough to pitch against the wind, the slope of the lonely garden. Mr

Leontes sets down his trug and listens again, his face, his ears tinged
red with the wind.

*

That was when the village started talking again. It must have been
two weeks ago. A young woman had arrived at the house, had pulled
suitcases from the back of the car as if she knew she was going to stay,
had banged the knocker until the whole house trembled. The village
gasped like fish in the muted light behind tweaked curtains. How could
it be . . . but it was . . . memories of white shapes on roads not yet
turned to black modernity . . . the murdered wife . . . Hermione . . .

And in these last days the scandal has come up again, although it
was Mr Leontes' daughter after all and not his wife, his dead wife, who
had come to pay an unexpected call on the old man. The scandal
flourished, a weed that pushed up in the crevices, burst out suddenly to
bloom at midnight in hushed, excited talk and red flowers the size of
lamps, casting shadows on the whisperers. The old friend of Mr
Leontes who had come to stay: he'd been a market garden king, how
they'd walked lovingly in the daffodils together! And the burst of rage,
violent as a thunderbolt, that came down like storms do in the West
Country, obliterating fields and hills with a blade-fall of rain, hanging
in black fury over church spire and meek row of cottages. How Mr
Leontes had seen his wife and his best friend – old Polyanthus, the
village called him affectionately, for his interest in flowers of spring –
how he'd seen them, from where you are standing now: holding hands
and kissing.

That rage had no meaning. It came to Mr Leontes from the world
he'd known, in the days before he retired to grow daffodils: the world
of men, of memos, the known world of telegrams and anger, oysters
and monogrammed shirts, counted and folded away by women like
blank, initialled letters that would go fresh every day over his heart.
The rage belonged to Mr Leontes, and could be used whenever he felt
so inclined. It was recognised that a select band of men possessed this
rage and that it was in their interest not to use it too often: the very
possession of it could be said to be a deterrent. But accidents do
happen – or these men must let off steam – and people get hurt. This
was how Mr Leontes came to kill his wife. This was how the whole

village saw a figure in a blanket being lifted into an ambulance and driven away. Then, as year came down over year, and Mr Leontes wandered in his eternal remorse among the daffodils, the rage faded again from memory.

*

The lost daughter walks in driven daffodils that are white as snow, piled up under the trees by the wind. You feel the eyes of the village on her, you stand aside yourself as she walks by. The whispers come on the wind, dance in falling lambs' tails at your feet. How like her mother she is, poor dear, how like Hermione. And it's true, Perdita could be her mother frozen in time, any daughter of any handsome mother, in her pretty face alive with love and thoughtfulness, against the trees and the rush of white and yellow flowers on the hill. The year has come round again, it is Hermione renewed.

Remorse. Mr Leontes has stood so long in the red splash of his rage that he can no longer feel the passing of time. The day his wife was taken from him was a day like today, a white sky that looked as if it would crack open and the contents of the vault fall out, a March wind blowing hell for leather in the flowers at the back of the house, a bare hill opposite, over the slope of the ambulance roof. But when brighter days come, and then the web of winter, pulling in the lines on old women's faces, puckering apples, taking in the tops of trees, like spiders in the mesh, Mr Leontes sees nothing but white flowers and the red stab of his rage. He sees his wife now in his daughter, that which is lost has been found. And in his face, the wintry pale of his face, it is not just the march wind that brings colour. The red blood returns, reigns, as it did in the days of his terrible jealousy and crime.

*

You walk down the side path by the garden and come out at the front, where Mr Leontes' cottage is just one of a row. A car draws up. An old woman steps out, on the arm of a nurse. A miracle!

*

It's cold in the pub down the street from the cottages at the side of the hill near the church. The whispers are steam, like ghosts photographed. It was his wife, it was Hermione. She was never dead. She had been mad. Now her daughter told her she was well enough to come back. He had been sorry long enough. He was so sorry and her madness must go, tucked away under his remorse. She had come back. Don't look out of the window, as they go in and out of their cottage, tidying the front step, placing pottery bowls of daffodils. Hasn't she aged, though, isn't she old?

*

Mr Leontes mourns. You can see him, when you go up the side path on the usual walk to the hill and the church beyond. The hedge is filling out, birds are thudding about in it, the daffodils are frail with age. But you can see him still, or his high, narrow head at least, as he plods up to the bonfire with weed. His daughter has gone. The white flowers have tipped over exhausted in a stained ballgown of green. This old woman coming up the garden is carrying a basket and shears.

*

Never believe – when you hear them say in the pub, Isn't it lovely? – never believe that Mr Leontes is a changed man now, a happy man since the reunion with his wife. Mr Leontes could no more let in the feminine than an old king, or a tycoon, or a general pondering the map of death. Shakespeare's dream, of man and woman magically together, of tenderness and love, is as much a dream today – or there would be no war, no misery.

Mr Leontes would have been perfectly contented with his daughter. She is a better age to be seen with, and a better cook. He can't think how he let her go, on that windy day in March when her mother fell out of the white sky, veined like marble and shaking with age.

At the spring show, Mr and Mrs Leontes won first and second prize for their daffodils. That was a year later, of course, when they'd had time to get to grips with the garden. All the year, as you walk up the side path in leaves, or in rich brown mud, or in snow that pushes down over the top of your boots, they work for the coming spring. You see Mr Leontes' sad, pale face as he sweeps and shovels. He is aspen-old, in the bare winter trees before the coming of spring. And Hermione, walking up the garden, stooping and saying when she reaches the top: ooh me legs!

WILLIAM BOYD

Extracts from the Journal of Flying Officer J.

Duke Senior   Stay, Jaques, stay.
Jaques   To see no pastime, I. What you would have
         I'll stay to know at your abandoned cave.
                                            As You Like It, V.iv.

Ascension

'The hills round here are like a young girl's breasts.' Thus Squadron
Leader 'Duke' Verschoyle. Verbatim. 4.30 p.m., on the lawn, loudly.

Rogation Sunday

Last night ladies were invited into the mess. I went alone. 'Duke' Verschoyle took a Miss Bald, a friend of Neves. At supper Verschoyle, who was sufficiently intoxicated, flipped a piece of bread at Miss Bald. She replied with a fid of ham which caught Verschoyle smack in his grinning face. A leg of chicken was then aimed at the lady by our Squadron Leader but which hit me, leaving a large grease stain on my dress jacket. I promptly asked if the mess fund covered the cost of cleaning. I was sconced for talking shop.

Verschoyle liverish in morning.

June 4th

Sortie at dawn. I took the monoplane. Flew south to the Chilterns. At 7,000 feet I felt I could see every trembling blade of grass. Monoplane solid as a hill. Low-level all the way home. No sign of activity anywhere.

Talked to Stone. Says he knew Phoebe at Melton in 1923. Swears she was a brunette then.

Friday. Lunchtime

Verschoyle saunters up, wearing a raffish polka dot cravat, a pipe clamped between his large teeth. Speaks without removing it. I transcribe exactly: 'Msay Jks, cd yizzim psibly siyerway tklah thnewmn, nyah?' *What?* He removes his loathesome teat, a loop of saliva stretching and gleaming momentarily between stem and lip. There's a new man, it appears. Randall something, or something Randall. Verschoyle wants me to run a routine security clearance.

'Very well, sir,' I say.

'Call me "Duke,"' he suggests. Fatal influence of the cinema on the service. Must convey my thoughts on the matter to Reggie.

Stone is driving me mad. His shambling, loutish walk. His constant whistling of 'My Little Grey Home in the West'. The way he breathes through his mouth. As far as I can see he might as well not have a nose – he never uses it.

Sunday a.m.

French cricket by runway B. I slope off early down to the Sow &
Farrow. The pub is dark and cool. Baking hot day outside. Slice of
joint on a pewter plate. Household bread and butter. A pint of turbid
beer. All served up by the new barmaid, Rose. Lanky athletic girl,
strong looking. Blonde. We chatted amiably until the rest of the
squadron – in their shouting blazers and tennis shoes – romped noisily
in. I left a 4d tip. Strangely attractive girl.

MEMO. Randall's interrogation

(1) Where is the offside line in a rugby scrum?
(2) Is Kettner's in Church Street or Poland Street?
(3) What is 'squegging'? And who shouldn't do it?
(4) How would you describe *Zéphire de Sole Paganini*?
(5) Sing 'Hey Johnny Cope'.
(6) Which is the odd one out: BNC, SEH, CCC, LMH, SHC?
(7) Complete this saying: 'Hope springs eternal in the –'.

Dominion Day (Canada)

Randall arrives. Like shaking hands with a marsh. Cheerful round
young face. Prematurely bald. Tufts of hair deliberately left unshaved
on cheekbones. Overwhelming urge to strike him. Why do I sense the
man is not to be trusted?

   Verschoyle greets him like a long lost brother. It seems they went to
the same prep school. Later, Verschoyle tells me to forget about the
interrogation. I point out that it's mandatory under the terms of the
draft constitution. 'Duke' reluctantly has to back down.

   NB. Verschoyle's breath smelling strongly of peppermint.

Wednesday night

Sagging, moist evening. Sat out on the lawn till late writing to Reggie,
telling him of Verschoyle's appalling influence on the squadron – the
constant rags, high jinks, general refusal to take our task seriously.
Started to write about the days with Phoebe at Melton but kept
thinking of Rose. Curious.

July –?

Sent to coventry by no. 3 flight for putting their drunken Welsh mechanic on a charge. Today Verschoyle declared the monoplane his own. I'm left with a lumbering old Ganymede II. It's like flying a turd. I'll have my work cut out in a dogfight.

*

   p.m. Map reading class: Randall, Stone, Guy and Bede. Stone hopeless, he'd get lost in a corridor. Randall surprisingly efficient. He seems to know the neighbourhood suspiciously well. Also annoyingly familiar. Asked me if I wanted to go down to the Sow & Farrow for a drink. I set his interrogation for Thursday, 1500 hours.

Bank Holiday Monday

Drove down to the coast with Rose. Unpleasant day, scouring wind off the ice caps, grey-flannel sky. The pier was deserted but Rose insisted on swimming. I stamped on the shingle beach while she changed in the dunes. Her dark blue woollen bathing suit flashing by as she sprinted strongly into the breakers. A glimpse of white pounding thighs, then shrieks and flailing arms. Jovial shouts of encouragement from me. She emerged, shivering, her nose endearingly red, to be enfolded in the rough towel that I held. Her front teeth slightly askew. Made my heart cartwheel with love. She said it was frightfully cold but exhilarating. Her long nipples erect for a good five minutes.
   July 21st – Boring day. Verschoyle damaged the monoplane when he flew through a mob of starlings, so he's temporarily grounded himself. He and Randall as thick as thieves. I caught them leering across the bar at Rose. Cleverly, she disguised her feelings on seeing me, knowing how I value discretion.

*

Randall's Interrogation

Randall unable to complete final verse of 'Hey Johnny Cope'. I report my findings to Verschoyle and recommend Randall's transfer to

Movement Control. Verschoyle says he's never even heard of 'Hey Johnny Cope'. He's a deplorable example to the men.

*

Note to Reggie: in 1914 we were fighting for our golf and our weekends.

*

Went to the zoological gardens and looked at the llama. Reminded me of Verschoyle. In the reptile house I saw a chameleon: repulsive bulging eyes – Randall. Peafowl – Guy. Civet cat – Miss Bald. Anteater – Stone. Gazelle – Rose. Bateleur Eagle – Me.

475th day of the struggle

Three battalions attacked today north of Cheltenham. E. went down in one of the Griffins. Ground fire. A perfect arc. Crashed horribly not two miles from Melton.

Dawn patrol along the River Lugg. The Ganymede's crude engine is so loud I fly in a perpetual swooning migraine. Struts thrumming and quivering like palsied limbs. Told a disgruntled Fielding to de-calk cylinder heads before tomorrow's mission.

Randall returned late from a simple reconnaissance flight. He had some of us worried. Claimed a map reading error. It was because of his skill with maps that he was put on reconnaissance in the first place. Verschoyle untypically subdued at the news from Cheltenham. Talk of moving to a new base in the Mendips.

*

RANDALL: Did you know that Rose was a promising young actress?
STONE: Oh yes? What's she promised you then?

As a result of this flash of wit Stone was elected entertainments secretary for the mess. He plans a party before the Autumn frosts set in.

63rd. Wednesday

                    On the Nature of Love
There are two sorts of people you love.
There are people you love steadily, unreflectingly.
People whom you know will never hurt you.
Then there are people you love fiercely.
People who you know can and will hurt you.

August 1st. Monday

Tredgold tells me that Randall was known as a trophy maniac at
College. Makes some kind of perverse sense.

August 7th

Luncheon with Rose at The Compleat Angler, Marlow.
Menu:
                    Oeufs Magenta
                    Mock Turtle Soup
                    Turbot
                    Curried Mutton au riz
                    Orange Jelly
Not bad for these straitened times we live in. Wines: a half bottle of
Gonzalez Coronation Sherry.

Sunday

Tea with the Padre. Bored rigid. He talked constantly of the bout of
croupous pneumonia his sister had just endured.
   Suddenly realised what it was that finally put me off Phoebe. It was
the way she used to pronounce the word 'piano' with an Italian accent.
'Would you care for a tune on the *piano*?'

Aug. 15th, 17.05

Stone crash-landed on the links at Beddlesea. He was on the way back
from a recce of the new base in the Mendips. Unharmed, luckily. But

the old Gadfly is seriously damaged. He trudged all the way back to the clubhouse from the 14th fairway, but they wouldn't let him use the phone because he wasn't a member.

*

Rose asked me today if it was true that Randall was the best pilot in the squadron. I said don't be ridiculous.

Read Reggie's article: 'Air power and the modern guerilla'.

500th day of the struggle

It's clear that Verschoyle is growing a beard. Broadmead and Collis-Sandes deserted. They stole Stone's Humber. It's worth noting, I think, that Collis-Sandes once played wing three-quarter for Blackheath.

Wed. p.m.

Verschoyle's beard filmy and soft, with gaps. He looks like a bargee. The Padre seems to have taken something of a shine to yours truly. He invited me to his rooms for a drink yesterday evening (one madeira in a tiny clouded glass as big as my thumb and two petit-beurres). Croupous pneumonia again.

On the way home, stopped in my tracks by a vision of Rose. Pure and naked. Harmonious as a tree. Rose!

Mendip base unusable.

21st. Monday

Verschoyle shaves off beard. Announcement today of an historic meeting between commands at Long Hanborough.

6th. Sunday before Advent

Working late in the hangar with young Fielding (the boy is ruined with acne). Skirting through the laurels on a short cut back to the mess I notice a torch flash three times from Randall's room.

Later, camped out on the fire escape and well bundled up, I see him scurry across the moonlit lawn in dressing gown and pyjamas with what looks like a blanket (a radio? semaphore kit? Maps?) heading for the summer house.

The next morning I lay my accusations before Verschoyle and insist on action. He places me under arrest and confines me to quarters. I get the boy Fielding to smuggle a note to Rose.

*

Visit from Stone. Tells me the autogiro has broken down again. News of realignments and negotiations in the cities. Drafting of the new constitution halted. Prospects of Peace. No word from Rose.

3rd day of captivity

Interviewed by Scottish psychiatrist on Verschoyle's instructions. Dr Gilzean; strong Inverness-shire accent. Patently deranged. The interview keeps being interrupted as we both pause to make copious notes. Simple ingenuous tests.

WORD ASSOCIATION

Dr Gilzean   Me
lighthouse – a small aunt
cave   – tolerant grass
cigar   – the neat power station
mouth   – mild
key   – kind
lock   – speedy vans
cucumber   – public baths
midden   – the wrinkling wrists of gloves

RORSCHACH BLOTS

Dr Gilzean   *Me*

'A queer nun'

'A new trug'

'A fucked hen'

Dr Gilzean pronounces me entirely sane. Verschoyle apologises.

First day of Freedom

Stone's party in the mess. Verschoyle suggests the gymkhana game. A twisting course of beer bottles is laid out on the lawn. The women are blindfolded and driven in a harness of ribbons by the men. Stone steers Miss Bald into the briar hedge, trips and sprains his ankle. Randall and Rose are the winners. Rose trotting confidently, guided by Randall's gentle tugs and 'gee-ups!' Her head back, showing her pale throat, her knees rising and falling smartly beneath her fresh summer frock, reminding me painfully of days on the beach, plunging into breakers.

   At midnight Verschoyle rattles a spoon in a beer mug. Important news, he cries. There is to be a peace conference in the Azores. The squadron is finally returning to base at Bath. Randall has just got engaged to Rose.

St Jude's Day

The squadron left today for the city. The mess cold and sad. Verschoyle, with uncharacteristic generosity, said I could keep the monoplane. There's a 'drome near Tomintoul in the Cairngorms which sounds ideal. Instructed Fielding to fit long range fuel tanks.

First snows of winter. Sow & Farrow closed for the season. A shivering Fielding brings news that the monoplane has developed a leak in the glycol tank. I order him to work on through the night. I must leave tomorrow.

p.m.

Brooding in the mess about Rose, wondering where I went wrong. Stroll outside, find the snow has stopped.

Observation: when you're alone for any length of time you develop an annoying inclination to look in mirrors.

A cold sun shines through the empty beeches, casting a blue trellis of shadows on the immaculate white lawn.

Must write to Reggie about the strange temptation to stamp on smooth things. Snow on a lawn, sand at low tide. An overpowering urge to leave a mark? I stand on the edge, overpoweringly tempted. It's all so perfect, it seems a shame to spoil it. With an obscure sense of pleasure I yield to the temptation and stride boldly across the unreal surface, my huge footprints thrown into high relief by the candid winter sun.

Cross Over

Only his feet were moving with any vigour and purpose through this inert landscape. They propelled him forward with such force that he was soon thinking that they were not his feet at all. After his experiences in this country – all of them fraught, tense and frustrating – to have feet such as these carrying him out of it with such positive energy was extraordinarily stirring. Were they part of a new self? Had the change already started to make itself felt, commencing with the feet?

In his times of most acute misery and self-criticism he had seriously wondered whether he would find the strength to leave his prison when the release was sent through. Would his soul rise to the moment? Would his mind be able to blossom? What he was hoping to find in the drab hills and plains as he tramped along was a complementing surge of energy to his own; life springing in grass or goat-games – but the land was barren and dead. Only his feet had the thrust of something new.

Under his breath he hummed a snatch from a Dunstable mass, a sweet Te Deum which he had first heard at Saint Paul's about the time of his brother Edward's marriage – a moment which remained mixed in equal parts of sadness and anger in his memory. Anxiously, with a glance over his shoulder, he pushed the ireful regret aside. This was no time to pore over old antagonisms. Those scores had been paid off now, in full.

Company was what he needed most now; someone to walk with and share his forthcoming happiness. Ahead of him on the road he had seen figures but they never seemed to get closer. Each time one appeared on a bend or over a rise it was always the same distance away. Behind him there were more travellers coming. Such was his desire for companionship that he had wasted precious time waiting by the roadside for them to catch up: but when he stopped they stopped.

So he was pushed back into his imaginings – what it would be like when he reached his destination. These were old dreams which had sustained him through the tedium and pain of many, many years. None of their colours had faded though. They could still flare up in his mind when bidden and cast a brilliant glow over his darkest, most self-destructive thoughts.

He knew what it would be like when he got there. He could see the sky, vast, open and blue; the rolling moors and deep valleys with tree-hidden streams. This is what he *trusted* would be awaiting him. He had never checked that it was the truth, never daring to think otherwise. From the best days of his childhood and young manhood he had culled this dream; in the wild green wastes of the north of England he would live again, humbly, unnoticed. However, he had never been guaranteed that this was truly part of Paradise. When the crisis had come and he had wished to cry aloud, cursing a cruel God and His perverted mercy, he had burrowed deep into this personal dream of heaven and kept silent. It could not be the truth – no man has the right to design eternity, he reasoned.

His left foot was starting to hurt again. He had noticed that after eight or ten miles along the road some of his old aches and pains returned, as if emerging from a warehouse of cares and cures. Some attachment to that other life had to be retained, a mark that he had been there, suffered and survived, scars and all. He was now starting to limp slightly but this only made him smile. He was glad to go lamely towards the frontier. He would crawl if need be. No matter what condition he was in by the time he arrived it would be as his new self; cleansed, purged, all reckonings paid. In this form he would be ready for the greater journey which must be undertaken beyond the frontier.

Ahead of him he saw a pool of clear water and a spring bubbling from the base of an outcrop of yellow, cloven rock. In the mud around the pool were thousands of footprints from other travellers who had preceded him. Squatting by the pool he cupped his hands to take water then caught sight of himself. He gasped, startled, falling back off his haunches on to his backside in the mud. Mirrors had been plentiful in the dull town where he had spent his sojourn in this country – in fact every other shop belonged to a trader in mirrors and reflecting pieces. Every day had been punctuated by frequent sights of himself. There was no part of his body which did not sicken him; it was a carcase of pungent fear, a world of doubt, an orb of anxiety, the face of dreaming death. His hair had enraged him. If hair could die but remain hanging on the head, that is what his appeared to have done. Now, reflected in the pool, it was black and bright. His eyes shone. Maybe it was a trick of the light but his pallor was going and there were roses beginning to glow in his cheeks.

Is that me? he thought. They would not deceive me now. That would be beyond the punishment I was awarded. I will look again.

There he was, smiling.

Happily he drank the cool water and splashed his face, washing away the fine dust of the broad road.

As soon as he had drunk he felt his heart beat stronger and new power infuse his limbs. The aches and pains of the journey fell away. As he stepped back from the pool he saw that all the old footprints of

past travellers had gone, smoothed over. Only his own dinted the mud.
Once back on the road he started to run.

*

It had been a cruel country to live in. His stay had been onerous,
labouring beneath a sense of waste. When the word had come through
that it was time for him to set out for the frontier he had thought that
all the monotonous tribulations and tests of his daily life were over.
For the first time in many years his heart had leapt and excitement had
stirred his blood. Now, as he left the pool and rejoined the road, he was
sure that beyond the next rise he would see the town which sat on the
frontier, sprawling on either side of the wall which separated the
different countries. From his calculation of the distance that he had
walked, paced out in thousands of his own short-of-a-yard steps, he
must be nearing it.

When he reached the crest of the mild rise in the road he only saw
more of the dead plain.

Fighting down his disappointment, he stood with his hands on his
knees, bent over, staring at the ground for a while.

'It is my fault,' he said slowly through gritted teeth. 'My steps are
shorter than I thought. Even shorter than short-of-a-yard. They must
only be half-a-yard. The old English mile is governed by God, not by
me and my twisted foot. If it is longer than I thought to the frontier,
then I must lengthen my thoughts.'

He strode out, quickening his pace until he was almost trotting. As
he progressed he went through his account, the paper which lay next to
his heart and which must be presented to the officials at the barrier. He
had read it so often that he could say it backwards, sing it in the form of
a plainsong, re-arrange the letters and numbers to create other words.
As he jogged along he played no variations on his account this time. He
left it plain and bold – the sum of himself and his suffering in this
unhappy country. There was the amount for his envy of Edward, a
brother whom he had adored – the golden king of the English. Richard
had seen him ruined by self-indulgence and his cunning wife, Elizabeth; watched him die of a common chill, bloated, sweating, afraid.
For his lack of compassion and his ferocious judgements on his
brother's failures he had been given a fistful of years to endure his own

frustrations; years in which nothing would go right, when luck had left him aside. Edward was the second largest item in his account. On his entry into this country the officials had explained to him that there was always sympathy for one who had sinned heavily against his own blood. It was a natural thing to do in the world.

From that account for Edward had come the third heaviest – the sins he had committed as king himself.

The officials had been serenely practical about the question of his right to the throne of England. That was almost a joke with them. In such a tangle of blood and necessity such a right hardly existed. There was only one true king and all mortal men who aped Him were but ephemeral fragments of His power. What the officials had looked for in Richard's performance as monarch had not been much to do with how he had seized the throne; that was as inconsequential to them as the manner in which a pack of wild cats select a leader. All sense, rhyme and logic had gone from the election of kings thousands of years before.

The first, heaviest item in his account was sharper in pain than the others. Whenever Richard had studied the paper, lying in his cot by the window looking out at the ever-grey sky, it was this item which had become a pointed stick digging into his conscience.

It was an unspecified sin of omission.

Something he had not done or said.

Richard began to run as the item and its heavy penalty of years on his soul pricked and twisted in his mind. That one sin had reduced him to despair before the battle in which he had himself been killed. With the self-knowledge that it brought, reinforced by the hatred of his enemies and the rumours, he had despaired of aspiring to a better age. By the time Bosworth smeared the green fields of Leicestershire with blood, Richard had accepted failure. He was as bad as Edward had become; worse than Henry Tudor, a man who could not live up to his own sense of values.

The officials had been sympathetic to this failure. It was, they had said, a common falling away among men of power. People often expected too much of themselves. but this business with your brother's two sons . . . that was a melancholy, bad, messy affair. There will be a substantial penalty to pay for that. But it was not the major sin.

He suddenly realised that he was running as fleetly as he had ever been able to. Ahead of him were those same officers who had regarded him so gravely over their desk-tops and whispered among themselves. After one hundred and thirty years, eight months and a day, he was returning to stand before them, all his penalties paid.

Much of his suffering had been on account of the mysterious sin which towered over all the others, worse than his envy or his treatment of his brother's sons. The officials had only hinted at its nature.

He shook with fear and resentment as he thought of all the pain that he had been made to endure in ignorance.

Being an unclassified sin, it might mean that the punishment shared this lack of definition. The sentence might be lengthened arbitrarily. The uncertainty of his position made him feel sick and hollow.

Rounding a bend in the broad road, he emerged from behind a low hillock and saw the town squatting on the plain, the wall running through its centre. He had run ten good English miles in such a rush, such a jubilant mood! Now the frontier was within striking distance. The town reared up out of the yellow ground, dark, towered, silent.

He paused. The town looked menacing and cold. It should have signalled warmth and welcome to him after such a time, returning with his slate cleaned. Where were the bells? The people?

As he looked at the town he saw steel glitter in its streets and flags furling and flying in a sudden hot wind that circled the plain. Horsemen began to appear coming out beyond the town's limits, followed by companies of foot-soldiers. From old practice and memory he interpreted the signs, colours and emblems of these distant warriors. There was Tudor! To his left Lord Stanley! To his right, approaching in a sweep down a shallow slope, Sir William Stanley. A mixture of friend and foe from the old days trudging and cantering over the dusty yellow earth.

What were they doing here, these shimmering armies?

A great sound made him turn. Behind him were drawn up the regiments of his supporters – Oxford, Norfolk, Surrey, Lord Ferrers, Zouche – all assembled under their banners.

He cringed, limping, unarmoured, weaponless before them. Every soldier stared out at him with sightless eyes. Now he was in an empty tract of ground between the armies, stumbling along. He was brought up short by a small, friendly man with a staff who steadied him with a firm grip on his shoulder.

Richard recognised him as one of the officials from the barrier.

'It's nearly over now but there is a final stage, dear soul,' he said gently. 'Men have always been poor at mathematics. Their calculations seldom equate with ours.'

'I have done my time,' Richard cried. 'Don't ask me to go back and live there again. My account has been paid.'

'Not quite. There is a sting in the tail of all lists whether they be of money, penalties, or orders of preference. There was a common saying in your day – seldom used now as the world has got slacker in its arithmetic, believe it or not – yes, you used to say that a man owes God a death. Do you remember that?'

'I do!' Richard panted. 'And I paid mine!'

'That little sum was always slightly out, dear soul. In fact you owe Him two.'

'Two!' Richard shrieked.

'It is the beginning and the end of Purgatory. Two deaths, one at each end. Then you are free for ever. I'm sorry that you were not made aware of that clause but we never tell anyone – it is too bitter a pill to take straight after the first death.'

The armies began to call and grumble, the harsh, witless roar clamouring in the eddying air. Richard shuddered. Once that sound had stirred his blood, made the hair stand up on the back of his neck.

'And God is the god of this?' he asked the official. 'These men are in His pay?'

'Of course, dear soul. He was always the god of battles. Who else should be able to balance out such a mass outbreak of pain with the peace of death?'

Richard's hands were clenched as if holding the helve of his axe again. His palms sweated as the grumble of the armies made his skull reverberate. This was the moment when he had felt most intensely alive. It was the instant of creation scattered onto sword-edge and shield.

'Evil,' he mumbled. 'How can I get out of it?'

'The peace that passeth all understanding has to be offset by the

equally mysterious pain,' the official whispered soothingly, taking
Richard's elbow. 'It all makes sense, dear soul.'

The ground shook as Tudor's army started to stamp their feet.
Clouds of yellow dust rose into the air.

'They want your blood again. They are calling you pig, hog, swine.
None of them know you, dear soul, but they wish to cause you pain,'
the official murmured. 'What do you make of that?'

'Monstrous!' Richard snarled, his right arm twitching through to
the hunch of muscle on his shoulder, the powerful hill of his battle
strength.

'And you asked your God to be so simple?'

Backing away from Richard, the official headed for a gap in the
armies and climbed a treeless knoll where he stood and waved. His
pale hand was caught in the circling glitter of steel and he shone with
the same light as the heaving phalanxes of soldiers.

'Am I not to have a weapon?' Richard shouted above the din. 'If this
is God's fight, let me do my best at least!'

The hot breath of the armies poured upwards and sucked in a wind
from the horizon which carried leaves, floating seeds, scraps of paper
and cloth from dying towns. A bullrush stalk spiralled down from the
sky and fell at Richard's feet, its bold brown head eaten by insects.

As he picked it up and flexed it, the enemy howled with delight.

Once he had loved that swing of his arm, how it rocked through to
the centre of his spine, making his brain burst into fire. It had been a
tangible, credible sign of war's glory – a lifting of self to a level of
savage power where the laws were different. It was a new world that
the warrior entered when the battle began. Richard had loved it, in sin,
so he thought, but now it was revealed to him that it was as much a
part of God's mind as the Crucifixion itself.

Richard stumbled across to the knoll waving the bullrush as if it
were a flag of truce.

Horsemen galloped round him, showing off their accoutrements,
prancing, shouting out boasts and challenges. Over the intervening air
came the stench of wine. These knights had been drinking since dawn
to drive their spirits forward. Richard's heart quailed as he remembered the cups, the stains on his breastplate, the stale taste of burgundy
on his tongue.

'Will it be exactly the same?' he asked the official. 'Will I have to die in the same way?'

'That won't be so bad now that you understand, will it?' the official replied with a kindly twinkle in his eye. 'In war God has all the weapons.'

'And this is all I may have to defend myself?' Richard complained, holding up the tattered bullrush.

The armies of Tudor and the Stanleys stood stock still and opened their mouths. Gales of wine-stench streamed over the yellow ground as the cry went up:

'Child-murderer!'

The official retreated, giving a final encouraging smile over his shoulder.

Richard was left between the armies in a sighing silence. In the faces of his allies he saw questions. Far off he saw the army of Northumberland, the poison of doubt in its eyes. From Tudor and Stanley there was accusation and hate.

'Child-murderer!' bayed his enemies again, the dust swirling up in wind-spouts from the draughts of their drunken, clamouring throats.

'Answer them, my lord,' old Norfolk begged.

'They have stirred up the earth against you, sire,' Oxford said from under his fluttering silver stars, 'and they have used a lie to do it. The drunkard in the ditch calls you that name, child-murderer; the ale-wife, the gossip take it up. Why will you not answer it? Tell them the truth!'

Richard stopped moving between the armies, and held up his hand. His allies leant forward in their saddles to hear him.

'I have nothing to say. Let the battle be as it was and my death likewise. I cannot unbend a truth that was never straight.'

There was a moan of disappointment from his friends, then Norfolk freed a white horse which galloped over and rested by Richard's side. He mounted it and took the head of his line, conscious of the dark disappointment which reigned around him.

Bosworth Field began again. Richard was betrayed by the Stanleys. He cast his force full tilt against Henry Tudor's front rank and was cut down, strokes and blows raining down on his head, bone crunching, blood leaping.

The agony was identical. The shame was the same. An animal's red wonder.

At the point of death the armies melted away from around his head and the land became as silent as before. He was standing on the road looking at the town which now was garlanded with flowering boughs, streamers and bunting. Birds of all sorts tumbled through the sky over the rooftops. Every door and window was open to the warm sun which shone brightly over the frontier. From tall churches came the sweet, clear voices of boys praising God for their innocence while lusting to lose it. At intervals the bells pealed out as if calling him to hurry in and join the general joy.

*

Richard had passed through the town in triumph, limping, holding his scrip tightly in his fist. He was alone in the middle of the street surrounded by cheers and applause as the dancing crowds swayed on the pavements. He could not smell them above the scent of flowers and apples. When he approached the barrier at the border the people fell silent, and watched him go into the low stone building where the officials were waiting.

It was cool inside and the light from the windows was as clear as quartz.

Four officials sat around a small wooden table. One of them was the genial official who had been at the battle.

'You see how it's never as bad the second time?' he said smilingly, holding his hand out for Richard's scrip. 'Let me have your account.'

Richard handed over his scrip. It was torn and frayed from his long journey and the battle.

'I did not answer my enemies on the charge of child-murder because . . .' he began to say but the senior official tutted and held up his hand.

'Should I not openly say what really happened?' Richard asked nervously. 'Am I not required to say it out loud?'

'Much of God's good work is done in silence, dear soul,' the senior official said softly.

Horrified, Richard shrank away, his face hidden behind his hands.

The officials let him be, busying themselves with their paperwork until he had recovered his composure.

'Feeling better now?' the senior official asked.

'What can be more important than the truth?' Richard demanded passionately, his fists crashing down on the wooden desk. 'Are you responsible to God here?'

'Calmly now, calmly. You must make these adjustments before you continue your journey beyond the frontier. Sit down, dear soul.'

With brotherly concern the four officials gathered around Richard and sat him down on a bench in the sun, taking their places on either side of him. They sighed, smiled, shrugged, indicating with their eyes that Richard should accept, not question, the queer system that was confronting him.

'Does it honestly surprise you that it is God and God alone who controls the deaths of princes?' the senior official chided him.

'Doesn't anyone want to know what happened?' Richard moaned, rocking to and fro in the crossed arms of the officials. 'Doesn't anyone care what I did?'

With a knowing smile the senior official unrolled Richard's scrip along his thigh and pointed at the first item – the unspecified sin of omission.

'What do you think that was for, dear soul? It was not for murder, not for failing to reveal some dull fact of death. Your heaviest penalty was paid for not believing that all men of power are in the grip of God. There has to be change, dear soul. God changes Himself. He is in a state of constant activity. He used you to shift the age into a harsher light. Honour, dear soul, had to make way for intelligence.'

The officials murmured approvingly, lifting Richard from the bench and setting him at the door. While he faltered there they filed his scrip in a vast oaken cupboard and locked its doors with a slim silver key.

Then they beckoned him to leave, wishing him luck for his journey.

At the barrier he waited for the gate to be opened for him.

Coming the other way was a man in his grave-clothes, his domed forehead gleaming with sweat. In his arms he carried hundreds of papers which kept dropping to the ground so that he had to keep stopping to pick them up. As he bent over the man cursed and swore under his breath, grinning, then frowning at the guards who were watching him.

Leaving the low stone building, the officials joined Richard at the barrier, aggressively eyeing the newcomer.

'See this case, dear soul?' the senior official muttered grimly. 'His will not be simple like your own. Here you see the greatest error of all, sin on two legs, the old Adam, still arguing.'

The man arrived at the gate and dumped all his papers by the side of the road, putting his foot on them to keep the wind from blowing them away. He stared at the officials across the barrier with alternating looks of pride and humility, waiting to be addressed. Eventually he sat down on his papers and clasped his knees to his chin, refusing to be the one who spoke first.

'And how are you, master?' the senior official called out suddenly, his serenity shattered by a fit of furious indignation. 'Are you ready to put us all to rights, thou animation of the sin of God Himself?'

'I have my explanations to hand,' the man replied. 'All I ask for is justice. It was never my doing to make the world an imperfect place.'

The guards opened the gate and showed Richard through.

When he passed the sweating newcomer one of his papers blew away from under his foot and fluttered along the road. As it turned in the air Richard saw the legions of alterations and erasures, the gaps, bog-holes of ink, tangles of alphabet, thorn-crowns of thought scratched on both sides of the turning page.

Together they watched the paper as it was sucked back along the bottom track by a dark, hungry wind: then Richard took the twisting road which runs from the honour of Man to the honour of God, leaving his debts paid, his sins atoned, and the stranger to fend for himself.

DAVID HUGHES

Rough Magic

A bloody great clap of stage thunder, typically Greek, woke Palmer up from a dream, probably of drowning, for it had a lot of his past muddled into it like avant-garde cinema. His face was wet because, Christ, his daughter's roof was leaking. He jumped out of bed into a puddle, no, the tiles were awash, then lightning sheeted green across the sea below the villa, a brassy glint on the icons showed them up streaming with water, and naked he sloshed over the floor unhooking them off the walls, throwing them on to the bed. Then he dipped under it to drag out his daughter Nellie's pornography and, God, the bottom dropped out of the cardboard box.

It was the fifth night of Peter Palmer's lonely tenancy, and he was daily expecting by post the promised guide-lines from his director in London. He had never worked with Kemp before; indeed this *Tempest* caper was his first proper go at the stage in thirty years of showbiz. He had grown to middle-aged stardom in the movies, playing men of action; now, unnervingly, he was into ideas. 'Go off some place,' Kemp had said, 'and think through the character.' To dig out of himself the resources he would need to play Prospero, such as understanding what the hell it was all about, his daughter had lent him this house of hers on an island two hours off the Greek coast. She had described the place as pure magic.

A caique connected it to the mainland once a day. Every morning Palmer's binoculars ranged the decks as the vessel curved under the headland into the bay where the island's only village bracketed a shallow harbour. Nellie, not a bad little actress, was supposed to be coming to help him; even alone he needed an audience. But however hard he willed her to materialise, she was never aboard. Nor were there any instructions from Kemp. The thunder rumbled away off the seas. In the small hours this small-time tempest – yes, Palmer saw the boring connection – had concentrated his anxiety, almost as if he had projected the blasted thing. The lights had failed too, and in the darkness the magazines on the floor slipped fishily through his fingers.

The storm blew itself out at dawn. The sun rose. The sea remained choppy, a hard purple. Heavy scents of earth and thyme entered the villa where newspapers, sent express from England to keep Palmer in touch, were sopping up the bedroom floor. To put off working, he went through the motions of shifting the furniture, icons, damp magazines, into the sun. Encircled by tubbed geraniums, the terrace now looked pristine, all the dust laid: utopia, a stage where nothing happened.

Walking to the parapet, leaning over to watch the sea unfurling on the rocks below, Palmer thought of the man who according to Nellie had stood just here for a piss one party night, all stars, and tumbled over, the twit. Was it suicide? Fishermen had picked his body off the rocks. Palmer turned abruptly to look at the savage hues of the bougainvillaea spattering the walls with reds, the bloody geraniums.

No wonder he couldn't work. The sun rose higher into its daily parabola of tedium.

Nothing had happened, no, not yet, the curtain refused to go up on his great new chance. What could he do? Under the bed he had soon found her dirty books, he had swum in the sea, eaten big claws of the craggy local lobster, but these were the only events in a rough paradise where nobody spoke his language and the hill swept upwards from the villa into tangles of gnarled olive where the asphodel grew, and from this moment on, as he stood waiting for her handyman Mikis and the mail and the day's provisions, it would grow too hot to move or think, let alone learn his lines. Only the sun had power; the rest was in thrall to it: a dead clatter of cicadas in bushes as dry as bone, the chuntering of the inarticulate sea a long way below.

Mikis came up the hill path with a sprig of sage in his mouth, leading a donkey on whose back the dead man had been conveyed to the village. Mikis was always on time, like the caique: the long day's only punctuation. Treating Palmer to an actorish display of his own language in rapid explicatory vocables, Mikis laid out on the parapet the treasure he had brought – fresh bread, a small fish, limp vegetables, an oil-can of wine – then went indoors to inspect whatever had gone wrong since yesterday's interruption, in fact the leak.

This was the chance for the donkey to take the stage. Hitherto as rigid as a frieze, he now planted a randy fearful eye on Palmer, then danced in a high-stepping seesaw across the terrace, kicking at flower-pots in brief hysteria and peeling back an upper lip to reveal foam. With a stab of a hoof he broke a ceramic mermaid, her scaly bottom upthrust to support a potted cyclamen which at once tumbled in smithereens of petals on to the terrace. When Mikis emerged the donkey was meekly back in position, batting flies with his ears. All this happened in seconds. Had Palmer imagined the whole thing? He longed to control the donkey, to punish it.

That there was no word from Kemp, no newspaper, and today no service from the mainland, became painfully obvious. Indeed, Mikis growled an imitation of thunder to explain why the caique wasn't coming. Nerves rippled along the donkey's flank.

In the pause of noon, too disturbed to work, Palmer lay back on the bed and flipped through the next of Nellie's magazines with a scorn

that slowly tensed into sexual rage. The shutters were shut, the
bedroom light strained. The paid faces vacuous with agony or pleasure, upended women frilled and stockinged gaping at him from the
page, enlacing him – they all grew disgustingly into his daughter,
because they were her property, her taste had collected them. He
squirmed at the thought of her intimacy, her letting him down like this.
How could he think of his work?

The fantasy of the afternoon seeped into Palmer's bones until he fell
asleep with his hand on the wrinkled paper. He awoke with a headache
which he still blamed on the wine being brought him daily in a polluted
can by the damn donkey. His brains felt numbed.

By habit, an hour before sunset, Palmer walked down the prickly
slope to the beach Nellie had recommended. It was a narrow rocky
inlet of clear water that held the light as if in aspic, an amphitheatre
without an audience. He donned the flippers, goggles, strapped the
breathing apparatus to his bare back, his body in the cooling air
clumsy. And then he was in the sea.

The freedom hurt, but as soon as he had broken through the shock
he felt in his element, purer than air, cleansed. A multitude of fairytale
fish came at him, paused, poised, darting from under his fingertips as if
he were spawning them, seemingly awed by this creature entering their
common world, to him of such fabulous novelty. The shallow rock
fluttered under him for a while, late sunlight snaking in shoals across
the weeds, and then, still with a sense that he was creating this dreamy
environment, he was stroking his way deeper into a declivity that
appeared to be bottomless. Here began the real sea.

And now, below him, like an icon touched by that second of
lightning, at the furthest reach of the sun, an image: the prow of a boat
sticking out of mud that swirled at his approach, then cleared – yes, a
distinct prow. Palmer flapped in shock around it, trying to reach out a
hand to touch the encrusted woodwork, but the oxygen closed in
spasms on his lungs, and the rest of the vessel had vanished into the
lower dusk, so that it was impossible in the faint play of light to judge
its size, date it, make anything of it at all, and the breathlessness of
finding something human in this element sent him rocketing upwards
for air, air to gasp in, air to normalise his discovery. For an hour, long
after sundown, he lay on the beach, drinking air, resisting the villa

where the script was, getting bloody cold. What was that object down below? Oh, yes, of course, ha-ha, the shipwreck of those mariners in the first scene. The only sane explanation was that he hadn't really seen it.

The next day repeated a perfect dawn, another chance of getting down to serious work on the play. He finished the bread and drank his coffee and gazed upon the magical view he owned by proxy. There seemed a lot of air activity high up in the blue; with every trail of smoke the promised letter was coming in to land. Endlessly the donkey was climbing the cliff path with Kemp's key to the secrets of Prospero, trembling to break free when Mikis turned his back. Insects whined in and out of the creepers all morning.

Then for a long time the boredom of the horizon was cracked, surely, by the gathering shape of the caique. Meanwhile Palmer had one ouzo, the cicadas thickening into whispers up the olive groves, then another ouzo, and nothing happened, no donkey or daughter happened, and Palmer went blindly indoors to check his resources.

There was enough for one more meal, a tin of sardines, an egg, but no bread. He felt hunger like panic and like hunger despair, but all disembodied in the heat, dissolved. He was not himself. The dead man stole over him in the dead sweat of noon, with only that lewd library or drink – one shot left – to keep his hold on the part he was supposed to be studying. With the binoculars Palmer scanned the view, but still the tight lips of sea and sky did not open. He ached for his instructions, hungered for his audience. The sunken boat's prow rose into the fluid of his mind, then escaped him. It was irrelevant.

Palmer ate the last egg hard-boiled and poured a few drops of wine out of the can. Then he rested in the bedroom gloom, fingering the pages. His daughter evidently had a taste for pain he had never suspected; backsides lifted nude out of seas of underwear, waiting for blows to fall. Had he brought her up like that? He rose to these images of her angrily, as to a bait: the stupid ferocity of putting her over his knee, all the icons back in place, and slapping her little bum. And then sleep, the one reality, people were always falling asleep in the play and no wonder, shut out the shuttered afternoon.

Later on he took the thorny path to the village. From some way off voices were crackling in the air, but no figures were visible. Windows of white houses stood open on the heat, and the disembodied voices, now and then backed with vicious distortion by a brass band, grew more martial at Palmer's approach, packing the little square with an unseen mob of thousands. As with the caique he had a momentary impression of something that was happening only in his mind, not to other people; either that, or he was manipulating the entire scene and had an audience in the palm of his hand.

The whole village was indoors. Everyone was listening to the wireless.

Palmer entered the bar. In the white-washed cavern with a cramped counter and the only telephone, two or three unshaven men, hunched over the dregs of wine, listened in lazy awe to the spasms of rhetoric rising and falling between bursts of gunfire in the background. He picked up the phone – he must ring someone at once, his daughter, his director, to find out what had really happened – and the receiver crackled gibberish into his ear, then went dead. Outside he then noticed a pair of sailors lounging on the quay, automatic weapons slung diagonally across their chests. Had they been there before? Three girls in black stood pretending to gossip, eyes on the sailors, in the pall of shadow cast by the white church.

What was going on, why, and where? Was all this fuss due to a coup on the mainland? There was nobody Palmer could ask. The village was absorbed in a noisy silence which he had no means of breaking. When he walked towards the sailors they strolled away, faded into the heat. The girls, as Palmer turned, lifted skirts slightly at the knee and hobbled up an alley, throwing back their heads as if in laughter. So he had no control, after all. Nor was there any sign of the donkey. If this theory of armed rebellion was correct, he must surely pack up and get out fast: but how? And he still had work to do, all the work. Only when he arrived back at the villa, panting from the long haul up, did he remember the hollow of his hunger. While he consumed some damp biscuits and the last of the ouzo, the sun sank.

The sun rose over his weak final cup of coffee. Palmer felt on edge, pining. He knew for sure that the donkey wouldn't come, or the caique. They had passed beyond his reality, engulfed by the incomprehensible voices of the revolution, or whatever it was, that gabbled on the air from the susurrating heat of the olive groves. He sat feebly among the untended flowers, the script upside down on his knee, eyeing the void of the horizon benevolently. A stunned hot peace had gathered him up. Who the hell cared what happened? He certainly didn't need the money. He'd rather retire and be himself for once.

Then suddenly his hand snatched up the binoculars. Far away a minute shape had caught his eye, Christ, yes, a vessel. At too great a distance Palmer saw his daughter bending over the rail, lifting her skirt at the knee, bitch, the prow of the boat shimmering in the haze as if under water. Doggedly the caique drew nearer. Faces swam into the clear of the glasses. They had moustaches, plump rounded faces with hair round the crack of a set grin, their bodies in uniform: soldiers. There were a dozen soldiers on the caique, armed. Their teeth showed white. Nellie's familiar shape which he had seen seconds ago was transmuted at closer quarters into a coil of rope, a kitbag, cargo. In his disappointment he turned *The Tempest* over on his knee. Its language was no comfort.

Dramatically, Palmer ate the remaining biscuit for his lunch.

In the late afternoon he tiptoed painfully down with the equipment to the beach where the wreck lay hidden. Once again a heightened sense of freedom, as if walking onstage, enveloped him in the purity of the element. The sun tongued under him in a language smoothly familiar. Bright fish glanced, then glanced away. He was in command. He dug deeper into the darkening water and for a while all was immensely still, as in a theatre, his memory losing hold of the reason for diving, but then, panic, he began tacking to and fro in the medium in a breathless effort to locate the wreck. And there at last, unmoved, was the prow, perhaps with a figure-head missing, maybe sunk in a classical war, ageless.

This time, remembering the limits of his resources, Palmer put a hand out for the prow, contacted it, then pulled. With a swirl of sand that levitated glittering into the upper light, the rowing-boat shifted at once, indeed surged up at him, then bottomed down. But in that instant, with a terrifying actuality, Palmer caught a hint of the shadowy idea that had been evading him all along.

In seconds he was at the surface, tearing off his mask, gazing at the fantastic sunset and retching salt from his guts. What had he latched on to, then lost? He sat shivering on hot sand, again wondering if what he had seen was true or of his own making.

And then he trapped the idea. All of it. In a bloody nutshell, old mate. He lay there on the beach and – was it out loud? – shouted, like making a speech: Christ, whether it's true or not, I've invented the whole shooting match. My power, the power I have to pretend to suppress on the boards, the ego that rages in me demanding an outlet wherever I am – yes, all this power has got itself jumbled up here, as in a dream. Soldiers and sailors arise at my bidding, I conjure black-skirted girls out of thin air. I am surviving on an island populated only by me – or at least by the anxieties I've built up over years, or by my real desires hidden from me by all the man-of-action parts I play, the wrong women, drink, haste, the mad concomitants of success. The fact is – why didn't I see it? – that the isle is full of silence. Perhaps a few animals stalk the scrub, yes, and the olive groves have old legends pacing them. But that's the lot. Otherwise it's all in the mind. The rest is me.

Yes, yes, he had said all of it aloud, without an audience, and the whole island now spoke the same language, with nobody listening.

Climbing away from the wreck, Palmer had a sunny sense, as blissfully obvious as a memory, that there was much more to explore. Beyond the village the land rose steeply to the inner mountains, where caves bit into the depths of the rock, and the resinous air was as rare as the sea. It was all his. Only mount that high and he would be able to see in every direction at once. He picked up his Shakespeare and began reading.

Waking next morning, weaker, walking on air, hungry, Palmer in no time moved down to the village. He thought he wanted to hire a vessel to get him away. Fluttering a wad of thousand-drachma notes under the noses of the soldiers, he pointed to the rowing-boats moored under the quay. Without interest, cradling their weapons, they turned aside to look out to sea. There was no escape, thank God. Palmer looked back at the square.

The middle of it was occupied by a long table fringed with lace under the dappled shadow of the few trees. It was heaped with copious helpings of food which Palmer hadn't observed in this country: sides of smoked fish, tinted pink, glistening in the sun, mounds of artichokes swimming in deep green oil, coral prawns in pyramids surrounding the vermilion of lobsters, cold ham on raised white dishes, pies, galantines – all rich, all ingredients of his favourite diet. In the shadows of the church two old natives in baggy suits were rolling out tuns of wine, which when tapped gurgled into jugs; they smacked their lips as they handed tumblers to the soldiers. A crackling fire of vinestocks plumed into the mauve air, roasting to a succulent brown an animal that sparkled with fat. An orthodox priest bearing an icon led a small procession into the church and closed the doors.

On to this scene now, a frieze touched into motion by the day's intense heat, danced the three girls Palmer had noticed, wearing this time some local costume in blue and white, their hair braided, springing out of schoolboy mythology: dryads, possibly, materialising from the glades above the village, drawing into the square a crowd clapping hands, stamping feet, the women shrieking a sweetly syncopated rhythm into the still air, the men growling a thunderous bass. All this had an air of art, artlessly pursued; a natural show that passed beyond nature.

Then with splendid appetite the entire village fell upon the food and drink, natives and invaders alike slicing off portions of meat with knives that flashed in the light, spitting out the scales of prawns, pawing pastry into their mouths, gorging ham, duck, salmon, cleansing their throats with the wine. Palmer gazed at it all in wonder, sharing their crude pleasure from afar as if he were providing it, longing to know what they were celebrating, what change, what revolution in their ways. It was useless to guess, impossible to find out. He merely felt their joy flowing through him, the impeccable use for a day, an end in itself.

A more steely light was now settling over the scene. Colours drained; black stood out more sharply from white. A faint rumble echoed off the horizon and a milky haze arched the sky, straining the sun, thinning the shadows. The long table had been cleared of food, but the dancing went on, soldiers entwined with girls, as the village eased back into the stupor of the afternoon, the women snoozing indoors, the men propped against the bleached walls in various contortions of body, clinging to the last of their wine. It looked like a tableau.

In the growing silence, as if hypnotised, Palmer watched the dance slow and darken to a halt, in a rhythm now sluggish the girls being gently pushed back against trees or bent over the table, backs arched, heads upside down, their skirts lifted to the shoulder to reveal white stockings to the thigh, and the men loosening their uniforms at the waist to make love to them, at first teasingly, then with increasing force, until the bodies of the girls were bouncing in their arms as loose as puppets, what a fine sight, their mouths gaping to utter a series of small warbling cries, oh beautiful, as if birds from the hills were descending unseen into the afternoon lull. One after another these tangled couples erupted into spasms of pleasure, then sank to the dust, where they lay drowsily as the sky darkened from the west.

Above the island empurpled clouds had gathered and thunder cracked inside Palmer's skull with the shudder of a knife on bone. He had all the time he wanted, every chance. As the whole of the village lay asleep, he backed to the edge of the quay, took a last look at the slack remains of the festivity, then dropped into the first of the rowing-boats, cast off, and sculled across the harbour that was already thrilled by a slight wind. A few blots of premonitory rain further uneased the surface of the water, but his desire to escape matched the risk. He must row away from this happiness before he lost it. And then he could start work.

His arms seemed weak against the oars, but they strengthened as he skirted the headland under his daughter's house where that fool fell to his death. Then suddenly, as if magnetised, the boat swinging beneath him, he turned into the teeth of the storm. A wind gushed, caught the high-standing prow, twisted it broadside shorewards. The sky was almost black, the sea a choppy white. Within seconds, as the boat bucked out of his control towards the rocks where he bathed and dived, Palmer knew with a rising elation that he was on his way. At that instant the boat somersaulted.

Still with a sense of freedom, he went under, the boat over him. He saw it outlined in luminous turbulence against the sky before he struck lower, on his back, breath held tight, with an impression that the boat was below him, wallowing in the stirred water, then settling. He expected the whole of life to parade before his memory in good order, but then his tight lungs forced him upwards, his head broke surface.

Water stinging his eyes, Palmer found himself buoyant with a sense that he had missed something, that as from a dream he was already forgetting what that something was, and that therefore he was ready to begin, he could confront the part.

The sea was calm again, Christ, as if by magic. God, the sun had come out, pouring down with a permanence that a minute ago had gone for ever. He struck out towards the shoreline and there on the beach sat a vision of a woman, his daughter, bitch, very neat, skirt tight over her knees, gazing at him in his straits with the familiar irony. She wasn't alone either. Kemp was with her, grinning broadly as if he had just produced a runaway success. They both clapped lightly as he emerged from the water.

'How the hell did you get here?' Palmer said.

'Helicopter – how else? The production's paying,' Kemp said. 'Didn't anyone tell you there'd been a revolution?'

'I know.'

'Darling, he wants me for Miranda,' Nellie said.

'You jolly well look the part, old boy,' Kemp said. 'You haven't shaved for days.'

'Haven't I?'

Palmer felt naked. He began shivering.

'I think I know how to play your father, Nellie,' he said quietly.

Elizabeth Troop

The Queen of Infinite Space

She dreams she is in infinite space, on an endless stage. There is no audience, just a girl, sitting on a chair. She feels feral fear, the words will not come, Will's words, the words she has lived by – words that have sustained her over a lifetime. After a long run, when the soul shadows left her, each time she had felt voided, empty – a nothing. Between engagements she had hardly existed, bereft of an interior life she could but crawl through an ordinary day, mouthing and having to invent for herself the platitudes most people exchanged.

She feels the heat of the spot upon her; there is a vast white light. The male figure who bends over her is not Prospero, not Hamlet, not Orlando. She cannot make out who it is.

The spot blinds her, and the voice, her trademark, tries to rise in her plastic-tubed throat.

I am between roles again, she thinks. I have never been more empty. A void. I should have chosen one part to remain in, finally. To hide in for the rest of my days. Yet I am aware it is too late. Like a needle stuck in a record groove I must revolve in this eternal nothingness of myself. Nothing to hold on to – oblivion. No words. It is not, it had never been enough to be Laura Tate. *Her* face, my face, she tells herself, my face moulded by the grimaces and smiles of applied artifice, formed by a hundred passing parts, is now immobile, it has become the mask of tragedy. The mouth turns down, the sockets weep.

Machines, she is sure, are registering her functions, her bodily performance, as an audience used to do. It is an audience of a sort. They do not applaud, she thinks they might have rigged up a little studio applause. She does not mind her spirit and flesh being monitored by robots. She is no longer in control of her performance.

Interviewer: Tonight we are honoured to have with us perhaps the greatest Shakespearean actress of our time, Dame Laura Tate. Dame Laura has just appeared as the Nurse in Romeo and Juliet with one of our national companies. Good evening and welcome, Dame Laura.

Dame Laura: Thank you. Good evening.

Interviewer: Your career, Dame Laura, started with Juliet, in the provinces, just before the War – now you have recently completed a run as the Nurse in the same play. How did it all begin for you?

Dame Laura: Like a lot of little girls in England, I began at dancing class. Church hall, tap dancing – Miss Entwhistle's Academy.

Interviewer: Amazing, amazing. A tap-dancing Lady Macbeth is hard to imagine.

Dame Laura: Not these days.

Interviewer: Soon after Miss Entwhistle's you played Juliet?

Dame Laura: I could hardly have played Hamlet. Yes, you are right,

one minute an ASM sweeping the stage, the next —
Juliet. I was fourteen, which you must admit is nearer
than most over-age juveniles are when they play it.
Sheer luck — the leading lady got herself knocked up by
a GI and rushed off to abort, silly old trout. I was
ready with the lines, I have always been a quick study —
and there I was. Wartime, you see. Emergency.

Interviewer: You learned your craft as you went along. No drama
schools for you?

Dame Laura: Well, as you probably know, Sir Miles was my one-
man drama school. After he read the reviews of my
Juliet, he invited me to join his fly-blown touring
company — all darned tights, orange make-up and bad
verse-speaking. It took me years to undo what that
man did to me — and I don't just mean on-stage.

Interviewer: Quite. And then, Dame Laura —

Dame Laura: Could we cut the 'Dame Laura' business; it makes me
feel like widow Twankey.

Interviewer: Would it be correct to say that the review you referred
to — er — Laura, was not only instrumental in your
future success, but also gained a reputation for the
young local journalist, Edwin Turner? He went on to
become one of our major dramatic critics.

Dame Laura: It would. But let's not talk about him. Whatever
happened to him? Still fixated on little girls, I expect.
Ruined him, you know.

Interviewer: I have some cuttings here — he went into rhapsodies
about your 'corncrake voice and knock-kneed
charm.'

Dame Laura: Besotted fool. I went into the cinema next, in spite of
the knock knees.

Interviewer: The ill-fated Hitchcock *Hamlet*?

Dame Laura: Disaster. Korda chasing me around the set. Alfred
hidden behind the arras.

Interviewer: He saw it as a who-dun-it, I believe?

Dame Laura: He did, but as everybody knows at the beginning,
there was no way it would work. Unfinished master-

piece, they say, as they show it at the NFT. I believe they are putting music to it now. Don't go.

Interviewer: Then there was your Miranda, to Sir Miles's Prospero. The critics found a touch of incest there, I note.

Dame Laura: Damn right. Then his Petruchio to my Kate – what gall the man had. Did you ever see him in doublet and hose? Petruchio with a prostate.

Interviewer: Then your scintillating Beatrice. The New Elizabethan Age – Festival of Britain time, and you its bright star.

Dame Laura: I got a goitre from the ruff. I left Sir Miles and ran off with Benedick. I wonder what happened to young Benedick? Hollywood, I think.

Interviewer: Cleopatra, that well-known hurdle for the mature actress – it was, if I may say so, a bit of a flop?

Dame Laura: I could hardly be blamed for that. The director was in love with Antony. It was clear at rehearsal which way the wind was blowing. Not on the Serpent of Old Nile, I can assure you. Still, we had some gaudy nights.

Interviewer: And you found time to marry and produce a daughter – three times married, wasn't it?

Dame Laura: Was it? Motherhood was a mistake. It happened when I was doing the Grotowski-inspired *Hamlet* for that Polish director . . . we were all being so acrobatic at the time. I was a plausible Gertrude, I think – it was hard to tell. I named my daughter Gertrude, for which she has never forgiven me. I think I was supposed to play Gertrude as Gertrude Stein. Hamlet was Hemingway. An interesting conception. My daughter bears the scar to this day. She is a structuralist critic, working on a study of sexual relationships in Elizabethan England with special reference to Shakespeare's heroines. As you know, they were all played by boys. She calls it 'The Androgyne Factor' – you should have her on your show.

Interviewer: We will, Dame Laura, we will. You, who have played nearly all Shakespeare's ladies, must be able to give her a great deal of help.

Dame Laura: I would if she would speak to me.

Interviewer: What is it like to live your life through the eyes of Rosalind, Beatrice, Desdemona?

Dame Laura: A damn sight better than working in a department store, or scrubbing floors, I can tell you. But aren't all women Portias, Beatrices, Rosalinds?

Interviewier: And start out as Juliet and end as the Nurse?

Dame Laura: Exactly, but you didn't have to point it out.

Interviewer: Thank you, Dame Laura, for a stimulating and out-spoken interview.

Dame Laura: Thank *you*.

Interviewer: Next week our guest will be Geoffrey Boycott, cricketer in crisis.

Producer's Note:

This programme was shelved owing to the untimely death of Dame Laura Tate a few days after recording. A revised verion may be shown at some future date. However, there may be legal problems owing to the extreme frankness of some of Dame Laura's remarks. Note to the interviewer: please contact the Head of Department.

*

The scene: an intensive care unit in a London hospital. The decor, white and stainless steel, is a set designer's dream for a futurist play.

A cast of two: the Nurse, Shakespeare's Nurse, Juliet's Nurse, beached like a white whale on the bed, festooned with plastic tubes in every orifice – and the nurse, small, neat and (almost as if for aesthetic effect) black against the white.

The patient breathes, just, activating instrument panels. The nurse breathes easily, relaxed, fully alive. There are black nurses, but no black Nurses – or indeed Juliets or Rosalinds. This does not bother the nurse. It will come, she is sure. She has in fact seen the Nurse, the patient, the beached whale, earlier in the month, but does not remember it. She yawned through Romeo and Juliet, and her boyfriend was annoyed with her. Tickets were expensive and hard to come by. He is trying to educate her.

'It's our story,' he had nudged her to point out.

'Not at all,' she had whispered back. Their mutual families approved of their future union, even though it was racially mixed. No drama there, just common sense. So much for silly plots, she thought. She prefers more ethnic culture, Fringe plays and reggae. A pragmatic female, she is geared to reality, which for her is interesting enough. It would matter little if she knew Dame Laura was a star; she treats all patients the same way. There are two forms of dedication in the room: one to fantasy, one to fact.

As her stomach rumbles delicately, reminding her she should be off-duty shortly, she notices with horror (in spite of her voodoo origins she is now an agnostic) that from under the oxygen tent's filmy curtaining, apparitions emerge. Women's faces are pressing against it; they resemble children peering through a window, willing to be released to play. One, younger than the rest, almost like the Juliet the nurse had viewed in that boring performance, edges out. It is not the Juliet she saw, but an old-fashioned one, with a frightful wig, and a nightdress dogging her tiny feet. She is pale as a surgeon's smock. The nurse puts out a hand to stay her, to question her, but just as suddenly as she appeared, she seems to melt into the sturdy rep curtains that keep the windows dark. From under the tent, voices rise, a cornucopia of words, rising and falling; it sounds, as far as she can gather, like speaking in tongues. But words rise, like ornate jewels, not the words of ordinary commerce, or the intricacies of medical obscurity, but the pure words of poetry. Golden, melancholy, honour, sullied, sumptuous, willow, hoar leaves . . . the nurse's head reels with the reiterated sounds. A red-haired girl/boy, in doublet and hose, long legs in white tights, bronzed shoes, and a cape of velvet beauty marches past and, before the nurse can object, is out of the door and away. A wailing woman, rubbing her hands together, bends over the patient. There is an odour of blood, but not the blood smell familiar to the nurse. She crawls under the bed, but when the nurse peers down to see her, she is a mere shadow. The nurse bends and puts her head between her knees. She must be ill. She has never taken drugs, but she is suffering what she knows to be drug-induced hallucination. An imperious woman, who looks Egyptian, tears the film sheet. She moves out, like a barge in full sail – a queen. The nurse is awed. She rings for help.

'I'm unwell – why all these gliding ghosts?'

The young nurse, feeling incoherent, is off balance in front of her superior. Sister goes over to the patient, and then silently to the machines. She switches off, as if terminating a radio programme. Brain death, the young nurse knows they call it. It is as strange a phrase as any she has heard this night.

Sister guides her to the door and suggests coffee and an early return to the nurses' hostel. Sister too is black, but from a different continent. It seems odd to the young nurse that they, once-colonial sisters of a sprawling Empire, should be here, in Shakespeare's land, succouring and tending the sick. She shrugs off the thought. The forces of order are restored in the canteen with its bright clatter, its machines buzzing, its words describing only poor reality, which is enough.

*

They asked me to do *The Times* obituary, but I refused. I am surprised they remember who I am: Edwin Turner, the Fleet Street hack and collector of theatrical trivia – and, I thought, long-lost to them. I hide away in my South London bed-sit, churning out theatre notes for the local rag. Injured pride made me eager to turn them down, I hang on to my injured pride. It is all I have, it keeps me going, along with the meagre handouts from the State. By the time I changed my mind and rang them from the urinal they call a phone box, it was too late. Some slick Johnny who didn't know her had done his mediocre best, calling Laura Tate (my Juliet) the bridge between the old style Shakespeare production and the new, as if she had been a plastic prosthesis propping up decaying teeth. Yet I could not have done it – I have betrayed her in this as in everything else. I am no longer able to visit those palaces of dreams she inhabited; she, the epitome of every fine line the Bard ever wrote.

The suburb I inhabit has a lone theatre, a Victorian relic among the office blocks, all gilt and plush. It devotes itself to TV names who turn up there for pre-West End runs. I donate to them drops of acid from my pen. I prefer the amateur groups in the church hall or social centre, fat housewives essaying Elvira in *Blithe Spirit*; bank clerks getting their adolescent Adam's apples around the punning felicities of early Stoppard. With them I am gentle, for they have nothing to do with Laura, or with me.

Laura has won. I lost my faith years ago when we parted. I lost my religious passion for the theatre as surely as Mr Joyce lost his for the church. For me there was one church, the theatre, one god, Will Shakespeare, and one actress, Laura Tate.

Youthful theatre, the fringe brigade, leaves me cold, with its accent on social change and theatrical ignorance, its desire to change the world by playing to middle-brow intellectual converts. I am sometimes tempted to attend the new concrete cathedral complexes where the ritual is practised these days, to genuflect in my old manner; but the heart has gone out of me.

What have I to remember of those days when I followed you like a cur (and was rewarded by you allowing Tynan to write your biography) and moved towards self-hatred as surely as you moved towards self-fulfilment? Those were the years when my purple-tinted prose was praised, the mass of readers not realising it was but a pale echo of what you inspired.

The first time, though; that is *mine*. A shabby theatre, a provincial rep. – a morning rehearsal, you with a mug of Ovaltine in your small hand. I, spotty and intense, promoted from funerals and jumble sales to the theatre column because old Perkins had piles – I was to take notes. And I did. As you began to speak, with that shrill-child yelp, marred by your nasal twang, my skin prickled. Magic had entered the arena. A virtual child had discovered herself, there on the bare stage, proclaiming the Master in a way all the touring hacks and has-beens could never do.

I went back and wrote my piece, and when the review of the actual performance came out (so inspired had I been) I was offered a better job, and then the *Manchester Guardian* beckoned. In your digs after the first night we had our first fumbling sexual encounter. You rhapsodised about the leading man, who spoke the verse as if written by Ivor Novello, and wore his tights the same way. You had never heard of queers, and I informed you, while trying to get my dirty fingernails into your softer parts. 'You are a fair viol, and your sense the strings; Who, finger'd to make man his lawful music, Would draw heaven down . . . to hearken.'

I sit in the suburban park, filled with the lonely, the dogs and droppings. I watch the nymphets on their yellow roller skates. I see in them, you, Juliet, as you were. The object of all my latent (and fulfilled) desires. I have profaned with my unworthiest hand many holy shrines since then, Laura.

*

No, I'm afraid I wouldn't be of any use to you on *Kaleidoscope*. We didn't get on. It was rather like directing a talented cow. A deeply talented cow. Yes, only once, thank God – Antony and Cleo. Loved him, hated her. My dear, that voice, pure Bacup. Refined of course by Sir Miles. How she *shouted*. Of course in England old ladies can do no wrong. There is nothing like a dame, dear. Sorry I can't oblige. Kind of you to ask.

*

I heard the news flash on the car radio, driving to one of those old studios that are now devoted to TV movies. Off to do another *Bestseller*; they say my carefully studied grey hair over my unlined old/young face gives class to dross. We have to keep it up, here, Laura, cosmetically and sexually speaking, in the City of The Angels, Los Angeles.

I am to play yet another suave businessman with a touch of viciousness. I specialise, Laura darling, I specialise. Where did I go wrong, Beatrice? You may well ask. I was an adequate Benedick, wasn't I? I stayed you in a happy hour? I cannot imagine you dead, though you died so many times. Not meant as a joke, my love. I myself am got up each day like an Evelyn Waugh corpse from *The Loved One*, a living corpse. I can still move, play tennis, flop in a jacuzzi, and get myself around the set. I often take out a lacquered blonde. It is a life of sorts, but not your sort, witty Bea.

I think of Golders Green in the rain (it almost beggars my imagination to do so) and wish I could be there. I wonder which thespians will throng the pews. Sir Miles is too decrepit, no doubt, and a lot of your other swains defunct or scattered. Like me, who am both of those. You, I hope, had a Shakespearean death, to save us all. 'Here comes

Beatrice. By this day! she's a fair lady: I do spy some marks of love in her.'
'Have a nice day, as they say here.'

*

'Gertrude, could you speak to someone from the *Daily Mail*?'
'No.'
'It's about –'
'I know what it's about. Tell them to get stuffed.'
Gertrude tapped out a heading: 'Woman and Ideality – Time, Change and Individuality in Shakespeare's Heroines.'
It wouldn't do. She tippexed it out. She was, she supposed, in her own convoluted way, paying tribute. That wouldn't do at all. She had hated it all, the theatrical effusiveness, the false bonhomie, the ignoring of herself as the plain child of a talented mother. She had also had to admire the sheer integrity of the career. No one could accuse Laura, mother, of selling-out, of cheapness. It was the last straw, to have moral virtue, as well as all the others. It was impossible to live up to.
She would not mourn. She had work to do. It was as difficult to force out a word as a tear. She thought she heard behind her that glittering laugh, the scent of musk and Leichner goo. Just like *her* to try and get in on the act, playing Hamlet's father's ghost.
'Stay dead, mother – damn it,' she said, and began again the staccato machine-gun rattle of the Olivetti, her only weapon.

*

Well, yes, dear child, I have outlasted you – if what I am doing can be said to be living. A vegetable, more or less, wheeled on and off this stage, the old actors' residence, by kind nurses. (I read the reviews of your Nurse; I always said your bawdy nature would out, in the end.) I never thought to see *you* out – I expected to exit first through that door whence no travellers return. I was old when we met, or you said so, in your rude child's way. True, I had one moth-eaten Elizabethan shoe in the grave even then. But you revived me, dear Shrew. 'Is this the way to kill a wife, with kindness?' do you remember? I tried to kill you with kindness (and overwork, and an old man's importunate libido). Forgive me.
What I gave you was all I knew, the tattered experience of a good

craftsman – the pre-War squawkings of the Bard as he was done at the time, in the convention. What you gave me was indescribable. To bring one's own qualities to the conception of character and verse, to transcend, to transform, and bring delight.

They wheeled me in to the television lounge to see you on the box – a chat show. I was tranquillised, in case my old heart gave out at the sight of you. But I saw a Miss Shirley Bassey instead. Cancelled, they said. And then the news of your death. What could I do? Howl, howl, howl. They gave me a sedative. I shouted: 'Wash me in steep down gulfs of liquid fire! O Desdemona! Desdemona – dead, oh, oh, oh . . .'

And then they gave me an injection.

*

Golders Green. A cold, blustery day. Not a bad turn-out. The ceremony, a stock one. The neat coffin sliding back behind the velvet curtains to a semi-religious muzak is an anti-climax. There is no great sense of occasion. The actors greet each other noisily, catching up on gossip. Those with matinée performances rush off, the ones 'resting' pretend they have appointments to attend. There are, surprisingly, quite a few drama students.

'Who was the tall girl with glasses who cried?'

'Her daughter. Some kind of academic.'

'Not like *her*, was she?'

'Did you see Sir Miles wheeled in? It was like seeing Irving.'

'It was horrible. I want to be buried.'

'Remember how she died as Cleopatra? Remember that.'

'Or Juliet, on that ancient bit of film.'

'I brought violets. But there is nowhere to put them.'

'We should say something.'

'You do it . . .'

'The barge she sat in, like a burnished throne, Burned on the water; the poop was beaten gold, Purple the sails, and so perfumed that The winds were lovesick with them, the oars were silver Which to the tune of flutes kept stroke, and made The water which they beat to follow faster, As amorous of their strokes. For her own person, It beggared all description.'

'That's it, then.'

'Let's go. I have a rehearsal.'

The Second Best Bed

'Shall I compare thee to a summer's day?' he enquires politely.

'No, thanks,' I said.

He smiled. He doesn't laugh a lot, Mr Shakespeare, my husband, on account of not liking to show those two black broken teeth he has at the front. But you can smile as much as you want without showing your teeth. So he smiles at me then. Crafty dog.

We were standing together on the bank by London Bridge. He was picking his nose. I was counting the heads of the traitors.

'Winter,' he mutters.

'What?'

'You're more like winter anyway,' he said.

I hit him. Not hard. I didn't have a fan.

'Thank *you*,' I said.

I was wearing my peachflower gown and those new green ankle-boots. Mutton dressed up as lamb, I daresay, but quite presentable mutton.

'Well, shall we say September to my June?' he suggested.

Now that's what he calls a metaphor. You mix up two ideas in one figure of speech to make yourself sound clever. In other words, a high-class compliment or insult. Thou shalt not commit metaphor, I say. Because this was no compliment. I'm eight years older than he is. He never lets me forget it.

So I paid him back the same clipped coinage.

'You flatter yourself,' I said. 'You are August at least. Besides, as your mother's always telling me, one is only as old as one feels.'

He smiles again. Only this time a bit sadly.

'In that case,' he remarked, 'I think I must be coming up to immortality tomorrow.'

'Thirty-four,' I said.

He glared at me. 'Thirty, Anne, thirty!'

The next day being his thirtieth birthday.

'Not your big head,' I said. 'Theirs.'

I pointed at the Bridge. At the grinning skulls stuck up on the poles of the tower.

'Thirty-three,' he said.

He was right, too. I counted them again. He's always right when it comes to things like that. His eyes might look half-shut but they never miss much. A most particular man, my Mr Shakespeare.

*

The swans looked grey as old geese on the Thames. It was a wishy-washy sort of a day for April. No sap in it. No sinew. Not like spring at all. I'd left the spring behind me in Warwickshire the day before, a spring in such a rush that the hawthorn had been out before the blackthorn was over.

But then London always struck me as a cold place. A cold place and a dirty. And unreal, somehow. Like a theatre, London. A make-believe city. I don't go there any more. Nor does he if he can help it.

Even the breeze chill off the river that late afternoon was like no wind that I'd care to call a wind. No wind like the wind in Arden Woods or up on Stinchcombe Hill. Just a swirling smoky stench of bad-cooked cabbage and garbage. It stuck in my throat. It made me feel sulky and sick.

No, you can keep your rat-packed flea-picked London as far as I'm concerned, and what my dear husband ever saw in its maggots I honestly couldn't tell you. Except, of course, the playhouses. I know that in those days he had to be near them for his trade.

I was shivering. Mr Shakespeare took off his cloak and wrapped it around my shoulders.

'Cheer up, little autumn,' he said.

'Is it far to go?' I demanded.

'Not far,' he said. 'Bishopsgate. By St Helens. And the walking will warm you. Come on.'

He took my arm and we set off for his new lodgings.

*

It was a splendid cloak, tawny, brocaded, velvet-lined, cut in the Spanish fashion. I noticed the rest of my husband's clothes. They were excellent too. A red silken doublet, well-padded, with close-set silver buttons winking down the front. Stiff white cartwheel ruff and foamy lace wrist-ruffs. His silk hose paned with canions. A copotain hat on his head.

This outfit must have cost a pretty packet, I reckoned.

I made no comment. You see, Mr Shakespeare hadn't exactly been sending sackfuls of rose nobles or gold jacobuses home to Stratford for the housekeeping. For years I'd been living on not much more than a diet of promises. Seven lean years.

He'd soon make his fortune, he said, when he first left me and the children and dashed off to London. Great prospects, he said. A sea voyage with Sir Francis Drake, no less. Another to Aleppo, he said, in a vessel called *The Tiger*. Such a shame that some shipwreck off the sea-coast of Bohemia left him poor again. Did he ever go to sea? I don't know. He's a slyboots. He likes to have his little secrets. I don't care. I asked him no questions. Maybe he told me no lies. But he never refers to sea voyages again. Not in my hearing.

Still, not to mince matters, let me tell you this. When I first took the coach to visit our fortune-maker I discovered that his only employment was holding the heads of the horses of the gentlemen who frequented the playhouses. By the next time I saw him – which must have been when he came home for the twins' fourth birthday, the February of '89 – he had worked his way up from the horses, and moved from the outside to the inside of the playhouses, to be something called a prompter's assistant. Or was it an assistant's prompter? I forget. But I do remember the main thing. The pay. You couldn't have kept chicks on it. I should know. We had three.

Then my husband got in with Mr Burbage – I mean Mr James Burbage, the manager, a good man of business – and he did a spell of acting. But Mr Shakespeare was never cut out to be an actor. He lacked what they call Stage Presence and his voice has no variety. He got stuck with what he called the hammy parts. Ghosts, heralds, third messengers and such. And even in these hammy parts he was hopeless. He admitted it. He'd forget his lines and have to make up alternative speeches.

But that gave Mr Burbage a great notion. He set his failed actor to work patching up other men's plays, taking stale stuff and revamping it, breathing new life on to old bones. The breakthrough at last, said my husband. He was pleased. As pleased as Punch. His Judy didn't quite know what to think. But, for a brief interval, things went swimmingly. He can work very damn fast when he wants to. He must have worked very damned hard, too. That Christmas he sent gifts home for all of us. I got garters of best silk of Granado. He sent this doll for Susanna, with arms and legs that moved. And a musical box for Hamnet and Judith, our twins.

More followed.

And not trinkets.

I mean: it wasn't just at Christmas he remembered us.

Alas, that died the death in '92. The plague hit London again. The playhouses were shut down, them being pits of infection.

He wrote me a letter. So many were dying, he said, that the sextons wouldn't even toll the bells for burials, because the tolling would have gone on night and day.

I thought he might come home then. But he didn't.

I hadn't a clue as to what he'd been doing since. I knew he hadn't died himself, that's all. Certain small sums of money turned up regularly. Enough to keep us going, just about. But never a word to explain what was holding him in London. His letters seemed quite cheerful, if evasive. He'd write of tennis-matches, tobacco, the price of pens. No more about sextons and burials.

For all I knew he might not have been in London . . .

For all I knew he could have been spending his enforced leisure-time hopping to Norwich in company with that clownish crony of his, Will Kemp. Turning their backs on the plague. Fitted out with their own little belis. Footing it merrily. Drinking all the way. Stopping at every whorehouse. Counting ten miles as but a leap. Morris-dancing mad-caps! More like St Vitus Dance, if you ask me —

Not so. No way. When it came down to it, I couldn't possibly picture in my mind's eye the image of Mr Shakespeare hopping from London to Norwich. Lord, he wouldn't even walk the mile or so west to my father's farm at Shottery in the early days of our acquaintance. Not if he could beg or borrow a nag to ride on.

Besides, my husband's life is his writing. And it's hard to write on the hop, I should say.

Now he had lured me up to London with this letter full of sudden grand vague talk of having something to celebrate as well as his thirtieth birthday.

Well, all right, the plague had abated and I'd heard that the playhouses were soon to be opened again. And he'd mentioned in his letter that Mr Burbage now required him to write plays of his own. Comedies, he said. Comedies and histories. But he hadn't said anything about payment in advance for these comedies and histories. And even if he *had* touched Mr Burbage for a bit on account, I was sure it wouldn't have been sufficient to splash out for a suit like the one he was strutting in. Let alone that Spanish-style cloak which was keeping me cosy and warm.

My arm linked in his, I fingered the texture of his doublet and I wondered where he'd got it. I was puzzled. How on earth could my out-of-work husband afford such dandy clothes?

*

Mr Shakespeare has always been good at guessing what I am thinking.

As we came out of the shadow of the spire of St Clement Danes and trod our way into the offal pudding which is Gracechurch Street, he suddenly glances at me sidelong, sly-eyed, and announces:

'That cloak. Someone gave me that cloak. I didn't buy it.'

'I see,' I said.

He scowled. 'You don't,' he said. 'Let me explain. That summer's day comparison. I was joking.'

'Oh, thanks again,' I said. 'Thanks very much.'

'No, no,' he snapped. 'A joke at my own expense. I was quoting myself. Something I wrote. A sonnet. I wrote this sonnet comparing someone to a summer's day. The person I wrote the sonnet about gave me the cloak.'

'Must have been a good sonnet,' I said.

'It wasn't too bad,' he said modestly. 'I've done better.'

I considered the peacock feather in his hat.

'Did you get your whole wardrobe from sonnets?' I asked him.

He starts blushing. My husband has always been a great blusher. Surprising, really.

He turned aside to kick with alacrity at this passing cur. 'You saw that?' he growled. 'It was going to bite you!'

My husband has never been what one might call a dog-lover.

'Yes, I saw that,' I said. 'Well, *did* you?'

The blush spread. It resembled a rash now.

'More or less,' he admitted. 'But I didn't write the sonnets to get the clothes.'

'Of course not,' I said.

'I just got the clothes for the sonnets.'

'Of course,' I said.

'I only wrote the sonnets because I *had* to.'

'I understand you perfectly,' I said.

*

Mr Shakespeare seemed relieved. As if he had got something off his chest. Unpacked his bowels of some worm that was poisoning him.

The blush faded.

We strolled on without speaking for a while.

Then he stops a pedlar woman and he buys me a handful of red cherries.

I ate one.

It tasted of London and the woman.

'Sonnets,' I said. 'Written many?'

'Must be more than a hundred,' he said. 'Yes. A century plus.'

'Fancy,' I said.

I didn't eat any more cherries.

'That's nice to know,' I said. 'Nice you have someone you have to write so many sonnets for. *And* get paid in kind.' I smiled at him. 'More than a hundred,' I said. 'She must dote on sonnets. She must be a real addict. A sonnet-freak.'

My husband returned my smile sweetly.

'It isn't a she,' he said.

*

I tripped on the hem of my gown. I trod in a heap of horse-manure.

'Did it rain?' I demanded.

'What?' he said.

'That summer's day sonnet. Was there rain in it?'

Mr Shakespeare frowned. I could see that he was actually running through his sonnet in his head, actually trying very hard to remember.

'I don't think so,' he said, at last. 'No. No rain.'

'I see,' I said.

He stared at me. 'What the hell has rain got to do with it?'

'I just wondered,' I said. 'I just wondered if your sonnets were written to advertise cloaks. It crossed my mind that your patron might perhaps be a cloak-maker.'

My husband let go of my arm.

'As a matter of fact,' he said, 'he is of noble birth.'

'Rich?' I asked.

He shrugged. At least, I think he shrugged. The shoulders of his doublet were so puffed that what I took for a shrug may have been only a twitch of embarrassment.

I linked my arm in his again.

'Don't fret,' I said. 'I'm pleased for you.'

'Are you?' he said doubtfully.

'Yes,' I said.

'Really and truly?'

'Really and truly,' I said. 'There's no money in poetry. Any poet's wife knows that. Poets need patrons. You've been lucky to find one.'

'Henry's more than a patron,' he muttered. 'He's my friend.'

'Henry?'

'Henry Wriothesley,' he said.

We paused to let a cart turn into Leadenhall without killing us. I took the chance to drop the rest of the cherries down a drain. Then we walked on up past the Cornhill, arm-in-arm.

'Earl of Southampton,' my husband added pompously.

'Hang on,' I said.

'What's the matter?'

'I want to scrape this horse-shit off my boot-soles.'

Mr Shakespeare watched me while I did it.

'*And* Baron of Tichfield,' he says, rubbing his long nose.

My boots cleaned, we resumed our way towards Bishopsgate.

'Some patron!' I remarked.

'I told you, Anne,' my husband snapped, 'Henry's not just a patron –'

'I haven't forgotten,' I said. 'He's more like a summer's day.'

*

My husband's lodgings were over this wetfishmonger's on the corner of Turnagain Lane. Outside was all fish-heads and fish-tails and tubs of live eels. The inside seemed decent enough, but it did smell of mackerel.

At the foot of the back stairs, he kisses me, and then he's unwinding this silk sash from the sleeve of his doublet.

'What's the game?' I demanded.

'A blindfold,' says he. 'I'd like you to wear it. I know what's up there and you don't. I want to make it more of a surprise, that's all.'

'Couldn't I just shut my eyes?'

'Not the same.'

'I have to be blindfold?'

He nods.

Mr Shakespeare has never been what I would call a handsome man, but now his face was all at once boyish and eager.

I admit it: I felt this shiver of excitement run down my spine.

The blindfold bit was teasing. It suggested some strange treat.

So I humoured him. I gave in to his whim. I let him tie the sash around my head.

Then he takes me by the hand. He leads me upstairs.

His hand was hot and sticky. It was shaking. It was shaking so much I thought he must have the fever. And he had. But not any kind of fever doctors cure.

Those stairs were steep. They creaked as we climbed up them. Otherwise the place was silent as a tomb. But a tomb that stank of fishes.

We climbed right up to the top. I heard him unlock a door. Then we went in. He locked the door behind us.

'Just a minute,' he whispers.

I heard the rattle of a tinderbox.

I smelt brimstone matches.

Then he took the blindfold off me, and I saw it.

*

That bed.

'Jesus!' I cried. 'It's like some Papist altar!'

*

It was a gigantic four-poster, each post as thick as a man, with heavy crimson velvet curtains hanging down to the floor from the canopy, and fat gold cords that dangled like bell-ropes. When you pulled the curtains back you could see the bed itself was decked out with a silk coverlet, black as night, all crusted with embroidery of stars. It had half a dozen white pillows stuffed with swansdown by the fat soft look of them, and lots of bolsters, and mattresses piled so high you needed a small step-ladder to get to the top. As for its sheets, they were huge and begilt and gorgeous as sails ripped off some Spanish galleon of the Great Armada. There were these seven black candles burning in silver sockets all along the bed's headboard, and the headboard itself was carved over with nymphs and things like goats. Only they weren't goats, I saw that at once. They were more devils.

*

My husband was standing leaning against one of the bed-posts, grinning at me, his eyes as bright as beads, his face pale with tiny seeds of sweat trickling down it. Candlelight flatters him, but his head looked as usual two sizes too big for his body. His lips were dry and cracked, his tongue flicking in and out between them like a viper's.

'Not an altar,' he said. 'A theatre.'

He starts stroking his bony nose with the door-key. Then he's tickling his little moustache with it.

*

Now you might think I don't need to tell you what Mr Shakespeare had in mind. Nor what happened in that bed that night. And the next day, his birthday. And the next night. And all the nights and days of the week that followed. But I do, because it wasn't exactly the usual. And it not being exactly the usual is the point of my story.

*

I'd brought him a gift up from Stratford for his birthday. Now I chose to unwrap it.

It was a jacket of black and white lambskins to keep out the cold.

Not a seasonable present perhaps, nor at all fashionable.

Yet there was a certain wifely loving-kindness in my choice, seeing I didn't anticipate him being at home with me the following winter, or for any other winter for some time to come.

It was a handsome jacket. Well-stitched. Lined with sarcanet.

I held it up for his inspection.

'Did you make this with your own hands?' he enquired.

'I did,' I lied. 'Happy birthday.'

My husband kissed me then. Then he took the jacket and kissed it.

He knew such tasks were not to my taste at all.

'Try it on,' I suggested.

He did. He put on that lambskin jacket.

Then he stood there, still grinning foolishly, beside the big bed.

That grin was a mistake. I could see those two broken black teeth.

He was twisting strands of his thin hair forwards to hide the baldness at his temples.

'I'm a wolf now,' Mr Shakespeare says. 'A wolf in sheep's clothing.'

Then he took off my gown and my linen smock and my stockings, and he laid me down on that bed and we made love.

*

The love that we made wasn't good. This didn't surprise me. Right from the start, even that first time at Welford by the millpool, it was always the imagined, the longed-for relish that enchanted his senses. His palate when it came to it was what you might call watery. He feared the act. The nectar. He lacked thirst and bite. All the same, he got me pregnant with Susanna by that pool. I was the three months gone when we were married.

*

'O my love,' he says. 'O my life.'

'O my life,' I say. 'O my love.'

*

Love? No, it was not love we were making. He couldn't. And I wouldn't. And that's all. My husband had always been less than a man should be in the labours of love. I tell you the plain truth now. The unhappy fact of the matter. As God is my witness, our marriage bed never had been good. Why, even that first time, in the long grass, when first he tickled trout then tickled me, when you'd think perhaps the novelty might have inspired him . . . Well, it didn't. I'm sure the trout had a better time than I did. He proved no ardent wooer that afternoon at Welford. No great shakes when it came to it. Ha! His very name a joke. Mine too, mind you. Because, you may be sure, I had my way of him. I mean: It was me that did the hard work, or most of it, to untie my own unwelcome virgin knot. O, he was excited all right. Quite giddy with expectation. But then there was always this impediment in him which came between desire and its performance. How can I put it? Mr Shakespeare was a sweet lecher but he was not a lusty man. His function in my department was not sufficient. And now that night on that bed, that night before he reached his thirtieth birthday, I thought at first it would be the same as ever. The spirit willing but the flesh too weak. Lord, his action was no stronger than a flower.

*

'Anne?' he cried, anxious.
'Yes,' I lied, bored.

*

He rolled over on his back. He starts smoking this long pipe of tobacco. I lay there staring up at the canopy and the candles. There was black wax dripping down over those gross carvings.
'This bed,' I said. 'How many sonnets did this bed cost?'
He didn't flinch. He didn't bat an eyelid.
'No sonnets,' he said. 'Just two poems.'
'Long stuff?'
'Longish. Look, I'll show you.'
Then, setting his pipe aside, he goes delving under one of the swansdown pillows and comes out holding a book in each of his hands. A couple of slim gilt volumes, quarto size. He presses them on me, looking quite proud of himself. *Venus and Adonis*, one was called. The other, *The Rape of Lucrece*. Each book had the name William Shakespeare in bold print on its title page. And each bore a dedication to the Right Honourable Henry Wriothesley, Earl of Southampton and Baron of Tichfield.
'Venus,' I said, 'I know about. But who's this Lucrece?'
My husband reached for his pipe again.
'A Roman lady,' he said.
'A Roman lady who got raped?'
'Full marks,' he said.
He started blowing smoke-rings.
I propped myself up on one elbow to watch him.
'Who raped Lucrece?' I said.
'Another Roman.'
'Another Roman lady?' I said.
That made him cough.

'Of course not. A Roman *man*. A prince. One of the Tarquins. Sextus Tarquinius.'

'Sextus,' I said. 'That's a nice name.'

He frowned at me. 'You think so?' He looked puzzled.

'Sextus,' I said. 'Yes. I like the sound of Sextus.'

'Well, he was a villain.'

'No doubt. But I still like the sound of his name.'

My husband shook his head, sucking at his pipe. But he found that the pipe had gone out.

'So what happened to Lucrece?' I asked. 'I mean, after Sextus had raped her . . .'

'She told her husband. Then she stabbed herself.'

'And Sextus?' I said.

'He was driven into exile.'

'Is that all?' I said.

Mr Shakespeare fumbled with his tinderbox.

'What do you mean?' he demanded. 'Is that all?'

'It just seems a pretty feeble ending. Exile. Wouldn't it have been better to have had the husband kill him?'

'But he didn't. You don't understand. The basis is historical. A true story.'

'I thought poets were allowed to lie,' I said.

I lay back and considered the burning candles.

'So who gets raped in the other one?' I said.

My husband dropped his match. 'I beg your pardon?'

'Does your Venus rape your Adonis or your Adonis rape your Venus? Of course, if it's purely historical, or – what's the right word? – *mythological*, then –'

'It's not all rape,' he protested.

'Come on,' I said. 'I know a bit about that story. It's the woman rapes the man in that one, isn't it?'

Mr Shakespeare sighed.

'Venus is a goddess,' he said. 'She falls in love with Adonis, a mortal. She detains him from the chase. She woos him. But she cannot win his love.'

'Promising,' I said. 'But how does it end? Does Adonis go into exile?'

'He gets killed by a boar,' my husband snapped.

I giggled. I laughed out loud. I couldn't help it.

He removed the pipe from his mouth and glared at me.

'What's so funny?' he demanded.

'I'm sorry,' I said. 'But your poems sound ridiculous. All rapes, or attempted rapes, then exile, boars, and nothing.'

'Their plots are not important,' Mr Shakespeare said earnestly. 'It's the verse. It's what I make of the material. Let me just read you this passage –'

'I'd rather you didn't,' I said. 'I already have a headache.'

*

We lay side by side on that bed. Not touching. But I was naked. And those candleflames now seemed like hellfire.

I didn't have a headache.

It was strange.

This crazy conversation had made me ache elsewhere. All kinds of images were racing through my mind. Lewd images. Voluptuous. Unspeakable. Some comic. Some not comic at all.

I kept staring at the candles and the carvings.

The devils and the nymphs. What they were doing. I fancied that they moved. I could see them at it. That was a trick of the candlelight, no doubt.

But it was real enough that two of the candles had joined together, melting.

I kept stroking the black silk coverlet. I fingered its stars.

I could not turn to look at Mr Shakespeare.

His breathing was deep. But I knew he'd not fallen asleep.

Perhaps he was reading my mind. I don't know. If he was, that might go some way to explain things.

But my husband didn't need to read my mind.

Because, before long, I said softly:

'Henry Wriothesley.'

'Yes,' he said.

'He gave you this bed for those poems.'

'No. He gave me money. I bought the bed.'

'Money,' I said.

'Yes,' he said.

I hesitated.

I still couldn't look at Mr Shakespeare.

Then I realised I was sniffing at the sheets.

'This bed,' I said.

He said nothing.

'This bed,' I whispered. 'Has *he* slept in it?'

*

My husband wouldn't answer. So I knew that he had.

'Jesus,' I said. 'Jesus.'

I couldn't take my eyes off those candles.

'What do men do?' I whispered.

No reply. My husband drew his breath sharply, as if he was in pain.

I whispered:

'Good is it?'

He sat up. He was taking off the lambskin jacket. Then he reaches out for one of those ropes and closes the curtains all around us.

'Henry Wriothesley,' I said. 'Earl of Southampton. Baron of Tichfield.'

That bed was now like a room within the room. A secret place.

'Money,' I said. 'You whore,' I said.

The wax dripped down from the headboard. It was staining the sheets.

I whispered:

'How much did he give you?'

My husband muttered something.

'*How much?*' I said.

Then Mr Shakespeare spoke it clear and coldly.

'A thousand pounds,' he said.

*

I stared at him.

He did not smile.

He looked hard at me.

'What did you do?' I breathed. 'What did you do that was worth a thousand pounds?'

He was naked now.

His member stood up stiff as any poker.

'You really want to know,' he said.

It wasn't a question. It was a statement of fact.

'I want to know,' I whispered. '*What did you do?*'

Then:

'This,' said Mr Shakespeare.

And he did it to me.

*

It hurt me at first. Then it didn't. Hurt or not, once he'd started there was no stopping him.

'Good?' he cried. 'Like it?'

'No!' I cried. 'No . . .'

But after some more of it:

'*Yes!*'

When we'd done, my husband started talking about the money. That bed hadn't cost so much, he said. He had plenty of the thousand pounds left over. He was going to buy shares in a new playhouse Mr Burbage was building in Bankside. His plays would be performed there, he said. That way he'd get paid for the plays, and also get a percentage of their profits. Money made money, he said. Soon he'd purchase property as well. The day would come, he said, when we'd live in the finest house in Stratford . . .

*

I touched him.

'You want it again?' he asked wonderingly.

I wanted it.

And Mr Shakespeare proved more than willing to give it to me.

*

I fell asleep at last. He was still talking about money when I fell asleep. But it wasn't about money that I dreamt.

*

Next morning I was woken by this braying.

I looked round.

I saw the Devil standing by that bed.

'He-haw,' brays the Devil. 'He-haw.'

The Devil was stark naked save for this donkey's head.

'He-haw,' he brays again. Then: 'Ha! Haw!' And he's laughing.

The Devil's member was thrusting towards me.

Very hard. Very upright.

I reached out for it.

'Ha! Whore!' laughs the Devil. 'Can't get enough of it now, can she?'

Mr Shakespeare buggered me wearing his donkey's head.

*

That bed would blush if it could tell you all the strange things we did in it.

My husband had compared it to a theatre.

Amen. So it was.

A private playhouse where we acted out his fantasies.

O, and I was a willing accomplice, a wanton actress.

What we did was as I liked it.

Because I'd now found out that I liked what he liked.

Liked it? Adored it. Doted on the act.

And all of our secret plays had that one carnal ending.

*

Often I dressed as a boy and he dressed himself up in my clothes. He had costumes as well in a trunk he kept under the bed. Gowns, crowns, masks, wigs, skulls, daggers, and suchlike. Sometimes we used these. But usually just words were sufficient. His words.

He'd start talking as he lit the black candles. Then he'd pull the curtains around us and shut out the world, him still talking, and we'd act out his dreams.

Once he made me believe that the bed was an enchanted island where I was the daughter of this magician called Prospero. Miranda, he called me. He called himself Caliban. Caliban had very beastly lusts.

Then I had to be this shrew called Katharina and he was some peculiar Veronese gentleman, one Petruchio, whose delight it was to tame me of my shrewishness. Guess how . . .

Another time I was the Queen of the Goths, Queen Tamora, and he was a Roman named Titus who killed my two sons and baked their remains in a pie. I didn't much care for that one. Because he got a real pie, an eel-pie. He bought it down in Turnagain Lane and he made me eat it with him on the bed. I felt sick. But I ate it. I wanted Mr Shakespeare. I needed him to do what I knew he would do when we'd eaten it.

Then, another bizarre one, when I was this Italian girl, very young, Juliet he called me, and I had to pretend I was lying dead in a tomb (that bed) from a potion given to me by a friar. And Mr Shakespeare was my lover, name of Romeo, and when this Romeo thought his Juliet was dead he went and drank real poison. Only Juliet wasn't dead. The friar had only given her a sleeping potion. So when I woke from my trance I saw Romeo's body lying there beside me and I had to act out seizing his dagger and killing myself for grief. Then Mr Shakespeare kissed his dead Juliet and did that other thing to her.

Then he made me some Lady Macbeth walking in my sleep and trying to wash imaginary blood-stains from my hands. Then, another night, the lady-love of a Prince of Denmark who goes mad, and I had to wander about the room singing and strewing flowers and then act out that I had strayed to the banks of a stream and been drowned. The bed was the stream. Mr Shakespeare jumped into it after me. I might say that he had me drowned face-downwards. Which is, of course, quite contrary to nature.

Then he was a blackamoor called Othello in the service of the Venetian state and he pretended to smother me with a pillow on the bed because of my being unfaithful with his lieutenant. He made up a lovely bit of a song for that one, when we were doing what we did after the smothering. Something about a weeping willow. That and the other activity brought tears to my eyes, I remember.

And then I was Cleopatra of Egypt with a make-believe snake which I had to call my baby, saying it sucked me to sleep as its teeth were dispatching me. And, another time, Mr Shakespeare was Antiochus or something, the King of Antioch anyway, and I was his daughter. But I won't speak of that one –

Enough.

*

Infinite riches in a little room.

That's how my husband described what we got up to.

I couldn't put it any better, myself.

*

The week passed quickly.

It was on the last night in that bed that I said to Mr Shakespeare, as casually as I could:

'What's he like?'

'Who?'

'You know who. Your friend.'

My husband smiled.

'You whore,' he said.

I smiled back.

'Well, that makes two of us,' I said. 'Come on. Don't be a spoil-sport. You can't really expect me to turn round and go home knowing nothing about this rival of mine except that he's rich and his name is Henry Wriothesley.'

My husband was biting his fingernails.

'I suppose I could let you read the sonnets I wrote about him,' he muttered.

I pouted.

'That's cheating. You know I can't understand poetry. Just tell me in plain words. What's he look like, your friend?'

Mr Shakespeare stops biting his fingernails. Now he's rubbing his belly as if he felt an ulcer coming.

Then he frowns and says:

'The strange thing is . . .'

He stopped.

'Go on,' I prompted.

He reaches out with his hand. He starts stroking my hair.

'Maybe it's not strange at all,' he murmured thoughtfully. 'He's just about the opposite of you.'

'Ah, yes,' I said. 'I was forgetting. He's summer to my winter.'

'I didn't mean that,' says my husband.

'Well, what then?'

'Everything.'

'All right. Tell me.'

So he did.

A lovely boy, he said, with a fair complexion. Just twenty-one years old, he said, and a rose-cheeked Adonis. His breath sweeter than violets, he said. His hair like the amber buds of marjoram, he said. An angel. A spirit. A saint.

So he said.

I yawned.

'Sounds too good to be true,' I remarked.

Then I led Mr Shakespeare to think and to feel that I'd lost interest in the subject.

*

'Your eyes,' he said, 'are nothing like the sun.'

'Oh, thanks,' I said.

It was the morning of the day I left Mr Shakespeare's lodgings in Turnagain Lane.

I was looking at my own face in the looking-glass.

He comes and stands behind me.

'I mean it as a compliment,' he explains. 'Poets, as you say, lie. They make far-fetched comparisons. I was just being truthful for once. You're worth the truth, Anne.'

I painted my pale lips.

I rouged my cheeks.

I said:

'The truth is I look worn-out, and no wonder.'

I started brushing my hair.

Mr Shakespeare took the brush from my hand.

He brushed my hair for me.

'In the old days,' he says, 'black was not counted fair.'

'I can't help being a brunette,' I said.

'As black as hell,' he says, brushing. 'As dark as night.'

'There you go again,' I said. 'Far-fetched comparisons!'

I stood up.

My husband took me in his arms.

'Don't kiss me,' I said. 'You'll ruin my paint.'

Mr Shakespeare smiled.

He reached for his lambskin jacket.

'It's all right,' I said. 'I can make my own way. You get on with your work now.'

He did. And so did I.

More's the pity.

Because that bed, now I come to look back on it, would have been big enough for the three of us.